Religious Reason

Religious Reason

The Rational and Moral Basis
of Religious Belief

RONALD M. GREEN

New York, Oxford University Press
1978

Library of Congress Cataloging in Publication Data

Green, Ronald Michael.
  Religious reason.

  Bibliography: p.
  Includes index.
    1. Religion—Philosophy. 2. Reason. 3. Ethics.
  4. Religions. 5. Kant, Immanuel, 1724-1804.
  I. Title.
  BL51.G727   200′.1   77-26156
  ISBN 0-19-502388-9
  ISBN 0-19-502389-7 pbk.

Selections from Immanuel Kant: *Critique of Practical Reason,* translated
by Lewis White Beck, copyright © 1956 by The Liberal Arts Press, Inc.,
are reprinted by permission of The Bobbs-Merrill Company, Inc.

In memory of my father, Daniel David Green
To my mother, Beatrice Green

Acknowledgments

I want to thank Professors Fred Berthold, Bernard Gert, Robert Gimello, Steven Katz, Hans Penner, and Charles Stinson, colleagues in the Departments of Philosophy and Religion at Dartmouth College, for their assistance in the writing of this book. Their counsel and criticism have influenced almost every page I have written. Where I have gone wrong in my understanding of aspects of moral theory or religious belief it is almost certainly because I have not listened to their advice.

I also owe a special debt of gratitude to Professor Paul Ramsey of Princeton University and Professor John Reeder, Jr., of Brown University for their attention to the manuscript during its early stages. Though the approach to religion and ethics I take here differs substantially from their own, each of these men has been a source of encouragement to me.

Pat Golin of Oxford University Press has my appreciation for her careful editorial work on the manuscript.

Finally, I must thank my wife, Mary Jean. It would be difficult to itemize the many ways she helped me in the writing of this book, but if I were to choose one, it would probably be her

Acknowledgments

acceptance of responsibility for a Dartmouth language study program in Blois, France, during the academic year 1974-75. By doing this, Mary Jean provided the tranquil setting needed for the actual preparation of the manuscript. Walter Lippmann once remarked that happiness is writing a book that fascinates you and traveling south with someone you love. If residence in the Loire Valley of France is a reasonable substitute for travel south, I want to thank Mary Jean for those months of happiness.

Norwich, Vt.   R. M. G.
February 1978

Contents

Religious Reason

Introduction

Since the early nineteenth century there has been a common tendency within the study of religion to set religion and reason at odds with one another. Rationality, defined in its broadest sense as the objective comprehension and control of reality, has been opposed to religion, which has been characterized as a pre-rational, non-rational, or anti-rational phenomenon. The early positivists, for example, viewed religion as a rudimentary attempt to control nature, but one destined to be replaced everywhere by the rational methods of science. Feuerbach, Marx, and Freud were much harsher: for them religion is a delusion, an ultimately irrational and dangerous distortion of reality, and the elimination of religion stood high on all their agendas for rational human progress.[1]

More recently, a series of less hostile views has emerged. In differing ways, functionalist thinkers, phenomenologists, and some analytic philosophers of religion have acknowledged religion to be an abiding, and possibly important, feature of human existence. It is viewed as appearing at the limit points of life beyond the boundaries of ordinary rational activity, and it is seen to express deep human emotional or psychic needs. As such, it is neither rational nor irrational. But the hidden assumption, especially among the functionalists, is that religion cannot really retain full authority in the face of reason. Its most important effects must remain "latent" or hidden from the consciousness of believers themselves. It is no accident, therefore, that the sociology and anthropology of religion have focused so much on the elderly, the uneducated, or those otherwise outside the mainstream of modern life. Religion is seen to flourish where reason holds least sway.[2]

The purpose of this book is to call this separation of reason and religion into question. My fundamental claim will be that religion is a fully rational activity. It is the effort by reason to comprehend the totality of conditions that reason itself requires to make possible the understanding and control of reality. Behind this claim is the assumption that reason has three recognized employments related to one another in a progressive fashion. The first is theoretical reason, which seeks to construct an objective and universally acceptable picture of the world, to know the world, as it were. The second employment is prudential (or deliberative), in which reason, on the basis of the objective understanding of reality furnished by theoretical reason, governs the choices made by individuals or groups for the purpose of maximally satisfying the desires of the choosing agents. The third employment is moral. This also involves choice—it is a form of prudential reason—but here the ends or satisfactions pursued are not those of particular agents but of the whole community of rational persons.

To these three aspects of reason, my aim is to add a fourth: religious reason or reason in its religious employment. Like the others, this stands in progressive relationship to the employments which precede it. Specifically, religious reason arises because of an important conflict between prudential and moral reason, and it represents reason's effort to bring its own program to a coherent conclusion. Thus, the term "religious reason" should not be a source of confusion. It is the same reason operative in the other employments, but it is called upon in this special case to resolve a distinct set of problems in its general task of comprehending and organizing our relationship to reality.

All this remains to be explained in detail. Obviously, very much depends upon how reason, morality, and religion themselves are understood. Part I of this book is devoted to an explanation of these terms and to a careful following of the progression of reason through its religious employment. But the essential point I want to stress here is that the progression toward religious belief and activity takes place within the operations of reason and is a part of the conceptual structure of every rational agent. Religion, therefore, is not opposed to reason, nor is it the result of non-rational needs such as those arising from human emotions. Strictly speaking religion has nothing to do with the specific and non-rational conditions of human existence. Since it is reason in its deliberative and moral employments that gives rise to religion, any rational entity capable of deliberative and moral activity would have to follow this progression to religion, whether or not it had human desires or needs. Thus, if I am correct, cybernetic persons (choice-making and morally responsible electronic computers) would have to engage in religious reflection and eventually hold religious beliefs.

The view I hope to set forth is not new. In broad outline it has been suggested frequently in the past,[3] and in its specific form it was stated almost two centuries ago with considerable precision by Immanuel Kant. Kant's three famous questions for philosophy, "What can I know? What ought I to do? and What can I hope?",[4] nicely trace the progression within reason's concerns, and Kant's most important writings represent a careful and rigorous exploration of reason's development through its religious employment. Unfortunately, Kant's groundbreaking work here has been relatively little understood or appreciated. There are several reasons for this. One is that Kant's understanding of religion proceeds from his ethical theory, and it is well known that Kant's ethical theory is hard to understand and filled with obscurities. As a result, the understanding of his philosophy of religion has suffered. Related to this is a second difficulty which results from the fact that much of Kant's thinking about religion seems contrary to his most fundamental assertions about ethics, so that not a few commentators have attributed the philosophy of religion to Kant's old age and loss of mental acuity. Finally, and somewhat ironically, Kant's own thinking about religion has been made inaccessible because that very thinking unleashed critical and negative tendencies in the interpretation of religion that have dominated the study of religion since his work. Many of those who responded enthusiastically to Kant's destructive and ground-clearing achievements in this area failed to appreciate or simply dismissed the more constructive insights in his work.

If we are now in a better position to reconstruct and appreciate Kant's thinking on religion, credit must go to recent work on his ethical theory. In particular I would single out John Rawls' important book, *A Theory of Justice*.[5] This volume is by no means a study of Kant's ethics, but as an original and creative effort to develop the rational foundation of the moral life it has had the side-effect of opening up some of the more important aspects of Kant's own rational ethics. Thanks to the work of Rawls and others, we are in a better position to appreciate Kant's ethical theory and to see why he insisted that moral reasoning must culminate in religious reflection and belief.

It should not be surprising that much of the argument in the first part of the book is addressed to Kant's philosophy. Despite this, I hope it will be clear that my endeavor is not meant primarily to be a contribution to Kant scholarship. My fundamental aim is to use Kant's work to illustrate my points and, in difficult moments, to advance my argument. My debts to other studies of Kant's ethics and philosophy of religion, as well as my differences with others' work, are therefore largely relegated to footnotes. I recognize, of course, that much of my discussion here has the character of an interpretive essay on Kant's ethics and philosophy of religion. While I hope that my treatment of Kant will have some value in its own right, the primary reason why I am led so deeply into Kant's work has to do with the needs of my own systematic argument. Unless Kant is saying what I think he is saying in crucial parts of his writings, my employment of his work for guidance elsewhere does not make sense. But I want to stress that my argument does not rise or fall with the adequacy of my interpretation of Kant. Should that interpretation be unacceptable, my argument would only be less Kantian and more nearly my own.

If the first half of this book is an attempt to penetrate and lay bare the basic and universal structure of reason which underlies religion—what I call "pure religious reason"—the second half is an effort to see whether actual historical religious systems display their adherence to that structure. Use of the name "applied religious reason" to designate this investigation as well as the religious systems which form its object seems appropriate. Here again I am retracing ground charted by Kant in his principal work in this area, *Religion within the Limits of Reason Alone*. Very commonly, this late work of Kant's is considered to be an effort at Christian (or Christian-Deistic) apology: an effort to uphold the rationality of this one religious tradition. While it is partly that, however, it is more fundamentally an effort at applied religious reason with Christianity chosen as the major illustration. My own effort in Part II follows upon and expands this kind of analysis.

In referring to Part II, I must warn the reader not to expect my treatment to serve as a complete introduction to the several traditions examined there, nor even to their ethical teachings. My purpose is not to introduce these traditions or their ethics, but to determine whether a method of understanding religion helps illuminate these traditions in a new way. I especially hope to clarify some of the more difficult aspects of these traditions' beliefs. My enterprise, in other words, is above all an application and test of the method I propose. At the same time, I have purposely avoided assuming a good deal of prior knowledge concerning these traditions on the reader's part. Because my aim is to suggest a way of approaching religion that renders religious belief intelligible, I hope that Part II can be read with profit both by students of religion as well as those seeking for the first time to understand some of the more puzzling aspects of religious belief.

The book, therefore, divides naturally into two parts. Part I develops the structure of pure religious reason. It begins with an analysis of reason in general, prudential reason, and moral reason. The focus throughout is on the concrete question, "Why should I be moral?" in all its nuances and implications. This part culminates on page 109 in the table of the "Requirements of pure religious reason." Part II works forward from this table. The effort is to see whether the major historical religious systems examined there can be understood as conforming to this table of requirements. I should add here that the choice of these traditions and the exclusion of others has no more basic explanation than the limits of my expertise. As a teacher of Jewish and Christian ethics, I obviously feel most comfortable in exploring how these traditions conform to the demands of reason. But, to suggest the universality of the understanding of religion I develop, I feel compelled to illustrate its pertinence to at least some non-Western religious traditions. The religions of India are sufficiently different from the Western faiths to serve this purpose.

The focus on these traditions in Part II does raise several important questions about the term "religious reason" itself. First there is the question of whether reason must always culminate in the kinds of beliefs associated with the historical religious traditions. That is, must reason always become "religious" in the narrow and accepted sense of that term, or could not other kinds of beliefs satisfy reason's demands? The answer to this question, I think, is both yes and no. Yes, in the sense that many kinds of belief systems involving transcendently grounded confidences of the sort—as I shall show—that reason demands could probably serve reason's immediate purposes. The twentieth century offers several examples of political systems able to motivate the most intense moral commitments. Yet, it seems to be the nature of these systems that they either fail after a short time or come to motivate actual violations of morality's commands. In opposition to this, the carefully drawn and tested metaphysical beliefs associated with the recognized "religious" traditions seem less subject over time to this kind of failure or distortion. In labeling the kinds of beliefs demanded by reason "religious," therefore, I avail myself of an accessible term and I suggest that the ordinary meaning of that term is an accurate description of what reason demands.

A second question is whether all those systems commonly designated "religious" can be understood as responses to the requirements of religious reason. Unfortunately, this is a question I cannot entirely answer. What I am prepared to affirm is that each of the traditions looked at here can best be understood as a response to these requirements. I would also extend this claim to include traditions closely related to any of these (for example, Islam). But for the time being, I must leave the determination of whether traditions other than these can best be understood in this way to those more conversant with those traditions. Particularly interesting in this connection are the religions of non-literate cultures whose study by means of rational and moral analysis seems promising but is only very little advanced.[6]

Finally, there is the question of whether this method of approaching even those traditions discussed in Part II really captures what is most essentially "religious" about them. Do the requirements of religious reason, in other words, most fundamentally explain, at least on the plane of human experience, why these religions have come into being? The answer to this question is complicated, as we shall see, by the fact that religious systems characteristically contain many more components than those strictly required by reason. And it is further complicated by the fact that no religion fully complies with all of reason's demands. As a result, it is tempting to see the rational belief aspects of these traditions as somehow secondary to more important or more essentially "religious" activity (cosmogonic speculation or ritual activity, for example). Only careful attention to the complexity of each tradition, I think, can finally resolve this question. If an understanding of religious reason can assist our comprehension of the central aspects of a religious tradition, especially those aspects that most defy other means of analysis, and if it can assist our understanding of the development of a tradition by showing that development to be an effort to improve the religion's response to reason's demands, then we have certainly identified something central to the religious enterprise, and "religious reason" becomes a description not of one aspect of the religious life but of something at its very heart.

I.

Pure religious reason

1.

Why should there be morality?

Religious reason comprises an extensive domain of thought but one which can be entered only by properly asking and answering a single complex question: "Why should I be moral?" If religion is virtually a universal phenomenon, it is perhaps because this is a question that every human being must sometimes confront. Actually, within this larger question there are two separate questions. The first may be phrased in several ways: "Why should there be morality? What is the sense of morality?" or "What reason is there for the institution of morality?" The second major question presumes a satisfactory answer to this first one. It may be phrased, "Given that there is a rational justification for the institution of morality, why should I myself be moral?"

These two major questions must be sharply distinguished, since the first question is rather easily answered while the second has no sure answer at all, and it is here that one finds the source of the deep internal conflict that forces reason to become religious. By ignoring this difference and collapsing one of these questions into the other, many persons have missed the whole problem. Some individuals, for example, have believed that a satisfactory answer to the first question necessitates or implies a satisfactory answer to the second. In their view, once a general rational justification of morality is offered there is no problem in justifying moral obedience on the part of the individual moral agent. For other thinkers, a negative answer to the second question involves a negative answer to the first. If it cannot be shown to an individual why he or she should be moral, then morality itself is without justification. The result is a radical nihilism or relativism, but the net effect is an elimination of reason's internal problem as well.

Only the first of these two major questions is before us in this chapter. What we seek is an acceptable rational justification of the institution or practice of morality. We are not after an explanation of morality, i.e., an account of why it has arisen or why it is a common human phenomenon. Rather, we want to know to the satisfaction of any rational person whether and why morality ought to exist. But in order to face those questions a clarification of terms is first in order. To begin with, we require an understanding of the terms "reason" and "rational" in their various uses, since these terms form the measure of the institutions or practices we will be looking at. Unfortunately, despite their prevalence in our ordinary discourse, these terms resist careful analysis. The best we can do is clarify the leading ways in which they are used. In particular, two different meanings or uses of these terms can be identified. One is the logical use as a measure of judgments, actions, and persons. This, in turn, involves the two sub-standards or requirements of sufficient reason and non-contradiction.[1] For a judgment to be rational in this logical sense, it is necessary for it to proceed from sufficient reasons or grounds of justification potentially acceptable to all persons of at least ordinary intelligence and intellectual capacity. Similarly, it must not contradict other judgments held by all persons of at least ordinary intelligence and intellectual capacity. And these same two criteria are applied, *mutatis mutandis,* to individual actions or to the behavior of persons.

The reference here to the forum of all individuals of ordinary intelligence and intellectual capacity must certainly seem strange, for when we employ the terms "reason" and "rationality" we do not commonly have such a jury in mind. Yet if we consider that judgments about rationality are, for us, necessarily based upon the assent of a community of minds, I think we will not be surprised at this implicit reference in our use of the terms. It should be noted, furthermore, that the reference here is not to some particular community or to a whim of majority rule, but to the unanimous assent of *all* those of at least normal intellectual ability. Whether such assent is ever actually obtainable and whether "normal" can be employed in any meaningful sense are problems that, though important, I will choose to bypass. The intuitive meaning of this standard of reference, I think, is clear enough, or at least as clear as it ever is in our actual use of this reference in judgment.[2]

In addition to this logical significance there is a second use of the terms "reason" and "rationality" that has become common in the social sciences. According to this a judgment (or, by extension, an action or person) is rational if it involves the selection of effective means to given ends or if it conduces to the maximization of a desired series of satisfactions.[3] According to this understanding, reason is purely formal in its activity. It does not determine which desires are to be satisfied or which satisfactions pursued, but on the basis of a given pattern of desires or satisfactions, it selects the optimal means of pursuing them. Actually, this neutrality of reason concerning desires is not absolute. Where a given series of satisfactions are in conflict with one another, reason as an optimizing or maximizing choice process can be employed to select that pattern of ends which will most likely satisfy the choosing agent. But even in such cases, reason establishes the weighting of desires on the basis of the actual or presumed importance of these desires to the choosing agent. In the end, reason authorizes the pursuit of any satisfactions so long as they hold out the objective possibility, overall, of maximizing the sum total of satisfactions enjoyed by the agent. Hume's understanding of reason as "a slave to the passions"[4] perhaps puts the matter too strongly, because reason rules desires in its effort to optimize satisfaction, but despite the exaggeration, Hume is close to expressing the essential aspect of this sense of reason. It should be noted, by the way, that this conception of reason also involves an objective reference, that is, an appeal to the unanimous judgment of the whole community of choosing agents. For a judgment or act to be rational, it must be such as could be seen as maximizing satisfactions not by any one individual, but by all persons of at least ordinary intelligence and intellectual ability. This forum of judgment, it seems, is central to reason in all its senses.

A very difficult question is whether one of these two important senses of reason is more basic than the other. These two senses can obviously be related to one another in various ways. Thus, the satisfaction of a person's desire is itself a sufficient reason for acting and the pursuit of satisfactions presupposes the principle of non-contradiction. But a strong case can also be made that these two logical principles follow from reason's practical and action-oriented maximizing function (clearly, an agent who made contradictory judgments or who acted without sufficient reason could not coherently pursue satisfactions). Whichever is more fundamental, I shall henceforth treat these two as equal and interchangeable expressions of what we mean by reason and rationality. When I say that a judgment or choice is rational, therefore, I mean that it is one that complies with the principles of non-contradiction and sufficient reason and—if some agent's desires are involved—one that conduces to the maximization of these desires. In every case, as well, I shall have in mind the forum of all intelligent persons as the referees of the application of these standards. Thus, when I use such phrases as "reason requires" or "reason demands," the reader should not be puzzled. I am merely making elliptical reference to the judgments or choices made by this community of intelligent beings, using these standards and on the basis of any judgments or choices they have already been presumed to make.

Against this background, the question of whether it is rational for there to be morality takes on new form. It can mean, Is there a sufficient reason for morality to exist? or, what is the same thing, it can mean, Does the institution of morality tend maximally to satisfy the desires of those individuals capable of availing themselves of it? In either of these forms, however, the answer to the question "Is morality rational?" depends upon what we mean by morality. Once again, there are probably many ways in which this term can be understood. But for the moment, to keep matters as simple as possible, I suggest that we think of morality as involving the ordinary rules of behavior generally recognized as moral. By that I mean the rules prohibiting killing other human beings or doing them physical injury, the rule requiring fidelity or the commitment to uphold one's word once it has been given, the rule of non-deception and honesty, and the general, if vague, rule of fairness in one's relations with others. Hand in hand with these I would consider, as part of morality, the recognition that it is permissible or even required to punish those who violate these rules. Such punishments can range from mere expressions of opprobrium to severe legal penalties. Whatever punishment is appropriate in particular cases, however, I take it to be a part of our sense of right and wrong that violations of these moral rules are deserving of some kind of disapproving response.

Now, it seems clear that human existence without these rules would not be pleasant. Whether Hobbes' description of it as a "war of all with all" is correct, life under these circumstances would be without many of the supports to security we normally expect. Thus, taking morality in this sense, and understanding rationality to involve the maximal satisfaction of desire, we arrive at an answer to our question: it is rational for there to be morality. In general, a society with a moral code will better permit its members to satisfy their desires than one without such a code. If one could choose to live in one of the two types of society, the one with a morality would generally represent a rational choice.

To this point my argument has rested on our received understanding of morality. But now I want to go deeper and suggest that our very idea of morality holds it to be a rational phenomenon. Indeed, that idea conceives morality as reason applied to the selection of social rules. The implication is that our original question, "Is morality rational?" or "Should there be morality?" is self-answering because the statement "It is rational for there to be morality" amounts to the statement "It is rational for there to be a rational method of selecting social rules." This does not mean that this particular tautology is uninformative, however. It would be so if any particular rational selection of social rules were defined as morality. But if it can be shown that the ordinarily received rules of morality must result from a strictly rational method of selecting social principles, then a tight logical chain has been forged from our conception of reason to our understanding of morality itself.

One way to perceive this logical relationship between reason and the ordinary moral rules is to imagine a society without a morality of any sort, that is, a society with no general principles recognized as governing conduct and no idea of right and wrong in behavior. Such a society would probably be characterized by persistent conflict, and whatever order prevailed would result only from fleeting coalitions of power and force. Such a society would not be rational in any sense of that term. That is, over any extended period of time the society would not be likely to maximize the satisfactions of its members, since continuing conflict and strife would impede almost every person's pursuit of his or her ends. Indeed, because it is force and power that determine the social arrangement rather than any coherent rational choice of objectives, the society would be excluded from the benefits produced by the productive instrumentality of reason. Finally, in the simplest logical sense this would not be a rational society because its activities would not be governed by reasons, universally acceptable principles, but by the sheer play of force.

Should it occur to the members of this society to set their relations on a rational basis in order to maximize their satisfactions, a course is open to them. They might try to agree jointly to a series of enduring principles to regulate their conduct and to provide a firm basis on which to establish their expectations. They might arbitrarily call these principles the "moral" rules and set about trying to formulate them. But what would be the nature of these rules? Would there be any characteristic they would have in common that would distinguish them from other possible rules that society might come up with? The most general answer to this, I think, is that these particular rules would be of the sort to which all members of the society could freely agree. This idea of unanimous agreement by free consent really follows from the idea of a principled and rational means of social settlement. For if agreement were less than unanimous, then for some members of the society the so-called moral rules would be merely a ratification of the existing power relations of the society, and the same would be true if some members' agreement was secured by coercion. In either case, the rules would not be recognized and acknowledged principles of behavior but a mere expression of the will of the strongest. The very concept of rule by principles, in other words, has within it the idea of free, unanimous consent by all those so ruled. For our imaginary society, therefore, the substitution of reason and rational principles for force requires those principles to be such as can receive the uncoerced assent of all.

Do any such principles exist? Given the differences in interest and the varying degrees of power that characterize most societies the answer is probably no. Thus, if a rule were proposed that really restrained the conduct of certain members of the society, those members would be likely to resist accepting it, however much it was in the interest of the society generally to prohibit that conduct. A rule prohibiting the killing of other human beings, for example, though desirable in the eyes of the vast majority of the society's members, might not be accepted by skilled gunslingers. Alternatively, those rules that could probably be accepted by all would be of an exceedingly trivial nature with little significance for regulating conduct. A rule requiring people to tip their hats to one another in greeting might be an example, although even here acceptance would require that nobody really minded the slight exertion involved. Then again, the sheer unimportance of such a rule might lead more than one member of the society to withhold his or her consent.

Note the curious situation we are led to here. The present state of this society is by no means satisfactory, since it is not rational in any sense. Moreover, through morality (rules facilitating a genuine settlement of conflict and free cooperation) this society could probably arrive at future circumstances far more satisfactory to all. Yet it is not necessarily rational for every member of this society to help bring about this rational social order. That is, if we recall our understanding of rationality as involving the maximal satisfaction of desire, it does not necessarily or clearly maximize the satisfaction of every member's desires to move out of the chaotic status quo. And this is why unanimous consent to significant rules is unattainable. We are, in fact, already touching here on the central problem of this book, a problem that plagues moral reasoning from beginning to end, and which we might tentatively call the conflict between particular and general rationality. For while it is generally rational for there to be a principled method of social settlement, it is not necessarily rational for every particular member to sacrifice in order to bring that method about.

Is there a way out of this dilemma? Can such a society ever arrive at significant rules that receive everyone's consent? We should observe that reason, in its most general survey of the situation, requires a solution, since the existing society cannot receive rational approval (cannot be approved of by the whole community of rational agents). In its very anarchy, this society is antithetical to the idea of reason, and reason naturally demands some way out of the problem. One possible solution is offered by John Rawls in his work, *A Theory of Justice.* To understand what Rawls proposes, we should return to the case of the anarchic society we have been looking at and imagine that all of its members have been gathered together into a vast conference hall which Rawls calls the "original position."[5] Once within this hall, each member of the society is informed of the conditions that will govern the selection of principles. Each member will have a single vote, and agreement on any principle will have to be unanimous. We already know the reasons for these conditions, of course, and the problems they create. Just before voting begins, however, a special procedure is employed. Each participant in the conference is made to pass behind what Rawls calls a "veil of ignorance."[6] This fictive and imaginary device has the effect of depriving each participant of the knowledge of all those particular features of his situation which distinguish him from the other participants at the conference. Each is prevented, for example, from knowing his sex, race, physical strength, or intellectual capacity. Each is also prevented from knowing the special circumstances of his birth, whether he was born into favorable or unfavorable social circumstances. And finally, each is prevented from knowing the special ends or values he wishes to pursue, what Rawls calls, his special "plan of the good."

As a result of this procedure each participant is rendered effectively identical to every other. Though participants may be permitted to know that certain differences exist in their society between persons, they are not allowed to know what is the likelihood of their being one kind of person rather than another. As a result, each participant is rendered radically impartial before the array of conditions and objectives that had heretofore distanced one person from the other. Now it may seem that under these peculiar circumstances it has become impossible for any participant to select satisfactory social principles. After all, if a person is prevented from knowing which special ends or needs are his, how is he to make a rational choice to maximize his satisfactions at all?

As formidable as it seems this problem is not really a decisive obstacle to social choice in this situation. For it must be remembered that each participant does retain all knowledge of those non-particular ends that are his. Thus, each person knows that he is a human being with all of the ends and needs associated with this condition—the need to be free from physical injury, to have a minimum of material goods to sustain life, and the need, on occasion, to secure the cooperation of his fellow human beings. Also, though one does not know what his ends are, he knows that he does in fact have objectives of some sort and that he desires a maximum liberty eventually to do what he wants to do (whatever that may be). Thus, despite the limitation on particular knowledge, it becomes possible for the conference participants to select principles that are maximally to their advantage in the condition in which they find themselves. These principles take the form of general rules governing behavior. They include a prohibition on killing or inflicting physical injury on other persons; a rule prohibiting various forms of deception and dishonesty; a rule of fidelity requiring the upholding of agreements into which one has freely entered; and a rule of fairness requiring one to do one's part in the maintenance of mutually beneficial cooperative arrangements. In other words, the choice process eventuates in agreement on the very rules of received morality I mentioned before. It is not necessary here to spell out the strict link between these specific rules and choice under the circumstances I have described. That has been done by others in far greater detail than I can allow myself.[7] Nevertheless, it should be reasonably clear why rules of this sort, and only rules of this sort, could emerge from the choice situation of the original position.

It might be objected at this point that it has still not been shown that the possibility of unanimous free agreement on social principles can be realized. For while it is certainly true that such agreement would be possible behind the veil of ignorance, there is no reason to believe that disputing members of a society would ever agree to this particular constraint on their ability to choose. After all, if they refused to relinquish their special ends and advantages in the first place, why should they go behind the veil of ignorance, which has the same effect upon their interests? The answer to this is that they probably would not do so. For the veil of ignorance is just a device for eliminating the particular interests we could not originally overcome, and we should not be surprised that resistance should finally crystallize against this device itself.[8]

Still, the idea of the veil of ignorance and the strict impartiality in the choice of social principles that it implies is very important. In fact, we can now see that such an idea is logically and necessarily related to the task of securing universally acceptable social rules, or what is the same thing, the rules of morality. Without this impartiality, the unanimous agreement on social rules which reason requires could not be secured, and without these social rules, there would be no strictly rational ordering of social disputes. Thus, a logical relationship exists between the succession of ideas we have looked at: reason requires the free acceptance of principles by all participants in the social order; free unanimous consent requires the imposition of strict impartiality (of the sort made possible by the veil of ignorance) on the choosing agents; and choice under such circumstances leads logically to the selection of principles corresponding to the most basic rules of received morality. Graphically expressed, this series of connections looks something like this:

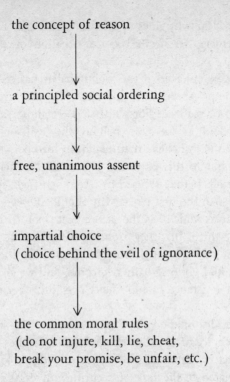

the concept of reason

↓

a principled social ordering

↓

free, unanimous assent

↓

impartial choice
(choice behind the veil of ignorance)

↓

the common moral rules
(do not injure, kill, lie, cheat,
break your promise, be unfair, etc.)

We can see now why the question "Is it rational for there to be morality?" is self-answering. But we can also see just how complex the concept of morality really is and what steps are required to arrive at the moral rules we so take for granted.

None of this, of course, helps us with our problem of whether members of our imaginary society would ever agree to moral principles or to the constraints that the choice of these principles requires. That problem, once again, arises from the fact that what is generally rational is not always necessarily rational for every individual in every particular circumstance. Though we can certainly describe the overall situation of our anarchic society as irrational, in other words, we cannot decisively say that each member of that society is being irrational (is minimizing his satisfactions) in refusing to agree on principles

or the constraints necessary to generate them. This disparity between what is generally rational and what is rational for particular individuals not only animates this book but is the basic reason why few, if any, societies ever achieve their higher states of
harmony and cooperation merely by free agreement on the part
of their members. Generally, such harmonies are imposed from
above by a will or wills for whom harmony is advantageous, or
from without by the threat of domination. Occasionally, such
harmonies do come about when events produce transient states of
equality in power and ability between members of the society,
and it is then that the model of free consent is most nearly
approximated.

The resistance to general rational organization on the part
of individuals also illuminates the truth and the falsity of the
idea of an historical social contract as the basis of any real social
order. This idea is false because, given the perpetual differences
in power between individuals, it is unlikely that any society was
ever constituted in this way. But it contains an element of truth
in recognizing that any society which considers itself moral or
just must be constituted in this way, on the basis of the free consent of all its members. Rawls himself makes this point when he
insists that the original position in his contract theory must not
be thought of as some actual historical event but as a test or
standard against which all actual political constitutions can be
measured.[9] At the same time, by clearly expressing this understanding, contract theory today has lost something that has long
been of political and moral importance. To understand this, one
must recall that contract theory has traditionally been a theory
not only of how social principles came into being but of moral
obligation as well. The implicit idea is that I should obey the
rules of my society because I have consented to do so, have obligated myself, by freely entering into some compact in the past.
This idea is filled with problems—how, for example, can I be
held responsible for my ancestors' commitments?—and Hume
did the whole idea in when he asked, What is the source of the

presumed obligation to uphold contracts on which the theory of obligation rests? He rightly observed that this obligation could not itself be the result of a contract, since then one would be involved in an infinite regress. Rather, the idea of obligation had to rest on some idea of reason itself, which, for Hume, was the principle of utility.[10] Rawls assumes this criticism when he stresses that our obligation to valid moral principles derives from reason, although not the kind of rational considerations that moved the utilitarians. But although this view is certainly correct, it throws into high relief the very problem that the older contract theory (in the cunning of ignorance) sought to efface: that it is not always rational for an individual to do what reason generally requires. Thus contemporary contract theory, and for that matter all contemporary rational ethical theory, has had the effect of exposing both the logic and grave difficulties that underlie moral reason itself.

Putting this problem aside for the moment, we have seen that reason and morality are logically related to one another. Morality may be thought of as one of two basic ways of ordering social disputes. One way relies upon the play of force and is the antithesis of reason. The other way relies on principles to which all could agree. It generates those principles by the single method of impartial rational choice, and the principles themselves are the basic ones of ordinary morality with which we are familiar. These ideas are not terribly new, although recent ethical theory has served to bring them out more clearly. The essential ideas have long been intuitively recognized by many people. The utilitarian tradition relied upon similar conceptions, despite the fact that the utilitarians were confused about just how reason arrives at principles. And in a very precise way Kant was able to draw the link between reason and morality almost two centuries ago. Indeed, since my subsequent argument throughout Part I of this book draws heavily on Kant, I want to spend some time comparing Kant's understanding of morality with the one I have just set forth.

Explaining Kant's ethics is no easy task, and the job is made harder by Kant's own dense philosophical style. His tendency to alternate passages of lucid clarity with others that are almost incomprehensible has given rise to many misunderstandings of his position, most of them frequently repeated by students in introductory philosophy courses. Still, I think the major lines of Kant's view are so fundamentally sound that if his thought is once opened up by getting past the more difficult initial obstacles, his entire position becomes remarkably clear. By simply rectifying any of the more common misapprehensions of his position, for example, one is led to perceive the essential coherence of his thinking. Thus, there is the matter of Kant's presumed antagonism to happiness and to basing ethics on considerations of happiness. As Kant insists again and again in the opening pages of his major writings on ethics, happiness cannot be the fundamental aim of the moral life. Happiness for myself, for others, or even for all, is not, he says, a morally acceptable object of pursuit, nor for that matter are any of the other common values that human beings pursue, from the most base of pleasures to the noblest love. This rejection of a host of values as morally acceptable ends culminates in his well-known statement that the only unqualifiedly good thing is the morally good will.[11]

Kant's repudiation of values has always lent a priggish or puritanical cast to his ethics and it has reinforced the common interpretation that his moral thinking primarily reflects a Prussian or narrowly sectarian background. This impression is further strengthened by Kant's opposition to allowing happiness or any other commonly pursued values to serve as the "determining ground" or primary motivating consideration for the moral life. If I ask why I should do something, says Kant, it is not satisfactory to reply "Because it will make some persons—or even very many persons—happy." The only morally permissible consideration is whether duty requires that I do it. For Kant, the voice of duty is stern and takes precedence over the pursuit of any other values.

In view of this unremitting attack on the values people normally pursue and consider worthwhile, it is important to ask what is going on here. Is Kant really the tight-lipped ascetic that many commentators have made him out to be? Does he really believe that happiness has no place whatever in human life or in the realm of ethics? The answer to these questions, I think, is no. In particular, Kant is not unaware of the importance of happiness. Thus, he defines man—and all similar finite living beings—as a "being of needs" whose very existence is bound up with bringing into reality the objects of his desires.[12] He further defines happiness as the state where all desires are satisfied, or as he puts it more colorfully, the state of a being in which everything goes according to its "wish and will."[13] Thus, in Kant's understanding, man's very nature inclines him toward the pursuit of happiness. But even beyond this matter of definition, a strong case can be made that a fundamental purpose of reason for Kant is to facilitate the happiness of rational agents. Kant himself distinguishes between two different senses or employments of reason. One, the theoretical, aims at knowledge of the world, at organizing experience into lawful, predictable regularities. The other employment, the practical, seeks to utilize this knowledge in order to satisfy the desires of the rational agent. Indeed, the will—that faculty which acts on desires—is sometimes equated by Kant with practical reason.[14] Thus, there are substantial grounds for holding that Kant believed that a goal of the whole cognitive and rational process is the realization of objects or states desired by rational agents, or what is the same thing, happiness.[15]

Why then is happiness, if everyone desires it, not unqualifiedly good or, even more strongly, the only thing that is unqualifiedly good and worthy of moral recognition? The answer, it seems, is that while everyone agrees that happiness is good, almost no one agrees on what the content of happiness is.[16] John wants Martin's wealth and Martin covets John's wife, and they are not prepared freely to exchange. Each has the same end: hap-

piness. But beyond this misleading generality their goals are radically different, and the state of things, if each were to achieve
his ends, would be quite different. If John were to succeed, we
would see a wealthy John with his wife and an impoverished
Martin. If Martin were to succeed, John would be without wife
or wealth and Martin would possess both. The generality that
everyone wants to be happy should not obscure the fact, therefore, that everyone really wants quite different things.[17] To put
this another way, happiness is not good without qualification.
Each state of happiness is not good in itself or good without
question but must be followed by the qualifying explanation of
for whom it is good. It is a mere extension of this to say that no
particular valued object or state, however much it is cherished
by some or many persons, is unqualifiedly or universally good.
Diamonds are good, but only for those who happen to like
diamonds.

The essential heterogeneity of desires explains why, in the
search for a basis for morality, or for what Kant calls a supreme
"determining ground" for every person's will, happiness will
not do. For if every agent were to pursue happiness, people's
pursuits would be constantly at odds with one another. Just as
John's pursuit of happiness must conflict with Martin's, so would
all persons' efforts to secure values of interest to them or their
group end up in a state of continuing contradiction. With private
or particular ends as the supreme determining ground of each
person's will, moreover, no one's pursuit of ends would be secure
and a harmonious satisfaction of desires would be ruled out from
the beginning. We see here, in other words, that Kant's uneasi-
ness with happiness or any other particular value as the supreme
end of morality is related to the idea I suggested earlier of morality as a non-coercive method of settling social disputes employing
principles capable of eliciting the free consent of all. This idea of
universal consent is contained in his claim that any morally worthy
end or any morally worthy motivation must be good without qualification, good not for this or that rational agent but good for all

rational agents. It is also suggested by his insistence that moral imperatives are not hypothetical but categorical. That is, they do not derive from the assumed wishes of any particular agent ("If you like diamonds, then . . .") but are predicable of any moral agent whatsoever.[18] Only universal acceptance, we know, can guarantee a principled settlement of conflict, and it is this objective that Kant clearly has in mind.

But if Kant will not accept happiness or any other particular value as the supreme determining ground of a moral agent's will, what will he accept? The answer, we have seen, is duty, which Kant gives a more precise expression as the willingness to submit all of one's volitions and actions to the rule of the categorical imperative. This latter rule receives several different formulations in Kant's writings, but the most representative and important for our immediate understanding of his position is the one found in the *Critique of Practical Reason:* "So act that the maxim of your will could always hold at the same time as a principle establishing universal law."[19] To understand Kant's position, therefore, is to know why this special rule should usurp the place of all other guides to conduct, or why it should take precedence over the pursuit of widely cherished values.

The answer to this question is as simple as it is surprising: the categorical imperative is the only end that all persons could freely accept, and therefore the only adequate moral ground for conduct, because it amounts to nothing more than the requirement that all objectives and behavior be capable of receiving universal assent. It is, in other words, a purely formal principle stipulating that condition which any policies or actions must meet if they are to be identified as moral. In itself the principle identifies no end as moral. It merely lays down as a supreme condition the conformity to morality itself.

It may be objected here that while it is interesting, this interpretation appears to have nothing to do with what Kant himself says. After all, though Kant's formulation of the categorical imperative does speak about maxims (individual policies for willing and behaving), he says nothing at all about these maxims being required to elicit the free consent of all persons. What the categorical imperative merely seems to require is that anything I will to do (my maxim) be capable of becoming a universal law. But is this not just an expression of the logical rule that I be consistent and not will for myself what I refuse at the same time for others? How does consent enter into this? I do not seem to require anyone else's approval if I am prepared to raise my volition to the level of a universal practice. Thus, if I wish to lie or cheat or steal, all that the categorical imperative seems to demand is my own willingness to have others do the same with respect to me.

This is certainly a common interpretation of Kant on this point, and for many who have read him in this way it has been a grounds for rejecting his position. Not that these individuals have disagreed with the importance of consistency in ethics or any other activity. But they have denied that consistency is a sufficient condition for the production of morally acceptable rules. After all, they point out, any principle or policy can be both logically and volitionally universalized. There are liars, cheats, or killers who might be more than willing to have their volitions elevated to the level of universal law.[20] True, some have tried to defend this kind of universalizing position by claiming that consistency does impose a real restraint on behavior, presumably because persons with particularly pernicious volitions would not be prepared to act upon them if others could do the same.[21] Nevertheless, these arguments have always failed to be absolutely convincing, since exceptional cases are easily identified.

Whether favorable or unfavorable to Kant, however, these interpretations, I believe, tend to miss his essential point by reducing it to a simple demand for consistency in volition. For the best that demand could produce in Kantian terms is uniformity of behavior, not a law. But it is a law that the categorical imperative requires a maxim to be capable of becoming. And law for Kant is always a rule of behavior constituted by reason and, as such, valid for and accepted by every rational being.[22] This is true of natural laws for which, according to Kant's epistemology, reason has the job of organizing the raw data furnished by experience, but it is doubly true where the behavior of rational beings is concerned. Since their behavior is never a brute fact but is free (capable of being abstained from), that behavior is exposed to the censorship of reason even before volition becomes action. In other words, reason does not have to accept any patterned behavior of rational agents as given, but can ask before action is manifested whether it ought to be. This question, in turn, amounts to asking whether the whole community of rational agents can long tolerate and accept a particular uniform pattern of behavior in their midst. Thus, the regularities created by human beings are always regularities that presume universal consent. For a volition to become law it is not enough for one individual to be prepared to universalize his course of action. That course must itself be of the sort that could be freely accepted and approved by every other rational agent. It must be such that they could tolerate as a regular occurrence among themselves, a natural law, as it were, which they have created.[23]

If further support for this interpretation of Kant were needed, it could easily be found in the constant motifs of social contract theory present in his thought, which reflect his deep debt to Rousseau. Nowhere is this clearer than in the formulation of the categorical imperative in the *Foundations of the Metaphysics of Morals,* which defines that imperative as the law for a "realm of ends."[24] Kant understands this realm as a community where every member's ends are mutually respected and where no person's will is arbitrarily subordinated to another's. In this kingdom, each person is an "end in himself," not in the sense that all his desires are always respected (that is impossible) but in the sense that each person has a final say in the moral legislative process. Since Kant offers this formulation as equivalent to the other formulations of the categorical imperative, there is substantial reason for maintaining that uncoerced, universal assent to policies is the key feature of his total moral view.

I might also point out here that this interpretation is supported by that formulation of the categorical imperative which defines rational nature as "an end in itself."[25] We have seen that the selection of universally acceptable principles requires the choosing agents to be rendered radically impartial by being stripped of their particular self-knowledge and reduced to their generic or common nature. Kant's conception of rational nature as "an end in itself," I would argue, expresses this idea by identifying the one generic nature we share with all other possible members of a moral community. In promoting ends of such a generic nature we necessarily reach a point of agreement with all other similar moral agents. I realize that the categorical imperative has often been interpreted differently than this. But it is no small support of an interpretation of Kant, I think, that it helps bring some order to the diversity of formulations he gives to ethics' most important principle.

According to this interpretation, the categorical imperative remains a purely formal principle. In itself it does not stipulate whether any particular kind of behavior is morally acceptable, nor does it single out any end as morally worthwhile (except the willingness to obey its dictates). Presumably, any behavior or values drawn from the realm of human experience are suitable candidates for moral approval if they can pass the imperative's test. We see, therefore, that nothing could be more mistaken than to interpret Kant as being opposed to the pursuit of concrete values and objectives or the various forms of happiness which human beings cherish. These are the very stuff of moral experience.[26] If he is opposed to these, it is only when they are offered as morally right instead of being seen as the raw material which, instance by instance, must pass before the bar of impartial reason.

Kant's thinking thus expresses all of the important awarenesses we developed earlier: the need for universal assent if conflict is to be eliminated; the importance of impartial rational choice; and the priority given to the dictates of impartial reason. At times, it is true, Kant is rather sparing in his explanation of important details in his position, and there may be moments when he is positively confused in trying to illustrate his points.[27] Yet the essential simplicity of Kant's position is striking, and is perhaps its greatest strength. Above all, Kant would insist that morality is a direct expression of reason. As the categorical imperative in its most basic formulation makes clear, morality is the rule of non-contradiction applied to the exercise of wills. As a result, Kant's claim that the categorical imperative is known a priori because it derives from reason is not an empty one. The purpose of this chapter, to press home the rationality of morality, is thus reinforced by an understanding of Kant.

Before concluding, one point I have just made must be repeated and underlined. This is the fact that Kant is not opposed to happiness. It is the great virtue of his position to have emphasized that reason must finally organize the pursuit of satisfactions even to the point where, from an impartial standpoint, it may require certain desires not to be acted upon. Kant's understanding of this leads us, in fact, to the brink of the problem that will occupy us in the chapters immediately ahead: the problem that reason, in order to facilitate happiness, must occasionally suppress happiness. This is true not only for the choice of those rules that bear on social relations (the moral rules in their most precise sense), but also for rules of individual prudential choice. Thus my own happiness as a rational agent, prudence's aim, sometimes requires that I suppress the pursuit of particular satisfactions because reason dictates that pursuit cannot cohere with other, more important objectives I may have. However tempting the invitation to a party may be, for example, I must turn it down if going to the party interferes with other aims and satisfactions I value: in this case perhaps passing an examination important to my career.

In most respects, therefore, moral and prudential reason are similar and the suppression of satisfactions is involved in both. But there is one important difference between these two distinct employments of reason. In the case of prudential choice, reason only suppresses one or several of my desires in the name of a greater total satisfaction of all my desires—my happiness. But in the case of moral choice, what is sometimes suppressed is my happiness itself. Where impartiality before my own desires can lead me to subordinate some of them, impartiality before the social array of desires can cause all or most of my desires—and the most important among them—to be suppressed. We shall look at all the implications of this difference between prudential and moral reason later. But for now it is enough to observe that this difference is not unimportant. It is, in fact, the difference that propels reason beyond morality into religion.

2.

Why should I be moral?

For many persons proof of the general rationality of morality may provide an adequate answer to their question, "Why should I be moral?" These are individuals who respect morality but who are troubled by the suspicion that they may be dupes. They are aware of the corrosive attacks by social critics who hold received morality to be an instrument of group interest or class domination. And they want to know whether morality really can be justified. Once shown this they are presumably content. But there is another sort of person—perhaps the same one thinking a bit deeper—who may not be satisfied by this justification. This is the person not willing to lend support to anything unless perfectly adequate reasons have been given for doing so. He may accept the argument that, in general, morality is rational, but he wants to know whether it is always rational for *him* to be moral. Put differently, this individual wants to know whether it is always rational for him to support an institution that it is generally rational to want. He is aware of the impartial reasoning that leads to the moral rules and wishes to know whether it is always in his interest to regard matters in this way. His question is

"Why should I be moral?" in the sharpest and most personal sense.

It seems that proofs of the general rationality of morality render this type of questioning even more pressing. So long as morality is not seen to be an expression of human rationality, there may be all sorts of reasons why human beings would find it rational to obey its commands. Thus where it is believed that morality is instituted by a powerful God for his pleasure and derives its force exclusively from his will, the question "Why should I be moral?" has a rationally defensible answer: "Because if you are not moral God will punish you." Or, where it is believed that morality derives from some original contract which we or our representatives actually entered into, the question may also find a ready answer: "Because you have so obligated yourself." This answer, as I observed earlier, only displaces the question since it can be asked "Why should I do what I have obligated myself to do?" But that does not alter the fact that in the absence of careful scrutiny, historical contract answers have often served to ground moral and political obligation. We can see, therefore, that the general rational justification of morality only serves to sharpen the question of personal moral obligation. To show that morality generally most satisfies the desires of rational beings, and indeed that that is the very purpose of morality, only serves to render more pointed the question "Does moral obedience really satisfy my desires?" or "Is what is generally rational always rational for me?"[1]

In isolating this question, we must be clear about what is being asked. For unless the question is put as sharply as possible, the difficult task before those who would seek to answer it is not fully appreciated. At the close of the preceding chapter I indicated that morality by its very nature must sometimes require rational individuals to suppress the satisfaction of their own desires, to interfere with their happiness. Thus, an individual may sometimes have to forego certain satisfactions to comply with moral obligations, as when a promise must be kept despite my inclination not to do so. In many cases such brief suppressions of satisfaction pose no particular problem. In this case I might reason, for example, that promise-keeping is generally useful, so that my temporary sacrifice will be amply compensated for by others' keeping the promises they have made to me. But there are other, very real cases where morality's suppression of an individual's satisfactions can be virtually complete and can make it impossible for the individual to be happy at all. To illustrate what I mean let me offer the following rather strongly drawn case. Only after presenting the problem in this extreme instance will I try to indicate how really prevalent the problem can be.

Imagine a small, democratic nation engaged in a war against a cruel and aggressive tyranny. All the citizens of the defending nation know that if they lose the war they will not only sacrifice their normal freedoms but for at least a time will be exposed to systematic programs of torture and extermination. Based on the past behavior of this tyrannical neighbor-state, it is estimated that up to 20 per cent of the defending nation's population may lose their lives in the persecutions to follow. Imagine further that successful defense of the nation rests, finally, on the retention of a vital bridgehead, which depends, in turn, upon the willingness of a handful of soldiers placed there by the random play of events to fight to the death if necessary. Now, assuming the defensive efforts of this nation to be morally just, the question "Why should I be moral?" in this context becomes "Why should I, if I become one of the defenders at that bridgehead, do my duty?"

Let me explain this example a bit further. In the preceding chapter we saw that the principles of morality arise from the free, unanimous agreement of impartial rational agents. Normally, this community of impartial agents is universal in that it includes all those beings capable of a moral settlement of disputes (since if any such beings were excluded, a rational procedure for ordering our relations with them would be lost). But in matters that concern only a specific community, and that do not infringe upon the universal rights of its members or their obligations to others, moral settlement need involve only the members of that community itself. Thus in the case before us, the rules of conduct among citizens in the war represent moral rules generally, and they can be thought of as being decided upon freely and unanimously in a legislative process prior to the conflict. Of course the citizens need not seek to establish such rules. They can forego morality and declare that when the war begins every man can look out for his own interests. But such anarchy is not generally rational, since it probably ensures the worst outcome for everyone. Thus it is generally rational to adopt rules on the basis of free, unanimous consent.

In the case before us the rules are likely to be numerous. But some among them would certainly cover bridgehead-type situations of the sort I have described. Assuming such situations to arise, and assuming the burden to be randomly distributed (impartiality probably prevents any other distribution of the burden), the question is What rule should govern the conduct of those who find themselves in situations of this sort, those who, as it were, have become losers in fate's lottery? The presumption here is that as the community collectively decides, each individual will feel obligated to act. Free obedience to whatever rules are decided upon, of course, is in everyone's interest. Now, one possible rule is that in such situations each combatant may act as he pleases and flee if he feels his life to be endangered. But clearly that is not a rational rule for impartial persons in the legislative process. So long as they do not yet know who will have to shoulder the burden, this rule is in fact irrational, and this can be shown mathematically. If we assume, for example, that the maximal chance of being a bridgehead soldier is one in one thousand, then this represents the worst possible risk each impartial legislator runs if he requires the soldiers to hold fast. But if the soldiers are permitted to flee, then each deliberator's risk (in view of the mass exterminations to follow) may rise to one in five or more. Taking rationality to require choice that maximizes the expected or likely sum of satisfactions, therefore, these legislators have no rational alternative in this case but to insist upon strict obedience.

We may imagine that every citizen goes forth to war understanding this rule and resolved to respect it. What happens now when any one individual finds himself, gun in hand, a part of that small contingent at the bridgehead facing a formidable foe? Each member of that contingent has lost in the lottery of fate. And the question "Why should I be moral?" becomes for each of these soldiers, "Why should I now uphold the rule that was rational for me while I was still an impartial legislator?" To point up the force of this question, we should observe that the conclusions of a rational calculation from this point of view are easily the reverse of those made in the impartial standpoint. If a soldier now stands fast he knows that the chances of his survival to pursue his happiness are very low, possibly nil. On the other hand, if that soldier runs, he stands a good chance of being in the fortunate majority who will survive the rigors of the period of domination ahead. Thus, where obedience to duty gives him almost no chance of happiness, disobedience may raise his prospects to nearly 80 per cent. Rational calculation naturally favors flight. As a result, when the question "Why should I be moral?" is asked by our soldier, it is with the profound awareness that he is seeking reasons for doing what, from his personal vantage point, it is actually irrational to do.

In attempting to answer this question, we can begin by observing that there are probably many answers to this question that the soldier can give himself, but which will not be fully satisfactory either to himself or to those who depend upon him. That is, they are answers which will, on occasion, lead him to do what, impartially considered, he ought not to do. For one thing, he can conclude that he will be punished if he fails to do his duty. But the effectiveness of this answer depends entirely upon the adequacy of the punitive machinery that has been set up. It certainly cannot always provide an acceptable answer for those who find themselves in his situation, and, more importantly, from the point of view of the impartial legislators, it is an answer that eliminates the whole idea of moral obligation. If this is to be the reason why people do what it is generally rational to want them to do, then why even insist that people be morally obligated in the first place? If each individual's ground of obedience to the moral rules is fear of punishment, then every collective rule freely agreed to by the community of impartial persons would require complete coercive support. In the process the whole idea of social cooperation based upon freely accepted principles would vanish to be replaced by rule by coalitions of power.

Similarly unacceptable both to the soldier and his impartial compatriots is an answer based upon particular interests he might possess. For example, one reason for the soldier's standing fast might be his concern for his wife and children behind the front lines. As a normal, loving father he might be prepared to sacrifice his life in order to ensure the survival of those he loves (this being a very important part of his happiness). The problem with this kind of answer—at least from the point of view of his countrymen—is that national survival would depend upon the marital status and family feeling of those at the front lines. Only those soldiers with families might be expected to hold fast. More troubling, just as this answer will not give every soldier a reason to fight, it will not always give even those soldiers with families a reason to fight. For consider: a soldier at the bridgehead may well decide that his loved ones' best interests are served by his living on to protect them. He may even conclude that his family concerns take priority over his objective moral obligation. The point is that particular reasons for being moral can as easily become reasons for being immoral, since the correlation between morality and these reasons is only contingent and transitory.

As a result, those in the position of this soldier cannot be satisfied with answers of this sort. Neither can the moral community that relies upon them. What both they and this community want is something that will surely eliminate the conflict between what impartial and prudential reason command. What they want is a reason or reasons that will lead those who find themselves in such circumstances always to do what morality requires. There is, of course, one answer that meets this demand, but it proves unsatisfactory in several different ways. This answer bases moral obedience on a love for the whole community of moral agents. Thus, in this case, if a soldier cared deeply for the welfare of all the members of his community, he might find his own happiness served by obeying their moral requirements. Nevertheless, to be a fully satisfactory reason for being moral, there are several things this answer may not be. It may not simply be a form of patriotism, since love of country (love of its history, geography, ideals, or most of its citizens) can frequently interfere with a genuine moral respect for persons either within or without the nation's boundaries. And it may not be a love for persons that hinders obedience to what morality requires.[2] For example, if defense of the bridgehead requires a soldier to sacrifice the lives of several of his fellow combatants, his concern for these countrymen must not interfere with his performance of his duty. Put differently, his regard for his fellow citizens must not be a concern for specific flesh and blood persons, but for their wills as impartial agents. In fact, it must be a love of morality itself. As such, this love can be a fully adequate reason for being moral, but to hold it an individual would have to be prepared to place this rather odd attachment to the impartial will of all above any real attachments he might have to persons. To suggest this as an answer to the question "Why should I be moral?" therefore, is really to raise anew the question of why any real, rational person should set the will of impartial agents, morality, above all the other ends he may have.

In just a moment I want to look rather searchingly at the point of view of those who hold that the whole question we are raising here is nonsense and cannot even seriously be asked. But before doing that, we might consider the objection that the problem, whether real or not, is unimportant since the case that illustrates it is rare. Certainly, it may be argued, the question "Why should I be moral?" can be a very pressing one for those stationed at bridgeheads or caught in overloaded lifeboats on high seas. But do cases like this really illustrate a deep and persistent problem of the moral life? Is this really a serious problem that confronts and disturbs each of us in our day-to-day existence as moral agents?

Without denying that the preoccupations of daily life muffle this problem or that the conventional institutions of society (law, the pressure of public opinion) remove the stark choice between moral obedience and self-interest for most individuals, I want to suggest that this is a problem that really assaults us, whether gently or abruptly, at every turn of the moral life. Indeed, our case of the soldier only vividly points up the circumstances that must obtain for any individual to be propelled to ask "Why should I be moral?" in a serious way. Simply put, the gains to the individual in refusing to obey what morality requires must be great relative to the losses he risks in refusing to obey. In our soldier's case, these circumstances clearly obtain. By fleeing he saves his life, and though that flight causes enormous evils, they are tolerable for the soldier in view of the alternative. But we do not have to construct bridgehead situations to find similar circumstances. They obtain in many situations that conduce to marital infidelity, for example, and they are especially prevalent in business or political life. In all these instances, individuals may find certain morally impermissible acts (sexual cheating, dishonesty, or taking bribes) to be enormously profitable to them in terms of satisfactions, while the evils they risk, usually because of the ease of concealment, are slight. Those who perform acts of this sort may freely concede them to be wrong. (I do not deny, by the way, that many adulterers or politicians who take graft think that what they do is, all things considered, right. But I am not speaking about them.) Nevertheless, in such circumstances rational individuals commonly find it very hard to uphold standards that they concede to be morally valid. Indeed, it is a partial indication of how difficult it is to answer the question "Why should I be moral?" that sexual infidelity or graft sometimes attract the best of persons.[3] Thus, our bridgehead situation does not distort our understanding of the moral life but merely puts into relief a problem that is everywhere present.

Granted the importance of this question, there are some who think that to ask it is nonsense, that the question itself rests upon a faulty understanding of the very concepts it employs. John Hospers, for example, has observed that asking the question "Why should I be moral?" involves seeking reasons for acting. These reasons, says Hospers, can only be of two sorts: prudential reasons or moral reasons, "Why is it good for me?" or "Why is it morally good?" But interpreting the question in either one of these two ways must lead to absurdity. Thus, if moral reasons are sought for doing what is morally required, the questioner is involved in asking why he should morally do what he should morally do, and this is clearly nonsense. On the other hand, if prudential reasons are sought for always doing what is morally right, then the questioner is asking for something that cannot possibly be given. For it is the very nature of morality that it must occasionally frustrate prudence, that is, that on occasion it must subordinate the individual's pursuit of happiness and sometimes that it must do so completely. Thus, when an individual asks for prudential reasons for performing a particular disadvantageous moral act, he is in effect asking why it is in his interest to do what it is not in his interest to do. And in asking the question, Hospers concludes, this individual shows that he does not understand what morality is all about.[4]

Hospers' argument has the virtue of pointing up the fact that reason has two essentially distinct employments: the prudential (or deliberative) and the moral. It is the same reason, to be sure, but exercising itself in different vantage points. His view also has the value of underscoring the fact that one must choose which of these vantage points or employments of reason one is going to resort to in choosing to act. But, Hospers' position serves not to eliminate so much as to point up the problem facing the individual in difficult moments of moral choice. What this individual wants to know, and what we see his question now amounts to, is which of these two employments of reason furnishes decisive grounds for acting? If prudential and moral reason cannot be made to speak with the same voice, which voice ought one to listen to? Which reasons are best?

Another student of this problem, however, has declared even this question to be nonsense. For Kurt Baier, the question of whether prudence or morality furnishes better reasons for acting is not nonsensical, as it is for Hospers, because there is no way of settling it, but because the question answers itself.[5] It is the nature of morality, says Baier, that it provides the best reasons for acting. In an argument very similar to the one I set forth in the preceding chapter, Baier points out that morality is a means of adjudicating conflict between differing wills. As a result, whatever reasons individuals have for acting, moral reasons must always be judged as superior and controlling. If this were not so, Baier observes, there would be no such thing as morality and chaos would reign. Thus, the question "Why should I be moral?" is nonsense because it amounts to asking for the best reasons for acting on the best reasons. In the conflict between prudential and moral reason, to ask this question merely indicates that one has not fully understood the nature of morality.

Baier's viewpoint is initially persuasive, especially since it has the whole force of our concept of morality behind it. That, however, is just its problem. There is no question that moral reasons are superior to prudential reasons. But why are they so? Because it is generally and impartially in our interest that they assume this priority. That is, it is our very reason in its general and impartial employment—the same reason of which morality is an expression—that establishes this priority. But when an individual whose happiness is seriously jeopardized by moral obedience asks the question "Why should I be moral?" he is precisely involved in asking why he should act as he would impartially and generally recommend that anyone act. Put differently, he is asking why in this instance he should be rational in this general sense. And to tell him that if he were impartial he would recommend doing so is really to ignore his question.

I can put this in a different and more complicated way by saying that in this particular case of decisional conflict, our usual procedure of deliberation by impartial reason radically breaks down. If we think of reason in its maximizing function, we can see that it implies a movement beyond the desires of the moment or even the subjective evaluations of the individual. A person pulled by differing and contradictory desires who stops to reason and who asks the rational question, "What should I do?" in a prudential sense is clearly calling upon the larger community of impartial, rational agents for assistance. This is that community of all persons of at least ordinary intelligence and mental ability we earlier saw to be a part of our very concept of reason. From these other rational beings this individual wants the guidance of a more objective experience than his own, as well as the detachment from the immediate urgings of desire that press upon him. Thus, impartiality—objectivity in Kant's sense of a universal judgment—is a basic part of reason. But it is so because the retreat to impartial and general grounds of judgment is needed to assist the individual in the ordered and maximal satisfaction of his desires. Thus if it is asked "Why should I be rational and seek impartially grounded reasons for what I do?" the answer, ordinarily, is "You will not be happy if you do not" and this answer is perfectly sufficient. But when the question "Why should I be moral?" is asked, this general retreat to impartial reason loses its persuasive force. It is true that in assuming this vantage point the agent learns what is generally best for rational agents. But in this unique case, what is generally best is not necessarily best for him. His own impartial reason, in other words, is biased against him, and the moment he exercises his reason to seek further reasons for impartial reason's judgments, he knows this to be the case.[6]

Nor is there any way of resolving this difficulty by reason's ordinary procedures. Thus, if the individual perceiving the essentially biased nature of his impartial reason's dictates seeks to retreat to a still more impartial standpoint, reason in that standpoint is naturally prone to favor its kin, impartial moral reason. The problem is not unlike that experienced by individuals living under corrupt regimes who try to sue the government in its own courts. Here impartial reason always tends to favor impartial reason, so that the matter goes on and on in an infinite regress until the individual gives up asking altogether. Then again, at some point in this process impartial reason may itself take its bias into consideration and simply affirm itself unable fairly to judge the matter. Either way, reason's normal adjudicatory procedure will not work. In a sense, therefore, Hospers' point is correct. Moral reason and prudential reason are two irreducible, related, but potentially antagonistic expressions of human rationality. There is no higher or more fundamental employment of reason that can assist in resolving conflicts between the two, and when such conflicts arise reason is at an impasse.[7] This means concretely that at the moment of moral choice, whenever prudence and morality dictate opposing courses of action, the rational agent is rudderless. Neither prudence nor morality stipulate absolutely required courses of action—or more correctly, each stipulates such a course but the ordinary deliberative process is unable to determine which one should be followed. In the next chapter I want to look more closely at the implications of this conflict for rational action, and I shall explore the possibility of escaping this impasse. But for the moment it is sufficient simply to observe that a real dilemma appears to present itself here.

If we seek an explanation of just why human reason should be led to this curious position, however, we do not have to look far. The problem arises from man's own ambiguous and self-contradictory nature as a rational, finite, and social being. That is, we are looking at a problem that reflects man's, and by extension any rational, finite, and social being's ontological status. Let me explain this a bit more. As we saw earlier, reason in one of its most basic senses is a method of organizing and maximizing satisfactions. In biological terms, it is a sophisticated instrument for adaptation and survival. This means that it performs the task for man which on lower levels of life is performed directly and without rational deliberation. Among plants, for example, the survival and adaptation of both the individual organism and the species is assured directly by chemical or mechanical processes. Among animals, the mechanisms of instinct perform many of these same functions. (To simplify matters I neglect here those evidences of intelligence, if not rationality, one finds in some non-human species.) But in the rational animal, man, a great many of these more primitive mechanisms are replaced by rational deliberation. Thus, as far as the individual is concerned, the protective cushion of instinct is replaced by the capacity of seeking reasons for natural events and for the individual's own behavior. Surveying nature around him, the rational being seeks to determine necessary connections between events (causal relationships) in order to facilitate his prediction of future events. Regarding his own behavior and possible courses of action, this rational being is compelled by the same rational capacity always to act to maximize his satisfaction of desire—that is, always to act with a reason. This does not mean, of course, that the rational being is self-interested in a narrow sense, for he characteristically has many satisfactions that are altruistic. The more instinctually based satisfactions of family life are an example. But it does mean that reason holds tyrannical sway over the agent's desires: it recognizes and permits no action that fails to maximize the agent's satisfactions in keeping with reason's own objective judgment.

There is no question that as an instrument for adaptation and survival, reason is of unparalleled efficacy. The history of human material progress testifies to this: by dint of reason man has become substantially the master rather than the subject of nature. Nevertheless, with all its power, reason poses a problem that appears as soon as man's social nature is considered. We know, of course, that reason's mandate extends beyond nature to man's social relations. The individual is compelled by reason to ask not only how he may best organize nature to his ends, but how he should structure his social relations to maximize his satisfactions. It is perhaps conceivable that reason need not have extended itself to this sphere. Who knows whether there has not existed or could not exist a partly rational form of life whose social organization was regulated by purely instinctual mechanisms, with the reason of each member of the social group forbidden from analyzing or questioning that pattern of organization itself. Fortunately or unfortunately for man, he is the totally rational animal. This does not mean that he does not occasionally fail to be rational (alcohol's effects in this regard are well known), but it does mean that his reason is, and knows itself to be, the judge of all states and actions. There is no domain where reason is forbidden to enter or where the question "Does it maximize my satisfactions?" is not appropriate and required.

In exercising its sway and in questioning forms of social relation, however, man's reason necessarily provokes the crisis whose internal, experiential side we have been exploring. Indeed, it is precisely in extending itself to social relations that man's nature as a rational and social being reveals itself as the curiosity that it is. In a sense, in bringing into existence a being of this sort, nature has engendered a monstrosity. To see this we must keep in mind that finite social beings always stand in a tense relationship to their larger social group. The needs of the whole frequently demand suppression of the ends or aims of the individual member. Nothing makes this clearer, I think, than the frequently self-destructive acts associated with the reproductive process among animals. Here the species' requirement of self-perpetuation becomes an occasion for the individual's destruction.

Now on the level of plant or animal life, this conflict between the larger group and the individual poses no problem. Either the overwhelming play of natural forces is allowed to settle events, or, through the mechanism of instinct, the individual entity is necessitated to do what the species as a whole requires. But this is not the case for man. He is neither the victim of natural events in every case, nor is he exclusively motivated by instinct. It is his fate to be ruled rigidly by one question: "Does this—objectively considered—maximize my likely satisfactions?" But by its very nature this question must occasionally conflict with actions or ends that serve the larger human social group rather than the individual. Apart from the species' limited needs, such as reproduction, those actions or ends are the ones identified by moral reason, for we know that morality arises from the will of the whole community of rational agents. It is true that a rational individual can give himself reasons for obeying the rules of morality that serve larger group interests. For one thing, many of these rules can be directly related to his own expected satisfactions, as these are produced by the harmonious give and take of future social relations. And those other rules which demand possibly great sacrifice on his part or a possibly irreparable loss of happiness can to some degree be handled by reason. They can, for example, be explained in terms of their usefulness to the ongoing human community, or, what is the same, they can be justified by the individual to himself whenever he employs his reason in its usual, impartial sense.

Nevertheless, in all this reasoning the individual necessarily intimates that something is seriously wrong. For his commanding reason, which instructs him never to act to reduce the likely satisfaction of his desires, now has him doing exactly what it is meant to prevent. Small wonder that any rational, social being must be perplexed at such a point. The very conflict between self and society, the one and the many, appears at the heart of reason itself which, though usually a univocal guide to conduct, is here unable to order its own dispute. Nor is the explanation for this impasse any comfort to the rational agent. It is one thing to explain how the self-contradictory imperatives bearing on an agent have arisen—to show, for example, that the authority of reason in its different employments has a natural history. But it is quite another thing for a creature whose every thought and action is ruled by these imperatives to use that explanation to escape from his predicament. To think and to act, such a being requires not explanations but justifications. But it is precisely at the center of reason, the justifying agency, that the problem begins.

Despite its uselessness as a solution to reason's dilemma, however, this explanation of reason's difficulties in terms of man's ontological status has some value for our understanding of religion. If it is the case, as I shall argue shortly, that religious beliefs are required to resolve reason's internal problem, then we have gained some insight into the virtually universal prevalence of religion among human beings. Moreover, according to this understanding, religion finds its basis not in those aspects of human existence that are least developed, such as primitive instincts or emotions, but precisely in that aspect that distinguishes man from lower forms of life: his sophisticated rational ability.

3.

Why should I be moral? (continued)

The fact that religion can play an important role in the moral life by furnishing an answer to the question "Why should I be moral?" has long been acknowledged by both religious and antireligious thinkers. Adherents to one or another creed have frequently questioned whether people would be moral without the sanctions of religion. And not too differently, critics of religion have characteristically regarded it as a clever but vicious method of social control—a means of enforcing a moral code advantageous to some individuals or classes. Neither the critical nor the uncritical positions, however, have fully perceived the exact nature of the relationship between religion and morality. Pious belief, for example, has typically affirmed the entirely religious nature of morality and has tended to deny the role of reason in the moral life. For this point of view religious belief is not a rationally developed response to problems within a rationally developed moral code, but rather it is the very basis of that code, the source of its content and the ground of its authority. In Chapter 5 I shall try to suggest that even this deduction of morality from religion has a rational explanation and justification. But it is

characteristic of this religious position to deny every such interpretation of its claims.

The critical view of religion misperceives the relationship
between religion and rational morality in a quite different way.
Though it concedes that the connection between religion and
morality can be understood in anthropological, sociological, or
even economic terms, it typically refuses to grant any fundamental rational basis to that connection. Either, in a less critical vein,
as in some functionalist views, morality and religion are conceived of as the customary and contingent practices of particular
social groups, or, more critically, religion and morality are both
understood as anti-rational phenomena. Together they are seen
to be a complex means of coercive social control which is the opposite of a truly rational ordering of social relations. The views of
Marx, Nietzsche, and possibly Freud reflect this interpretation.
Here as well the strict relationship between rational morality and
religion is missed, and religion is instead judged to be non-
rational or irrational.

The aim of this chapter is to suggest an understanding of
religious belief quite different from these extreme viewpoints.
What I hope to trace is the way an independent and rationally
constituted morality is compelled to resort to one form or other
of religious belief in order to render its dictates coherent, and I
want also to emphasize the essential and inescapable rationality
of this: the fact that religion is a firm part of our entire procedure for making rational decisions. To understand this we must
begin with the problem identified in the preceding chapter, that
of individual moral obligation or reason's inability always to furnish a decisive answer to the question "Why should I be moral?"
We have seen that at the end of its deductive process, reason
seems to be in a state of frustration. In certain instances moral
reason commands strict obedience to certain rules, whatever their
implications for the individual's happiness, while prudential
reason seems to command disobedience. We saw, moreover, that
neither form of reason is capable in these circumstances of dem-

onstrating its unquestionable authority or priority as a ground for action. Moral reason cannot do so because all its justifications rely upon impartial reason, which in this special instance is rendered suspect even before the bar of impartial reason itself. But neither can prudential reason absolutely justify its authority. As convincing a case as prudential reason can make for the irrationality of moral obedience (a case drawing, perhaps, upon a natural scientific explanation and de-mystification of morality's compelling force), it cannot finally provide an absolute justification of a self-interested course of action. This is because in doing so it must, at some point, finally seek the support of impartial reason for its commands, and this it cannot ever unqualifiedly elicit. Thus, as much as he may feel in certain cases that he is being foolish in acting morally, the rational individual knows that a commanding side of his nature, his impartial reason, can never absolutely say this is so or that he should not obey the moral rule in question.

It is important to underscore the existence here of an apparently serious and disturbing dilemma for the rational individual. The fact that moral and prudential reason are equally balanced should not be taken to mean that the individual is permitted to be indifferent between these two, or that the matter of final decision simply devolves upon his free choice. For the fact is that reason necessitates the individual absolutely in both directions. As a consequence, if he should act on any one of these two aspects of reason, he must expect condemnation from the other.

The dilemma, then, appears to be absolute, and fully rational action in any direction seems stalemated. I say "appears to be" and "seems" because the dilemma may not in fact be complete or insuperable. It is true that no higher justificatory employment of reason than these two exists to resolve the dispute. There is, in fact, no third use of reason that can adjudicate the conflict between morality and prudence. But it may be that there is still another way of handling the dispute between reason's two employments, *one that involves showing that no dispute really exists*. That is, that the apparent conflict between prudence and morality is only apparent, so that on closer inspection moral and prudential reason must always counsel the same course of action. It is precisely this step in reasoning that Kant appears to take in several key passages in his *Critique of Practical Reason*.[1] Kant's argument is so important for our understanding of this dilemma and its resolution that it is worth taking some time here to wade through a thicket of Kantian terminology and concepts to see what he has to say. Though that thicket is sometimes dense, by following Kant's path we may be more easily led to a course that reason can follow out of this perplexing and unaccustomed impasse.

At the center of Kant's argument in the *Critique* and almost at the center of the book itself is the concept of the "Highest Good." Kant defines this as an idea involving the exact "unity" or "connection" of virtue and happiness such that each moral agent is to be conceived as necessarily being happy in direct proportion to his moral worth. Kant further insists that this "Highest Good" is the whole or entire object of pure practical reason: it is the state of affairs which the reason concerned with conduct (practical reason) must, in its "pure" (or moral) employment, hold as the complete end which it must bring into existence. Finally, Kant maintains that reason leads each rational agent really to believe that this end can be achieved.[2]

As one might imagine, all of these insistences on Kant's part have puzzled and disturbed students of his ethics. Kant's almost casual introduction of these ideas at a fairly late point in the *Critique* has puzzled some,[3] but most disturbing for many is Kant's claim that moral reason must hold happiness for worthy persons to be an achievable end. Is it not Kant, after all, who most notoriously banished considerations of happiness from morality? Is it not he who insisted so persuasively that happiness ought not to be the guiding motive or "determining ground" of the moral life? Why then does Kant here reintroduce happiness as something for which impartial moral reason must aim? Might not Kant, in a moment of confusion, have retreated from his earlier awareness; or is it not possible that for dubious motives—perhaps to reintroduce a religious position which his own critical philosophy had discredited—he has been led to renounce the essential points of his earlier writings on ethics?[4]

I hope that, after my exposition of Kant in Chapter 1, I do not have to devote much time to these initial objections to Kant's view. Kant's ethics, as we have seen, are by no means opposed to considerations of happiness. Indeed, with Hume and later utilitarian thinkers, Kant shared the notion that all rational agents seek their happiness. Unlike these other thinkers, however, Kant recognized that happiness, whether my own or other persons' happiness, cannot be the determining ground of the will in instances of moral choice, for if it were, the resulting chaos would almost everywhere impede the pursuit of happiness. Thus Kant insisted quite rightly that only one determining ground of the will could rationally be allowed: the fact that a policy could be freely accepted as action by all other rational agents, the position implicit in the various formulations of the categorical imperative. But, and this is crucial to observe, Kant insisted upon this in the name of happiness, so that happiness is the point of departure as well as the object of his whole analysis of moral reason.

Once we understand how important happiness is in Kant's thinking, and once we see the course that reason must take away from it in order to ground its pursuit more firmly, we can begin to see why Kant reintroduces the idea of happiness as one component of the Highest Good. Having demonstrated that reason assumes command in the name of happiness, Kant is now compelled to show that reason's command really does serve the purpose of happiness; that, indeed, to the exact degree that they comply with moral reason, persons can expect to be happy. This in turn involves proving that virtue and happiness are connected to one another strictly as cause to effect. This point is important. Kant recognizes that one way of showing the unvarying connection of virtue and happiness is by assuming that happiness is a necessary and sufficient condition for virtue, so that those individuals who succeed in satisfying their desires are to be considered worthy of moral respect. But, of course, it is the whole premise of his ethics that an individual's pursuit of his satisfactions is not itself right, that considerations that such and such act make a person happy cannot be the basic reason for its being right, and that neither happiness nor the ability to promote happiness can be the grounds for according someone moral respect. Thus, this way of relating virtue to happiness is totally unacceptable to him. If virtue and happiness are to be related, it must be as cause to effect. An individual's virtue, in the sense of a constant willingness to do what duty requires, must be the reason for the happiness he experiences.

So we are led quite naturally from Kant's ethics to his effort to connect virtue and happiness. And, offhand, it would not seem terribly difficult to bring these two into connection. Is it not the case, after all, that morality is generally conducive to human well-being? Are not the members of a community where justice and right prevail happier on the whole than those who live in a society marred by injustice, deception, or cruelty? The answer to these questions is probably yes. But we must note that it is not this sort of question that Kant asks or that is implicit in his argument at this point. What is of concern to reason, reason's "object" at this juncture, he maintains, is not a general or probable relation of morality and happiness, but their *exact* proportional correspondence.[5] The end that reason must hold before itself as an achievable state, the Highest Good, is the perfect bestowal on each and every moral agent of happiness in proportion to his virtue. Negatively stated, a world in which even one moral agent (not to say whole groups of agents) did not experience the happiness he morally deserved could not be accepted by reason. Moreover, if reason were convinced that such an imperfect world is all that is achievable, reason itself would rebel and dismiss the moral law as a figment of the imagination. For there even to be morality, the Highest Good must be really attainable, Kant appears to insist.

The important question at this point is why Kant makes this point so strongly. Why does the Highest Good assume such a central place in his ethics at this juncture? Certainly the effort to indicate the general value of morality does not require it. For that, only an overall connection of morality and happiness is required. Nor is this idea needed, as some have suggested, to ground a general duty to strive for the happiness of other persons.[6] It is true that striving for any end becomes pointless if that end is hopelessly beyond our reach. Thus if we are morally required, as Kant thinks we are, to exert ourselves on behalf of others' happiness, we must have some grounds for believing that we can succeed in our efforts. But certainly we do not have to believe that we will be perfectly successful in this enterprise. After all, I am morally required to refrain from injuring other people and the knowledge that I will to some degree fail in that end does not relieve me of that responsibility. Nor does it make it irrational for me to try my best to do my duty. The idea of the Highest Good and the real possibility of its attainment cannot, therefore, derive from a duty to promote others' happiness, and some of those who have interpreted Kant to be saying this have correctly shown the several faults in such a position.[7] But is this really the basis of Kant's insistence? Why, in fact, does he maintain so stubbornly that the Highest Good is reason's necessary and real object?

The answer, I think, lies in our earlier discussion of the question "Why should I be moral?" In exploring that question, we noted the final impasse reached by reason—even impartial reason—in its deliberations. Though reason can provide a general justification of moral obedience, it cannot justify such obedience to every individual in every case. But this amounts to saying that reason cannot furnish a complete justification of moral obedience at all. So long as every rational individual knows that in some cases, at least, it will be in some respect irrational to be moral, he cannot give his unwavering and absolute support to the moral rules, although that is just what morality demands.

Matters would be quite different, of course, if it were never possible for morality and happiness to diverge, if—as the idea of the Highest Good dictates—no cases of suffering as a result of moral obedience could ever arise. If that were true, reason's impasse would be eliminated and a coherent rational justification of all human behavior, prudential and moral, would be given. Not only would the individual's prudential reason always counsel moral obedience (it would have no reason to do otherwise), but impartial reason would command obedience without fear of opposition or contradiction from any corner. The Highest Good, therefore, is an idea of reason that can solve the whole problem of moral obedience by showing that the dilemma on which it is based does not really exist but is only apparent, and Kant's resort to this idea may reveal his deep appreciation of this problem.[8] But, it should be clear that this idea does not eliminate reason's dilemma so much as shift it to a different level. For now the question becomes not, as before, how moral and prudential reason can be reconciled, but whether the proposed reconciliation of these two (the Highest Good) is really possible. Is the achievement of the state of affairs identified by the Highest Good really something that a rational agent can count upon? Indeed, it is on just this question that Kant's whole analysis comes to focus. Kant's major effort in the latter part of the *Critique* is to demonstrate that it is possible to affirm the real achievement of the state of affairs suggested by the Highest Good. Since his reasoning here is a possible way out of the impasse we have identified, I want to look at it closely.

In approaching the question of whether the Highest Good is achievable, Kant believes it necessary to eliminate at the outset what he considers to be easy but false answers. These answers have the character of unifying virtue and happiness in such a way that their separation cannot even logically be thought. The two concepts become, as it were, analytically related. Historically, as Kant recognized, the most forceful efforts in this direction were made by the Stoic and Epicurean schools of philosophy.[9] The

Stoics, for example, defined happiness as that sense of well-being accompanying the performance of virtuous acts. The morally upright person, they maintained, is always happy because virtue is its own reward. Correspondingly, vicious persons are denied genuine satisfaction and are not ever really happy. Not too differently, the philosophy of Epicurus established a necessary connection between virtue and happiness. Epicurus, Kant maintains, is often wrongly interpreted as a crude hedonist. True, Epicurus believed that one should pursue pleasure above all else, but he also believed that the most genuine and refined satisfactions were those accompanying virtuous behavior. Thus while he and his school might have been guilty of inverting the motives that ought to guide the moral life, they nevertheless shared with the Stoics a high regard for morality and, like them, believed that virtue is its own reward.

If either of these views were accepted, of course, the possibility of achieving the Highest Good would be assured. For then, no one who is vicious would be really happy and all those who are virtuous, despite their occasional apparent suffering, would be consummately happy. But, Kant refuses to accept these solutions to the problem of the Highest Good, because in every such argument happiness is confused with what he calls "self-contentment."[10] This latter is the feeling of self-approval and agreeableness that accompanies obedience to the commands of duty. It is an important feeling in its own right, but it is not happiness or that state where everything goes according to one's wish and will. And it is happiness, not self-contentment, Kant maintains, which is united with virtue in the idea of the Highest Good.

If we return momentarily to our discussion of the question "Why should I be moral?" I think we can see the validity of Kant's view at this point. There is no question that each individual's reason, in its impartial employment, must register approval when that individual subordinates his own happiness to obedience to the moral rules. For it is obviously a function of impartial reason not only to identify these rules and to command obedience to them, but also to applaud all those agents (including the self) who willingly do what the rules require. But as true as this is, and as resounding as reason's approval might seem to the rational agent, the well-being generated by this approval cannot be accepted as an answer to his question "Why should I be moral?" For it is obvious that this approval derives from the same impartial reason, the same "interested" panel, which commands the individual to sacrifice his happiness in the first place. Viewed in the full light of reason's processes, therefore, this approval and the contentment it engenders are untrustworthy and an unsatisfactory answer to reason's question. What the individual wants to know is not whether impartial reason approves of what it approves, but that his own happiness, his ability really to satisfy his desires, will not ultimately be frustrated by moral obedience. This, I believe, is why Kant refuses to accept the kind of analytic solution to the problem of the Highest Good that these answers represent. "There is no branch of knowledge which so abounds in tautological propositions as ethics, offering as the answer what was in fact the question,"[11] Kant observes at one point in his writings, and this remark effectively explains his rejection of these "self-contentment" answers.

It might be added here that by extension the same reasoning also disqualifies as an answer to the question "Why should I be moral?" the argument from freedom employed (or suggested) by Kant in the *Foundations* and more recently offered by Rawls in *A Theory of Justice* in response to a similar question.[12] This argument holds that in being moral one shows that one's actions are not necessitated or determined by the particular desires or inclinations one might possess. Now since not to have one's actions necessitated is to be free, and since everyone naturally wishes to be free, the freedom experienced in morality is a reason for being moral. Looked at closely, of course, this argument does not stand up. It is true that all rational agents wish to be free in a general sense of this term. And it is also true that to be free partly means to be free from necessitation by impulse or desire.

But the freedom which all rational agents want is above all a freedom to pursue the maximal satisfaction of their desires. And the freedom from necessitation by impulse which clearly commands their respect is the freedom that enables each individual to rise above the whim or impulse of the moment to pursue his most permanent and satisfying ends.[13] When these implications and nuances of freedom are used to justify moral freedom, however, the whole context of their use is changed. For here the freedom from desire is not a freedom from one or another of my more impulsive but less satisfying desires, but a freedom possibly from all my desires, i.e., from my happiness. And the freedom I am being offered is not a freedom for satisfaction but a freedom from satisfaction, a "freedom . . . rather like death."[14] Thus, its allure, though initially beguiling, is fraudulent.

It is not hard, of course, to understand why this kind of fraud is perpetrated. Since our impartial moral reason is one employment of our prudential (deliberative) reason, it naturally uses all the methods and concepts of prudential reason. Nevertheless, it has been just my point that when prudential reason has objectively surveyed its situation, it cannot be moved by the blandishments of moral reason. Neither moral reason's approval, nor its promise of freedom prove genuinely satisfactory or move prudential reason to relinquish its claim. So Kant is certainly right in saying that it is not virtue nor any of its analytically related components that is needed to demonstrate the real possibility of the Highest Good, but happiness in conjunction with virtue. And this happiness must follow from virtue not logically but really and always as ground to consequent. It must be shown to be always connected with virtue in the actual experience of moral agents.

The dilemma of moral obedience as Kant appears to have constructed it is now fully drawn. Where I was content earlier merely to indicate the apparent opposition of moral and prudential reason, Kant has eliminated that opposition by means of a concept, the Highest Good, whose real possible achievement he must now prove. But in arriving at this formulation of the issue, Kant seems to have advanced no further than we did earlier. For in view of our experience reason seems just as much at odds with itself as before. Indeed, it is precisely in an oppositional fashion, in what he calls an "antinomy" of pure practical reason, that Kant expresses the dilemma in its final form. Since his formulation is crucial to understanding that dilemma's resolution, I want to quote Kant's remarks at length. According to him, two possibilities for the real and experiential connection of virtue and happiness present themselves; either

> the desire for happiness must be the motive to maxims of virtue, or the maxim of virtue must be the efficient cause of happiness. The first is absolutely impossible, because . . . maxims which put the determining ground of the will in the desire for one's happiness are not moral at all and can serve as ground for no virtue. The second is, however, also impossible since every practical connection of causes and effects in the world, as a result of the determination of the will, is dependent not on the moral intentions of the will but on knowledge of natural laws and the physical capacity of using them to its purposes; consequently, no necessary connection, sufficient to the highest good, between happiness and virtue in the world can be expected from the most meticulous observance of the moral law. Since, now, the furthering of the highest good, which contains this connection in its concept, is an a priori necessary object of our will and is inseparably related to the moral law, the impossibility of the highest good must prove the falsity of the moral law also. If, therefore, the highest good is impossible according to practical rules, then the moral law which commands that it be furthered must be fantastic, directed to empty imaginary ends, and consequently inherently false.[15]

Behind this elaborate conceptual structure and the perhaps inexact terminology (e.g., the moral law may be unjustified but not "false"), we can see that Kant has driven himself and his readers to the same impasse we arrived at earlier. On the one hand, impartial reason commands moral obedience and the occasional suppression of happiness, and it cannot allow happiness to be anyone's primary end. On the other hand, there is no evidence in experience for any causal connection between virtue and happiness. In fact, experience appears to indicate that those who are happiest are not necessarily those who are virtuous, but rather those who through skill or luck have been able to manipulate the natural and social environments to satisfy their desires. As a result, the complete justification of morality seems to fail.

Immediately upon having described reason's apparent impasse in these vivid terms, however, Kant begins to trace the way out, and his discussion is again worth quoting at length. Referring directly back to the two terms of the preceding antinomy, Kant states:

> The first of the two propositions, viz., that striving for happiness produces a ground for a virtuous disposition, is absolutely false; the second, viz., that a virtuous disposition necessarily produces happiness, is not, however, *absolutely* false but false only in so far as this disposition is regarded as the form of causality in the world of sense. Consequently, it is false only if I assume existence in this world to be the only mode of existence of a rational being, and therefore it is only *conditionally* false. But not only since I am justified in thinking of my existence as that of a noumenon in an intelligible world but also since I have in the moral law a pure intellectual determining ground of my causality (in the sensuous world), it is not impossible that the morality of intention should have a necessary relationship as cause to happiness as an effect in the sensuous world; but this relationship is indirect, mediated by an intelligible Author of nature.[16]

This is clearly a complicated passage and some interpretation is in order. To begin with, we should note that without compromising the absolute priority of duty, Kant has offered an affirmative answer to the question "Is the Highest Good really possible of attainment?" and since an affirmative answer to that question serves to eliminate reason's most pressing objections to moral obedience, he has also offered a concrete reply to our question "Why should I be moral?" The content of that reply is that morality is not necessarily opposed to happiness. It is true, as Kant observes, that our experience reveals no necessary connection between virtue and happiness. But our experience may not be the last word on this subject. For in addition to the causal sequences we see in this world, there may be an additional form of causality ruled by the strictest moral intention. And this form of causality may ultimately, in some way, rule over all other forms of causality and subordinate them to itself. If this seems impossible, says Kant, we cannot logically certify it as so, because we have no warrant for denying the existence of a form of causality other than that revealed to us by our own limited experience. More positively, however, in our own moral experience we actually do come into contact with a weak form of the kind of causality we seek. In each moral act we know ourselves to be rational beings free from strict determination by prior events in time and space, and we know ourselves capable, through free moral decision, of altering the future sequence of events to conform to "timeless" dictates of our reason. (We are thus "noumenal" beings in an "intelligible world.") Indeed, this certainty of freedom, as Kant notes, is given to us in the moral act, for the imperative power of our moral reason could not even issue its commands unless such freedom were assumed.[17] In morality we therefore have concrete grounds for believing that a form of causality might really exist which would differ from our own rational and moral causality only in its power and purity. Because of this, as rational agents we have reason to believe that our sufferings in the name of morality may not be the final condition we experience, that a perfectly moral power somehow supreme over all causation and for which the constraints of time and space pose no obstacle can in some way ensure that unhappiness, even death, prove only minor facets of our total experience.[18]

To one who has followed our search for an answer to the question "Why should I be moral?" this far, Kant's answer as it stands must seem odd and unsatisfactory. This is so, first of all, because Kant has not really shown the Highest Good to be achievable so much as shown that it is not necessarily unachievable. More troubling, however, is the fact, recognized by Kant himself, that even this answer is found "only at a distance," in a realm beyond all our empirical knowledge. But if there is one thing the modern mind cannot accept, it is a retreat of this sort beyond the bounds of empirical certainty into metaphysical speculation. The initial temptation, therefore, is to ascribe Kant's satisfaction with this argument to metaphysical or religious vestiges in his thinking, and to declare his whole solution unacceptable. But such a response, I think, does not do justice either to Kant or his argument. For Kant himself is not unaware of the difficulties in accepting this resolution of the problem. It was, indeed, the point of his whole critical enterprise that reason may not ordinarily trespass beyond the bounds of sense experience. If he is driven to violate his own injunction at this point, however, it is not for slight motive. In fact, it is precisely because Kant has recognized that the other alternative, the continuance in a state of profound rational dilemma, is utterly and absolutely unacceptable.

Earlier I suggested as much when I stated that within this dilemma an individual's reason not only counsels two contradictory courses of action, but from the side of its differing employments, actually condemns whatever course is finally taken. We might look more closely, however, at just what this means. Within the dilemma these condemnations take the form of declaring either course of conduct (morality or immorality) both imprudent and morally wrong. That is, prudential and moral reason condemn each alternative course of action and not merely the one opposed to its own dictates. We know, for example, that self-serving prudent behavior must be condemned unequivocally by moral reason. But it is also true that moral reason to some degree must condemn moral obedience. Since impartial reason knows itself to be biased, it must regard its own mandates to the individual as in some sense deceitful and corrupt, and it renders a morally condemnatory judgment both on its own counsels and on knowing, self-destructive compliance with them. The same is true when prudential reason is selected as the locus of judgment. That prudence must regard moral obedience as folly goes without

saying. But neither can it render a wholly approving judgment
on the course of immoral prudence. To understand this we must
keep in mind that the individual who chooses his happiness over
morality in an important sense chooses for all similarly placed
rational agents. That is, if his actions are determined by certain
reasons, these reasons must hold for others in his position. A consequence of each agent's decision to disobey the moral rules,
therefore, is the possible creation of a world in which morality
has been radically compromised and where, in all situations struc-
turally similar to his (or regarded as similar), rational persons
can refuse to do what morality requires. Of course, given his immediate choice, the individual may prefer to undergo the risk of
living in such a world (and he knows that his decision to be
moral does not guarantee the creation of a moral world). But he
cannot be sure at the moment of choice that this self-regard is
wise. Thus, while the saying "better a live dog than a dead lion"
may make some prudential sense, the actor must consider that his
decision may also make him a "dead dog," someone who reached
for happiness only to lose it in a perhaps unexpected way in the
resulting moral chaos.

These sharply opposing considerations paralyze rational action at the moment of moral decision. One caught in the throes of
this dilemma either will not act at all or will be propelled to act
in a way that he must consider impulsive, irrational, or wrong.
This does not mean that an individual cannot abandon the effort
of giving himself a rational, coherent justification of his behavior and act either on the immediate impulse for survival or in the
name of ideals he knows to be suspect. But in acting in either of
these ways, the individual knows that he is perhaps being irrational, and for a being otherwise ruled by reason, such a course
must appear filled with uncertainties and even terrors.

Small wonder that a rational individual in this situation, out
of desperation, seeks an escape from this dilemma. Surveying the
way out offered by immoral action, however, he knows that to be
closed to him. Not only does experience fail to guarantee that this

course is prudent, but moral reason, in its still authoritative voice (however much that authority has been called into question), can never permit this behavior and erects an insuperable wall in this direction. Kant clearly recognizes this when on one side of the antinomy he absolutely refuses to allow inversion of the motives of moral choice. Surveying the other route of escape, strict moral obedience, the individual finds it apparently blocked by experience, for there is no empirical evidence that virtuous persons are really happy or that their suffering is not final. But this obstacle is not as unyielding as it initially appears. Not only is it logically permissible to qualify our conclusion to read "as far as we know," but in our own rational and moral experience we have the sense that reason and morality both can rise above the ordinary necessities of nature. That is, the same reason which we are unwilling to renounce also furnishes us with a basis, however small, for that which we most deeply hope: that reason and morality may be the supreme facts of existence and that the universe may not be, as Kant puts it, an "aimless chaos of matter" engulfing all men, just and unjust, regardless of their deeds.[19] The rational individual, therefore, finds on this side a possible escape from his dilemma. This is the prospect that through the agency of a yet more powerful moral causality than his own (just how he does not know) neither he nor any other righteous person may have to sacrifice happiness in always being moral. Admittedly, this prospect furnishes only the narrowest escape from the dilemma. But—and this is the crucial point—since reason's dilemma is so thoroughly unacceptable, and since reason is driven urgently to escape from that dilemma, it profits by this slight aperture in its circumstances to work itself free. Kant's resolution of the dilemma may thus initially appear unacceptable to reason and experience. But before it can be rejected, a more plausible solution is required and none seems forthcoming. As Sherlock Holmes once observed, when you have eliminated all else, what remains (assuming it is possible), however improbable, must be true. It is the power of Kant's total argument, I think, to drive us to the realization that his own transcendent resolution, as offensive as it may be, is one to which reason is ineluctably driven.

There is no question that this aperture in the impasse before reason is very small. Kant himself fully recognizes it to be so. Moreover, he insists that it is impermissible in any way to widen the gap further so as to convert the slender possibility of fulfilling reason's deepest need into any form of cognitive certainty. In Kant's own terminology, speculative reason (what we, and sometimes he, call theoretical reason) has an "interest."[20] This interest involves never allowing our cognition to trespass beyond the bounds of sense experience. As such this interest is rooted in cognition's most basic purpose, helping us to gain sure knowledge of the actual conditions of experience and, at the same time, preventing us from distorting experience by flights of speculative fancy. In emphasizing this interest of reason, Kant clearly sides with the empiricist tradition and opposes himself to dogmatic metaphysics. Yet in distinction from empiricists before and after him, Kant refuses to isolate this interest and make it the sole or sufficient determinant of our reason. For, as he says, practical reason, the reason that governs conduct and the exercise of our will, also has an "interest." This is in determining the highest totality of conditions that make rational action possible. Concretely, it consists in establishing the real possibility of the Highest Good, for, as we know, it is the real possibility of attaining this end that is required for coherent prudential and moral action.

Now, Kant asks in an important passage following his resolution of the antinomy, what happens if the interests of speculative (theoretical) and practical reason are opposed?[21] What happens, in other words, if, as in the case before us, practical reason requires the real possible existence of a form of causality, proof of which appears to transcend our empirical knowledge? Does it not violate the interest of our theoretical reason to affirm the reality of this causal agency? Which interest, then, that of practical or theoretical reason, ought to take priority?

Kant's question here is clearly one that has bothered many thinkers since his time. Anti-religious thinkers have frequently based their opposition to religious or metaphysical belief on the conviction that empirical verifiability is the only sure basis for knowledge, and they have regarded any flight beyond the bounds of experience as nonsense or delusion.[22] In response, defenders of religion have sometimes attempted to show that religious statements and beliefs can actually satisfy the criteria of verification as well as most experiential or scientific statements can.[23] But the approach that Kant takes seems opposed to either way of regarding religious beliefs. Although he would presumably have no objection to efforts to defend the possible verifiability of morally-based religious beliefs, his clear recognition that such beliefs are opposed to experience and independently derived from the operations of practical (not theoretical) reason, would seem to render the matter of verifiability of very secondary concern to him.

Kant's response to the strict empiricist position is not waged at all on empiricism's terrain, the terrain of theoretical reason, but from the opposing side of practical reason. He does begin with a bid to empiricism by observing that when practical and theoretical reason conflict, the interest of theoretical reason must be respected as much as possible, and in several important ways. First, practical reason cannot ever be permitted to oppose the interests of theoretical reason for trivial purposes. Not merely any wish of a rational agent will do,[24] but only the most pressing needs of pure practical (moral) reason. Second, practical reason cannot ever be allowed openly to contradict the certain knowledge of theoretical reason.[25] It may affirm objects or states which lie beyond the bounds of sense experience, but it may not insist upon that which is clearly disproven by experience. If that were allowed, reason would be in contradiction with itself and could not function. Third, in moving beyond empirical knowledge, practical reason must keep its departures to a minimum.[26] If possible, for example, practical reason must content itself with the most slender grounds for basing its confidences and it must repress its wish for certainty.[27] Thus, in the case before us practical reason can be content with the affirmation only of the real possibility of the Highest Good and does not require absolute proof of its reality.

Finally, in moving beyond the domain of sure empirical knowledge, practical reason must be aware of what it is doing. It must recognize the fact that what it obtains is not knowledge in the strictest sense of that term (for that, experience is required), but a form of knowledge whose validity springs from the exercise of practical, as against theoretical reason. To distinguish this kind of knowledge from that produced by experience, Kant calls it "faith" or "pure rational faith."[28] The knowledge produced by practical reason is, of course, no less objective and valid than that produced through experience. Though it springs from subjective needs, these are needs of all rational agents. Moreover, the very needs of reason require that the beliefs it demands be accorded objective validity. Still, faith of this sort must be distinguished, according to Kant, from other kinds of knowledge by retaining a sense of its different origin.

Thus, the interest of theoretical reason commands a respect which in these various ways curbs the flight of practical reason. Nevertheless, in the final clash between theoretical and practical reason, the interest of practical reason must emerge supreme. This is so, says Kant, "because every interest is ultimately practical, even that of speculative [theoretical] reason being only conditional and reaching perfection only in practical use."[29] This is a rather cryptic remark and it is made even more so, as Lewis Beck points out, by the fact that nowhere in his writings does Kant take the reader by the hand and say, "Now I shall show you precisely why I think theoretical and practical reason differ only in being two applications of the same faculty."[30] Still, on the basis of some of our earlier discussion, I think we can see what Kant is trying to say. "Every interest is practical" merely expresses the fact that reason exists above all as a governor of action. It is, as I observed in the first chapter, a means of orienting our individual and collective behavior toward ends which will maximally satisfy desire. No less is this the purpose of theoretical reason. Its objective (its interest) is to comprehend nature's causal sequences in order to facilitate our command and control of the environment around us. It too serves the satisfaction of desire.

Seen in this way, theoretical reason's "interest" in giving sure knowledge of reality and preventing false knowledge is only conditional. Its "interest" forms part of its service to practical reason, and it may hold to this interest only so long as practical reason requires it to do so. For it to do otherwise would, in effect, represent an inversion of proper order. Instead of then contributing to the highest satisfaction of desire in self and society, objective knowledge would become an instrument of personal and social destruction, and, in the process, it would undermine the very grounds of its own continued activity. Now this clearly cannot be.[31] Thus, when (and only when) the matter is as clearly drawn as this, theoretical reason must bow. It must accept from practical reason those minimal beliefs that practical reason absolutely requires in order to render behavior coherent. In doing so it may, as Kant says, recognize those beliefs as "something offered from the outside and not grown on its soil." But it must accept those beliefs nevertheless, it must accord them a measure of objective reality, and it must, as Kant says, "seek to compare and connect them with everything it has in its own power as speculative reason."[32]

The reader who has patiently followed me through this difficult and sometimes circuitous argument can now relax. For though it may not be apparent, the question with which this and the preceding chapter began is now answered, and the important secondary objections that this answer may generate, in principle, I hope, have been set aside. That question was "Why should I be moral?" although it soon revealed itself as the deeper question,

"How, in situations where my happiness is jeopardized by moral obedience, can I act rationally at all?" The answer, we have seen, is that I can act rationally if I obey the moral rules and at the same time hold certain specific beliefs not supported by experience. These beliefs—they can be called, for convenience, metaphysical or religious—have the effect of persuading me that the course of moral obedience may not be imprudent at all, and they render that course an acceptable alternative. Finally, to the objection that my reason will not ordinarily permit me to hold beliefs of this character, the reply has been given that this case is not ordinary, and that in this special instance reason both permits and requires me to move beyond the domain of experience. Our initial question, therefore, has been answered to reason's entire satisfaction, and although that answer strains reason to the limit, it is better than the abandonment of reason, which is the alternative.

In the process of answering this question, reason has become religious, or, more precisely, it has begun to develop what I wish to call its religious employment. Passing from theoretical to prudential and finally to moral reason, impartial reason has been compelled, in order to render its whole enterprise coherent, to postulate certain necessary supra-empirical beliefs. It is true that at this point these beliefs are only skeletal in character and have very little in common with the kind of religious propositions with which we are familiar. Specifically, these beliefs required by reason include a belief in the possibly real existence of a form of causality, a causal agency, that is both perfectly moral and in some way supreme over nature. Impartial reason has led us to postulate such an agency in order to assure ourselves that the achievement of the Highest Good is really possible, although it has not required that anything more precise be said about the nature of this causal agency itself. In addition, reason has stipulated a series of constraints on this belief and on reason's religious or metaphysical employment generally. Thus, reason knows that its necessary supra-empirical beliefs must not contradict our sure experiential knowledge and that these beliefs must depart from experience as little as possible. Finally, reason requires the recognition of the qualitatively different source of these beliefs.

The reader who is familiar with Kant's own writings may ask at this point why, having followed his argument this far, I do not go further and maintain, like him, that this deduction culminates in the belief in that traditional religious causal agency, God. After all, it is well known that Kant's so-called moral argument was always advanced by him as a defense of theism. If I have not done this, however, it is because I believe that nothing that we have considered, nor for that matter anything in the *Critique of Practical Reason* or any of Kant's other writings, necessarily requires reason to affirm the possible existence of the personal kind of causal agency God is conceived to be. This does not mean that once we have all the requirements of religious reason before us we will not be able to construct a stronger argument (and one lacking in Kant's writings) for this kind of agency. But as the argument stands, all that is incumbent upon us to affirm is the existence of some kind of supreme moral causal agency. This can be personal, as is God, or impersonal, as is the agency of *karma,* which we shall look at when we examine the Indian religious traditions. But for now, reason seems strictly indifferent between these alternatives.[33]

This rather spare set of beliefs does not yet take us to the limit of religious reason's development. In the next chapter I want to turn to the problem of moral inadequacy and suggest several additional supra-empirical postulates. But before turning to that, I must add to an already long chapter by underlining and clarifying some points made in the preceding argument and by adding one other matter of importance for our understanding of the study of religion since Kant's day. First, it is important once again to stress that the resort to supra-empirical beliefs demanded here by reason is justified only because of the severity of the rational dilemma raised by moral obedience. As Kant himself makes clear, reason's theoretical interest prohibits such a resort for any lesser purposes. Now, if it is correct to assume that reason's essential demands and requirements are known to all rational agents, then we already have some grounds for believing that concrete religious beliefs everywhere are connected with the needs of social and moral life. This does not mean that human beings do not have other reasons for being religious or engaging in the kind of metaphysical speculation associated with religion. This kind of speculation, for example, seems frequently to be related to the exercise of theoretical reason—to the effort to establish a final why and wherefore for every event in nature. Occasionally, too, religious speculation has flourished in connection with purely personal or individual moral questions. Thus it has been common to argue—especially in our own day—that religion seeks to speak to the individual's quest for "meaning" in life or for something to organize and give point to his own activities and goals.

Without denying that these concerns may furnish important additional incentives to religious reflection, I want to suggest that they do not go to the heart of the religious enterprise. This is so because neither theoretical nor individual-prudential reason requires a final metaphysical or supra-empirical resort. Reason can comprehend nature well enough for action without engaging in metaphysics at all. Similarly, every individual can successfully organize his pursuit of satisfactions—happiness—without a metaphysical inquiry or search for the totality of conditions that govern existence. A character of Camus' who declares "Everything for happiness against the world which surrounds us with its violence and its stupidity!" reveals how satisfaction can be gathered out of an otherwise rationally meaningless context.[34] In contrast to these employments of reason, the moral life and our social obligations cannot be firmly grounded without resort to supra-empirical beliefs of the kind we have looked at. Only here does strict necessity obtain. And since the universality of a feature of rational existence is a function of its necessity, it is only here that we gain a possibly fundamental insight into the common enterprise of religion.

A second point that needs re-emphasis and clarification has to do with the necessary relation between reason and supra-empirical beliefs of the sort we have examined. It is very easy, I think, to assume that because reason requires such beliefs, an individual has no alternative but to hold them. But this puts the matter too strongly. It is true that if an individual wants to be moral, and if, at the same time, he wants his reason to speak coherently, he must hold beliefs of this kind. But no individual is absolutely required to be moral or rational. Every human being remains free to renounce moral obedience and with it strict adherence to reason. For that matter, every individual is also free to choose to be moral without holding beliefs like this even if that means that he ceases to be coherently rational in his position. Such positions may involve "arbitrarily stopping the process of thought,"[35] as Hastings Rashdall puts it, but it is certainly true that no one can rationally be required to be impartially rational. Impartial reason cannot require anything of one who perceives its essential bias and refuses to accept its authority. The decision to be entirely rational, therefore, rests on a free choice and a regard for reason itself. Once that choice has been made, an individual is required both to be moral and to hold those beliefs needed to render his reason fully coherent. But that is true only when the choice has been made.[36]

An important implication of this is that the kinds of beliefs demanded by reason to complete its activity—the specific supra-empirical beliefs that I have begun to indicate—may be thought of as an expression of respect for reason itself. No individual is strictly required to hold such beliefs, but to the degree that anyone does, it is an indication that he has chosen to opt fully for rationality. I cannot speculate here why anyone should decide in this way, although I can suggest that in reason and the life of reason, especially in its impartial or objective aspect, rational

agents characteristically perceive something of ultimate importance and worth. To each rational agent, in other words, a lofty
aspect of his own nature and a presentiment of a form of existence supremely worthwhile are reflected in reason's activity and
commands.[37] Less grandly, impartial reason may represent an inescapable aspect of our nature, an aspect which, as Thomas Nagel
suggests, it is not fully in our power to renounce. Whatever the
case, as a result of these considerations and at the end of a long
chain of deduction, religious belief emerges as an expression of
respect for reason.

No one, I believe, has perceived this more clearly than Kant
himself. His own thinking on religion reveals a constant movement between various traditional theistic affirmations and what
could be called a mysticism of reason—a profound regard for the
internal voice of reason and conscience. Some commentators, it
is true, have chosen to see two different religious positions in
Kant's thought, with the immanentist view coming to the fore in
his later writings to replace the earlier, more "traditional" position.[38] This interpretation, however, reveals a fundamental misunderstanding of Kant. It ignores, for example, the fact that the
theistic and immanentist positions are commonly expressed side
by side in the whole corpus of Kant's writings. More importantly,
it misses Kant's essential point that specifically religious propositions proceed from "a confidence in the promise of the moral
law" and, as such, are expressions of respect for the internal
voice of one's reason, especially one's impartial moral reason.[39]
These propositions are the result of a painstaking effort to give
conceptual clarity and coherent expression to something only in-
choately and ambiguously intimated by one's conscience and
sense of moral ideals.

A final point I want to make has less to do with the meaning
of Kant's position than with its impact on the study and understanding of religion since his day. In view of the complexity and
power of his view, it is natural to ask why rational analyses of
religious belief have not had more currency since his work. There

are probably many answers to this question, but one, at least, has a touch of irony about it. In a very real sense, Kant's own efforts to evidence the rational basis of religious belief have probably been a major cause of the post-Kantian separation of religion and reason. This is partly true because of Kant's critical destruction of the traditional metaphysics in the *Critique of Pure Reason*. By insisting on the rootage of our knowledge in sense experience, Kant eliminated the flights of speculative fancy associated with metaphysics and showed the tendency of these flights partly to reside in understandable, but not justifiable, impulses of reason. Kant, the "all destroyer," was aware of this negative aspect of his philosophy. But he was convinced that the traditional objects of religious faith could be given a firm basis in the needs of practical rather than theoretical reason. Religion, he insisted, arises in the first place not from the needs of speculative knowledge, but from the needs of man as a living, acting, rational, and social being. Moreover, he insisted, the objects of religious beliefs are not because of this to be regarded simply as the illusory projection of a human need. Rather, as we know, because reason itself requires we do so, these objects are to be regarded as objectively valid and at least possibly real.

Now, it may be, as one commentator on Kant's position has observed, that the whole temper of the modern intellect is "to deny that what ought to be true is necessarily true."[40] But Kant himself was not unaware of this. If he insisted that the objects required by reason be thought of as having possibly real existence, it is because he realized profoundly that reason would accept nothing else. Thus Kant effaced the simpleminded distinction between subjective and objective validity, and he boldly and rightly refused to concede that objects of belief created and postulated by ourselves are therefore necessarily false. Unfortunately, the subtlety of his thinking here was easily missed. From the emphasis on the subjective and human basis of religious belief, it was a short but careless step to the conclusion that the objects of religious belief have no objective validity because they are only the wishful projections of human need. This was the step taken by Feuerbach, who would collapse theology into anthropology, by Marx, who saw religion as reflecting nothing but the conditions of social oppression, and by Freud, who traced religion to social and psychological conflicts.[41]

In their own ways, each of these thinkers rested content with only a fragment of Kant's complex rational analysis. Going beyond this, each of these thinkers insisted that religion is ultimately irrational since it works against the ends of man as a rational being. Whether emotionally, as for Feuerbach, socially, as for Marx, or psychologically, as for Freud, religion was regarded as promoting maladaptation to the natural or social environment. This condemnation of religion as illusionary or irrational can be explained, of course, by the repressive and immoral uses to which powerful religious ideas have been put. But as far as the objective understanding of religion is concerned, the effect of this attack was to create the common assumption that religion and reason are necessarily opposed. Lost beneath the rubble of this nineteenth-century critique was Kant's insight that genuinely rational moral activity requires specific religious concepts for its coherence and completion. To retrace carefully the steps in Kant's argument, therefore, is in some ways to overcome the deeply rooted misconceptions of religion accidentally generated by Kant's own thought.

4.

How can I ever be morally worthy?

In the preceding chapters we saw that the difficulties which drive reason to a religious employment become apparent when some common questions of the moral life are asked. One is the question "Why should there be morality?" and the other is the question "Why should I be moral?" In this chapter it is again a common question that forces reason to a religious employment. That question, "How can I ever be morally worthy?" arises when reason becomes alert to the persistent fact of human moral inadequacy. Like our preceding question, this one eventually comes to generate the deepest anguish in moral agents so that finally, to remedy the difficulties this question brings with it, reason is compelled to seek a religious solution.

The problem I am referring to derives from two contradictory awarenesses of reason. One of these is the uncompromising imperative issued to each person by his moral reason requiring complete fulfillment of the moral law. This imperative derives from the wish of every impartial rational agent to secure full compliance with the mutually beneficial moral rules. The strictness of this requirement should not be taken to mean that morally legislative reason is itself uncompromising, that it refuses, for example, to make exceptions for special cases or that it does not consider the actual consequences of certain kinds of compliance with moral rules. That is an unrealistic and rigoristic view of the moral reasoning process. In making moral rules, reason takes circumstances into account, and it must always be prepared to make exceptions to the general rules in cases where strict obedience would seem clearly disadvantageous in the eyes of impartial rational persons.[1] Nevertheless, it is true that once reason has dictated a course of action—even if that course is itself an exception—strict obedience is not only required but assumed. For why should impartial reason mandate behavior and at the same time allow violations of its dictates? In that case, why should reason dictate at all?

An illustration may help make this clearer. The keeping of promises is something generally required by moral reason, and it is fairly easy to offer a rational justification for why this is so. Since the institution of promise-keeping generally advantages all impartial rational agents, and since the vigor of that institution depends upon each agent's willingness to accept the responsibilities its free employment entails, all are required generally to keep the promises they make. But this does not mean that promises may not sometimes be broken. Because impartial rational agents occasionally have other ends more important than the strict preservation of the institution of promise-keeping, they may choose to subordinate promise-keeping from time to time when it conflicts clearly with these more important ends. Thus, it is morally permissible to break a minor promise (to return a book to a friend, for example) in order to save a human life. Indeed, for impartial agents not to permit this kind of exception would probably be irrational on their part. Nevertheless, even when they permit exceptions like this, the commands of moral reason are absolute and always binding. Whatever final course impartial agents command must always be followed. In every instance of moral choice, in other words, the moral agent is required to ask

"Would impartial rational agents permit this?" and he must never violate their final will. Such an agent is never permitted to act merely as he wishes (unless of course impartial agents would so permit), nor is he allowed to will a general obedience to the dictates of impartial reason while reserving for himself, on occasion, the right to do merely as he wants. From the point of view of moral reason, any such reservation is fatal to its authority. Just as the solemn pledge to aid another ceases to be a pledge at all when made with the mental reservation "so long as I wish . . . ," a conditional commitment to morality is really no commitment at all. In this respect morality is an all-or-nothing affair. Either a person is prepared always to do what impartial reason requires (although this does not rule out impartial reason's making exceptions, some of which may even benefit the self), or he is not and is properly considered by all impartial agents (including the self) to be immoral.[2]

Now, it is when this first observation is juxtaposed with a second one that the problem of moral inadequacy arises. This second observation is that no rational individual can ever feel confident of his commitment to the moral law. Though every agent knows, and must know, that he is capable of making and sustaining such a commitment, he knows as well that in the course of his moral experience he will almost inevitably choose on occasion to will, not as morality requires, but as he merely wishes. He will, as Kant puts it, occasionally choose to invert the order of his maxims and give conduct merely desired by him priority over strict moral obedience.[3]

To understand why this is so, we must return to the question "Why should I be moral?" for the inability always to be moral grows out of difficulties perceived in trying to answer this earlier question. In tracing the reasoning of individuals in the difficult instances where prudence and morality conflict, I observed that on the terrain of reason and experience alone an impasse is finally reached where reason can dictate no one necessary course of action. It is true that in such cases the individual is required to act in each of two contradictory directions, but that is the same as saying that he is not absolutely required to act in any direction at all. It is also true, we know, that if the individual wishes to be rational and if he wishes to have his reason speak clearly, coherently, and without any contradiction, there is a course open to him. He can choose to be moral and, at the same time, to hold those supra-empirical beliefs needed to render his conduct rationally defensible to himself and to others. But this elaborate moral and religious move, though it is the only course that is fully rational, is not itself strictly required by reason, because to embark on this course presumes a prior choice to act fully as a rational being, or to respect above all that side of one's nature which reason represents. But the choice itself is free (not required by reason), because reason cannot compel until it commands coherently and until a free decision has been made to render it coherent.[4]

In the moment of moral decision, therefore, the agent is radically free to act as he chooses—to act for or against morality, for or against reason. Now, it is the nature of a choice that is not determined that it can and probably will frequently be made either way. It is true that an important side of the human experience, reason in its fullest expression, attracts choice in its direction. But it is equally true that another aspect of man's condition, the desire for physical survival and happiness, frequently exerts an opposite attraction. As a result, it is possible to say that human beings will occasionally violate the moral law. Either they will will to be moral but will reserve the right, on occasion, to violate the moral law, or they will will firmly to be moral but will occasionally find themselves willing the other way. Also predictable, and perhaps even more common, is the tendency to obscure the self's dereliction from duty by an occasional unjustified distortion of the moral rules. To understand this, one must observe that in addition to openly disobeying the moral rules, an individual can violate moral reason's commands by sometimes concocting, under the pretense of a resort to impartial judgment, special rules useful to himself.[5] Thus, when faced with the choice of keeping a promise or merely doing what he wants, an individual can justify the self-serving course as a valid exception to the rule of promise-keeping. He might argue, to himself or others, for example, that all impartial agents would support an exception in this kind of case. Clearly, this method of achieving one's ends has an advantage over outright immorality, since it has the effect of preserving the appearance of morality. Moreover, it trades upon the fact that in cases of valid exceptions to moral rules the agent's own interests are sometimes involved so that no entirely clear line can be drawn between exceptions that are valid and those that are not. Nevertheless, the impartial vantage point required by morality does permit a general distinction between permissible and impermissible exceptions, and though the individual knows himself likely to obscure this distinction in the future, he also knows that it is morally wrong to do so.

I should note here that if human beings were not the kind of finite entities they are, rational beings limited in time and space and in what they can will, none of these typical violations of morality would probably have to arise. If men were immortal, for example, they would have little reason to succumb to the allure of physical survival and immediate happiness. In choosing to be rational and moral, they would experience no enduring sacrifices, and, in time, they would be able to avail themselves of all the benefits that morality brings with it.[6] Nevertheless, human beings are not immortal and in their real condition they are prone to wrongdoing. But neither does this mean that their finite condition is responsible for their immoral choices. Despite the incentive to wrongdoing that the specific conditions of human nature may furnish, each agent is and knows himself to be free to opt for morality. This is true, above all, because no rational agent can ever be strictly required to do that which is contrary to reason. But it is also true in a very real sense because man's condition does not really furnish an incentive to immorality until it has already been rendered intolerable by prior immorality. Thus, it is

not simply death but the prospect of a life wasted through depri-
vation and injustice that forces the individual to grasp selfishly
for relief; and it is not nature's hardships or inequities that most
prompt men to immorality, but the indifference of their fellows
in the face of these problems. In a profound sense, therefore, immorality is its own cause, or, as Kierkegaard put it in religious
terms, "sin presupposes itself."[7] If the whole sequence of wrongdoing is to be traced back to a source, it cannot be found in
human nature but in an initial free choice of immorality.

Be this as it may, in the actual imperfect circumstances of
human life, each person knows that he can be led on occasion to
violate the moral law. More precisely, the very fact of his radical
freedom to be moral or immoral in conjunction with his finite
nature deprives him of the certainty that he can always do what
morality demands. As a result, as soon as the individual scruti-
nizes his conscience he is confronted with these two irreconcil-
able convictions. On the one hand he is required honestly to
will always to maintain the absolute priority of the moral law
over all considerations of mere self-interest. On the other hand
he knows that as a result of his radical freedom and his human
nature there always remains the possibility that he will reverse
this priority. Taken together, these two convictions must impress
each individual with a sharp sense of his moral inadequacy, for
as soon as reason is fully clear about what morality requires, it
will not tolerate even the admission of a possibility of wrongdoing. Thus, as a result of man's radical freedom a genuine
dilemma arises. Ordinarily, moral agents cannot be required to
do what lies beyond their power. "Ought" does imply "can."
But in this special case the individual himself knows that he is
required honestly and firmly to will something which he cannot
will with absolute certainty or conviction. In each moment of
time he is required to will an abiding commitment to morality
despite the fact that he knows he cannot guarantee such a commitment. If his inability to maintain a firm resolution of his will
does not in this case excuse him from the obligation to so will, it

is because this inability arises not from external forces or insuperable personal difficulties beyond his control, but precisely from the free and unnecessitated future exercises of his will. But moral reason can never admit these future lapses of the will as a reason for relaxing its uncompromising demand. Thus the dilemma of command versus the inability to comply with that command is a necessary outcome of the process of careful moral introspection.

The problem we are looking at here was also identified by Kant. This should not surprise us, since we know that the understanding of man's radical freedom to be moral or immoral was clearly developed by him in the *Critique of Practical Reason.* It is to be expected, therefore, that in his subsequent work, *Religion within the Limits of Reason Alone,* Kant turns directly to this problem which he discusses in terms of the radical (or root) evil of the human will.[8] Aspects of his discussion there can help enrich our understanding of the problem and its eventual solution. Specifically, Kant identifies three grave difficulties produced by every rational person's admission of the possibility of his immorality. Each of these difficulties is distinct, but all have a common origin in the fact that reason uncompromisingly requires what no agent can ever really give: a commitment never to deviate from the moral law.[9]

One difficulty identified by Kant goes directly to the heart of the problem. This is the difficulty that no agent can ever be sure of the constancy of his moral disposition. However much and however firmly he should will to uphold the priority of the moral law, no agent can ever be sure that on occasion he will not abandon this commitment. Kant observes that the sharper one's conscience and the more acute one's moral sensitivities, the more one must become aware of this problem and be troubled by it. Ironically, therefore, it is usually those who are laxest in their moral commitment who are most prone to believe their momentary will to be moral to be final. "Man is never more easily deceived," Kant observes, "than in what promotes his good opinion of himself."[10]

A second difficulty is provoked by the inherent unsatisfactoriness of any single moment of willing as a measure of moral worth. What morality requires, we have seen, is a life dedicated to the priority of the moral law and a pattern of deeds evidencing that priority. Yet the most any agent can offer up to morality is his firm resolve at any instant in time to create such a pattern of will and conduct. Now, if his will were related in this case to the full course of his life, there would be no problem. But the possibility that he will will to do wrong, the inconstancy of his disposition, renders his will at any moment suspect and differentiates it qualitatively from the course of life it should represent. Thus, since all an individual can ever do is will, how can he accept that will as a ground on which to judge himself morally worthy? The crucial and troubling question each person must put to himself, Kant says, is "how can a disposition count for the act itself, when the act is *always* . . . defective?"[11]

If the first difficulty arises when the individual looks to his will in the future and the second arises when he judges the worthiness of his will in the present, the third difficulty becomes apparent when the individual surveys the misdeeds of his past. It is the nature of these deeds, Kant observes, that they can never be put behind a rational agent. However much an individual might will to reform himself, his prior evil continues to inflict upon him the burden of self-condemnation. As Kant puts it, "Whatever a man may have done in the way of adopting a good disposition, and, indeed, however steadfastly he may have persevered in conduct conformable to such a disposition, *he neverthetheless started from evil,* and this debt he can by no possibility wipe out."[12] Offhand, Kant's claim seems peculiar. And it is rendered no less odd by the fact that Kant is not really concerned here with the matter of past injury done to others which might continue to bother the moral agent. What he seems to be speaking about are inoffensive past immoral acts committed by the moral agent and from which he has since distanced himself by reforming his will. Why should his past acts now matter? The answer, for Kant, I think, has to do with the radical freedom that underlies each departure from moral obedience. If the individual's past acts were now regarded by him as not fully free, if they were attributable to his past ignorance, inexperience, or the pressure of events, they might be laid to rest. But once the fact of freedom is fully appreciated, and once the sensitive individual comes fully to see how much each past act was not strictly necessary even as he performed it, how can that individual pardon himself? Just as he must ask punishment for any other person who freely opts to be immoral, so must he ask punishment for his past self, however much he has now reformed—indeed, perhaps to the very degree he has reformed and has become honest with himself.

Each of these three awarenesses, Kant concludes, forces the sensitive moral agent to carry with him an unrelinquishable burden of moral self-condemnation. At each moment, the agent remains fully responsible for his past, uncertain of his present, and unable to believe that his future will be any different. With uncompromising force, reason commands the individual to a state of moral purity which that same individual knows, on the basis of all his own moral experience, to be beyond his reach.[13] And the result of his total self-estimate is a deep moral despair— the sense that he cannot do what he must do.

So much for Kant's analysis. In a short while I shall look at his solution to this problem of moral reason. But before doing so, I think it is important to underscore the fact that what has been identified here is a genuine and pressing problem for real human beings, at least insofar as they are morally sensitive. The inclination of the modern reader on encountering a formulation of this problem or Kant's discussion of it in the *Religion,* I suspect, is perhaps to concede the force of this analysis on paper but to continue to believe that the problem is real only for those who share with Kant a particularly rigoristic sense of duty. This modern reaction probably has many roots, too many to trace here.

But it is certainly aided by our remoteness in everyday life from situations in which we bear a full and painful burden of moral responsibility. To make matters clearer, therefore, I want to look briefly at a case in which the necessity for precise and defensible moral choice confronts the individual with inescapable force and in which the slightest departure from moral uprightness carries with it the severest form of self-condemnation. The case I have in mind is once again drawn from the sphere of military activity. I use it, at the risk of appearing excessively preoccupied with war, because I believe it permits us easy entry into a whole realm of problems, military and non-military. Only after looking at the way our consciences respond to this extreme situation will I ask whether the conclusions drawn from it are applicable to or help illuminate less urgent forms of moral experience.[14]

The case I want to describe involves action in what is sometimes technically called a "partial compliance" situation, that is, a situation where to be moral an individual must perform a type of act that morality ordinarily condemns. Thus, killing another human being is ordinarily prohibited by our moral reason because no impartial, rational human being is prepared possibly to sacrifice his life simply in order to gain the liberty to kill. Nevertheless, despite the customary force of this prohibition, impartial rational agents are sometimes prepared to make an exception to this rule and permit, or even require, killing if this is the only way to prevent certain other persons, who have refused to comply with the prohibition, from killing. Here, of course, we have the rational basis for the permissibility of self-defense as well as the moral basis for police and armies. Nevertheless, while it is true that impartial rational agents can legitimate the use of force against aggressors, in doing so they are always careful to confine the liberty of action of moral agents to the very minimum force required for their purposes. Thus, the use of force must be a last resort and no more force may be used than is required to halt an aggression or prevent future aggressions.[15]

These restraints have their basis in each impartial rational agent's desire not to have an initial situation of partial compliance with the moral rules become an occasion for the total abandonment of moral restraint. That is, they are an effort to protect the general rule prohibiting killing from the erosion that self-defense might represent. As a result, acting responsibly in situations of partial compliance or non-compliance with the ideal moral rules requires considerable moral discrimination. Not only must the responsible agent resolve to do what in ordinary circumstances he would condemn, but he is required to act in violation of the ideal moral rules to the very minimum degree possible. He must find that precise line between excess and insufficiency, and he must do so while ignoring not only all the usual pressures of self-interest but also the natural resistance to doing what moral reason ordinarily judges wrong. That is, the fully moral agent must employ his impartial moral reason to suppress not only his immediate self-interest but also his general interest as an impartial person in upholding the ideal moral rules.

Against this background we might consider the case of an officer commanding a platoon of soldiers in a guerilla war. For our purposes we can neglect the usually important question of which side is right or wrong in the conflict as a whole and we can focus on an isolated military operation where the officer is called upon to lead his men against a suspected guerilla force. We can imagine that force to be possibly located in the environs of a small peasant village whose inhabitants the guerillas resemble, at least from a distance. Now as this officer leads his men near this village, he is motivated, if he is a responsible moral agent, by two countervailing considerations. On the one hand, he knows it to be his duty expeditiously to destroy the opposing military force and to do so with as few casualties among his own men as possible. On the other hand, he realizes that he must avoid any needless killing both among the enemy soldiers themselves and the non-combatant peasant population surrounding them. What these responsibilities mean concretely in this situation is that he must lead his troops as close to the village as possible, in order to verify the presence of resisting enemy soldiers, before he allows his men to open fire.

Confronted with this situation, I suggest, there is no way this officer can emerge with a good conscience. Whatever action he takes, whether apparently successful or unsuccessful, he must thereafter carry some burden of guilt and self-condemnation. Imagine the worst to occur, for example. Approaching the village, the officer perceives a group of figures, apparently armed, moving menacingly in his direction across the fields. Nervous and naturally concerned for the safety of his troops, he orders his men to open fire. Drawing nearer, he discovers a group of injured and dying peasants with only their work implements and no weapons at all. As he reviews his own decisions and actions in this case, can the commanding officer fail to condemn himself? Most obviously, of course, he must confess that he acted more hastily than was really required. He could have waited several seconds more before ordering his men to open fire. In addition, this officer must feel deeply uneasy about any self-regarding considerations that entered into his decision—however much some of those considerations might have seemed legitimate at the moment of decision. For example, he must entertain the possibility that what he considered a balanced judgment was one really distorted by fear—fear for his own life, fear for the lives of his men, or even fear for his reputation among higher-ups in the command. Narrow, self-regarding considerations were everywhere present in his decision-making process, of course. And, as a moral agent, he knew it to be his duty to overcome them when his impartial reason so dictated. But since it was he who had to make all the decisions and assume all the vantage points, including the impartial one, can he really be sure that he did not distort matters in his own direction? If this officer is honest with himself, and if he openly recognizes how prone he can be to see his own interests as more pressing than impartial reason can always allow, I suspect he cannot fully acquit himself of culpability for the tragedy that has ensued.

Of course, the officer can try to deny all this. He can ignore any self-centered motivations he might have had and he can declare himself always the master of his selfish inclinations. Or, he can endeavor to excuse himself by saying that it was just not possible to act more judiciously than he did in the circumstances and that no one can be held fully responsible for decisions made in such trying moments. But I suspect that no genuinely responsible person will be entirely satisfied with these excuses, least of all as made to himself. Indeed, it is probably the case that a genuinely responsible person, one aware of both his ever-present tendencies to egoism as well as his radical freedom always to resist these tendencies, would find these excuses not only unacceptable but actually reprehensible. Viewed impartially, they become efforts at self-deception which only compound the sense of guilt.

Nor is all this very much changed if the officer's decision has a happier result. Imagine, for example, that he orders his men to hold fire and, at considerable risk, restrains them from shooting until the opposing group is readily distinguished as peasants. In this case, the officer has avoided casualties on all sides. But is his conscience completely clear? Does he consider himself fully worthy of the praise his men lavish upon him? The answer to these questions, I think, is no, because to the officer this situation is probably not totally different from the more tragic one I just described. Here, too, possibly impermissible self-regarding considerations can be identified by him as interwoven in his moral reasoning process, and it is virtually impossible for an individual to affirm that these played no part in his decision.[16] Perhaps in this case it was a desire for a "clean" military reputation, perhaps even a disconcern or dislike for his men. It is true that in this situation the objective outcome seems to support the officer's judgment. But "seems" is the appropriate word. For just as unfortunate objective outcomes cannot absolutely be attributed to bad judgment, so a good outcome cannot be considered absolute proof of good judgment. And in view of the egoism he knows to have infected his reasoning, the officer is likely to consider himself more lucky than wise and to some degree, at least, deserving of condemnation.

This happier outcome is, of course, the exceptional case. Somewhere between it and total tragedy lie an enormous number of outcomes where the officer's harsh judgment on himself must be more or less supported by the objective circumstances. If we ask, therefore, why there is no way an agent can emerge from a situation like this with a morally good opinion of himself, why he must eschew all praise and assume a burden of guilt, we find our answer in the role of the ego in the whole reasoning process. It is the nature of this kind of partial compliance situation, we know, that the individual must seek to find that precise point where his will as an impartial agent to uphold the ordinary moral rules is outweighed by his will, also as an impartial agent, to permit or require an action that normally violates these rules. Under the best of conditions, of course, this task of impartially weighing vitally important and conflicting interests is difficult, since the agent must get beyond his own desires or inclinations and seek to achieve a truly impartial viewpoint. But the task is enormously complicated when the agent is an actor in the situation, with vital personal interests cropping up on all sides. In such moments, the morally impermissible but extraordinarily easy and tempting possibility of bending one's judgment to suit one's purpose is always present.

None of these considerations prevent an agent from knowing in advance that a morally acceptable judgment is achievable— even in cases where choice involves some breaking of an ideal moral rule. It is not the less-than-ideal quality of most moral choices that poses the problem, but the fact that, whether choice is hard or easy, in the moment of choosing, the individual is prone to give improper weight to purely self-regarding considerations.[17] This is partly because the interests of the self are among the most visible at such moments, but also because the anxieties of difficult situations naturally provoke an individual to magnify the claims of his own ego. Whatever explanation the individual might offer himself for his behavior, however, cannot remove the sense of wrongdoing experienced after the act. For each individual, in his radical freedom, always knows that *he could have acted otherwise than he did,* that whatever degree of ego-assertion manifested itself in his act and judgment need not have been there. There is, therefore, a fundamental opposition between the self's awarenesses as an impartial moral legislator and the self as it is involved in difficult moments of moral choice, or, as Reinhold Niebuhr has put it, between the self in contemplation and the self in action.[18] In contemplation, either before or after the event, the self knows what ought to be done and it knows itself capable of doing it. Yet, in the moment of action, the self never acts without some ego-regarding considerations that it must eventually come to judge improper. Before and after each act, in other words, the self is always free to envisage a more perfect possibility of action, one where the ego's claim is reduced, which it seems never to accomplish in acting.

Nor is this opposition between the self in contemplation and the self in action confined to the difficult case of partial-compliance action we have looked at. It is true that this kind of case, where evil is countered by evil, magnifies the problem of choice because even the slightest movement away from strict impartiality is likely to bring tragic results. We and our officer would probably be less troubled if no human lives, one way or the other, rested on the outcome of his decision. But in a real sense the same kind of moral difficulty crops up every time one is called upon to make an exception to a moral rule. In fact, behavior in non-compliance cases of this sort is really only a special instance of exception-making. Exceptions are demanded whenever an individual in some specific circumstance seeks a permission from all impartial rational agents for behavior different from that ordinarily required and allowed by moral reason (whose expression is the moral rules). Furthermore, like our special case, all exceptions involve situations where the individual's ego is typically an interested party to the outcome, so that there is a constant temptation to inflate the ego's claims. Carrying forth our analysis in the non-compliance case we can see that the same factors can work together whenever an exception is made to produce a sense of self-condemnation. This is especially true when the exception immediately benefits the deciding agent or those he cares about. However much the agent may justify his exception as impartially acceptable, he knows that his judgment and actions can rightfully be impeached as self-regarding. After he has acted, for example, this may take the form of an awareness that he cannot really justify what he has done "now that the pressure of events has passed." Prospectively, it may take the form of a resolve "to do better" next time.

Actually, the self need not even apparently profit by an exception for this kind of judgment to occur. For whose particular and private interests are not directly affected one way or another by the making of exceptions? Certainly the party who will immediately benefit by an exception has a private interest in the outcome. But no less so does the "impartial" bystander who seeks to judge the legitimacy of the other's behavior. For it is the nature of exceptions to general moral rules that however legitimate they may be, they tend to erode respect for the moral rules themselves.[19] When someone breaks a promise in order to save a life, for example, his act partly undermines the institution of promising by rendering further promises less trustworthy or by encouraging others to make promises with a less sincere commitment to keeping them. As a result, however much an exception may advantage a single individual, and however much it may receive the support of impartial agents, the larger community does experience some loss as a result of allowing it. For this reason, members of this larger community are never fully impartial but are always interested parties to the exception-making process. A distant illustration of this truth may be found in the fact that in our day it is the crime-beset, but not characteristically criminal, members of the middle class who are the strongest opponents of judicial leniency. This opposition to relaxing the strict application of the penal laws, however widespread it may be, is certainly not based on fully impartial considerations.

This logic leads us now to the unqualified assertion that every instance of making an exception to a moral rule must carry with it, for the sensitive moral agent, a price in terms of self-condemnation or guilt. In every such instance, the fully responsible person knows that he has perhaps illegitimately exaggerated his interest in the matter at hand and has either denied a valid exception or made an exception too readily. This self-condemnation, it is true, is rarely as acute as in our military case, where grave evils were involved. But the difference between this and other cases of exception-making is, at best, only a matter of degree, and all cases are a function of the conscientious sensitivity of the agents involved. We complete our understanding of the extent and gravity of this whole problem, moreover, if we keep in mind the fact that the making of exceptions is the very stuff of the moral life. The general moral rules—the rules of non-injury, fairness, fidelity, and the like—are easily recognized by reason independently of experience. But the moment a person begins to act he is called upon to weigh rule against rule, since, in experience, most of these rules are incompatible.[20] Thus, it is often impossible to avoid injuring others if we refuse to be dishonest, and similar conflicts crop up all the time between other moral rules. To act, therefore, is to subordinate one moral rule to another under the guidance of impartial reason, but that is merely another way of saying that to act is to make exceptions. And it is just this process, we now see, that brings the morally sensitive person a constant sense of moral inadequacy and guilt.

In the consideration of our military illustration we have wandered a long way from Kant. I hope, however, that this illustration has made the human significance of what he says a bit clearer. The chief problem identified by Kant, we saw, is the tendency, deriving from man's radical freedom, to invert the motives of the moral life: to place self-interest above impartial moral reason. The recognition of this tendency produces, according to Kant, the awareness by each individual of the inconstancy of his moral disposition, serious uncertainty over the worth of any present moral disposition, and a pervasive sense of culpability for every past immoral act. If we think back a moment to our military officer, I think we can see the pertinence of Kant's analysis. In this officer's perception of his own egoism at the decisive moment of moral choice, we see the possible inversion of motives of which Kant speaks. Hand in hand with this is the officer's awareness of the inconstancy of his moral disposition in that his prior will to do what duty required, although sincere, was perhaps not strictly respected at the moment of action. Then, too, there is the sense of culpability for the tragedy that ensued, the feeling of deep personal responsibility which no excuses or acts of repentance can fully relieve. Indeed, it would not be surprising for a conscientious officer in such circumstances to see subsequent reverses suffered by himself as fitting punishment for the wrong he has done. This may even be true if the first encounter had a successful outcome. In that case, future, less successful military operations may be received as a punishment and be attributed by the sensitive officer to his corrupt volition in earlier, more outwardly successful circumstances. Whatever the outcome, of course, the officer can gather from his experience the resolve never again to accede to his ego's illegitimate demands. But the sheer force of his ego and its sudden eruption from an apparently firm moral disposition must render perilous any confidence in that resolve or in what Kant calls the constancy of his moral disposition.

Kant's analysis of this entire problem really manifests its truth in moral experience, therefore, and this supports the conclusion that no thoroughly honest individual can feel content with his moral virtue. Every such person is eventually driven, in troubled fashion, to ask the question "How can I ever be morally worthy?" Those who fail to perceive just what morality requires, or who succeed in covering their failures with the excuses offered by themselves or others, may feel satisfied with their apparent moral achievements. They are, as Pascal put it, sinners who believe themselves righteous. But the person genuinely dedicated to morality and ruthlessly honest with himself knows that whatever his outward appearance, a radically immoral tendency infects his will, which, at best, only awaits the circumstances to show how really condemnable it is. Indeed, as I have already suggested, to an individual whose conscience is this acute, the ordinary hardships or sufferings of experience may come to be viewed as earned punishment for his hidden moral corruption.[21] No doubt this extreme of self-condemnation and blame can frequently be associated in the lives of real persons with all sorts of diseased and aberrant psychological tendencies. But it is a mistake to attribute all such blame or willed self-punishment merely to irrational forces in the psyche.[22] For whatever the psychological forces with which it may be associated, self-condemnation can be a valid product of reason—indeed, if what I am saying is right, it is a necessary product of reason. Moreover, this means that such self-condemnation can only finally be relieved on reason's own terrain—with a satisfactory answer to the question "How can I ever be morally worthy?"

This brings us once again squarely back to the question with which we started. We can see now with what urgency it can be asked. And we can perhaps also see why this question must be answered. For unless it is, each individual is necessarily driven to despair. He finds himself required to pursue a moral perfection which he can never achieve and which his most intense efforts may serve only to distance further. Thus, this despair can propel an individual to abandon moral striving altogether, with the curious effect that self-condemnation is thereby increased, or it can drive the individual into new and frantic efforts at moral perfection which must always eventually lead to self-condemnation and which, in the process, can so distort moral judgment as to actually produce violations of the moral rules.[23] Either way self-condemnation is increased. Now, since no individual can function in despair of this sort, and since reason will not permit the abandonment of a full moral commitment, the individual is compelled to seek an answer to his question that will once again make the objective of an upright will a realistic goal.

The logic of this position, I should note, roughly parallels that of the dilemma we explored in the previous chapter. There, in connection with the question "Why should I be moral?" we saw an imperative demand of reason (recognition of the absolute authority of the moral law) opposed by an awareness drawn from experience (that moral persons are not necessarily happy so that it is not strictly rational to be moral). We also saw that reason, in order to remove the contradiction this involved and to facilitate the moral life, was required to postulate and affirm a series of beliefs which went beyond experience to overcome the difficulties experience presented. Now here, too, we see something of this pattern. In this case, the demand of reason (that to be judged morally worthy we always maintain an upright moral disposition) is opposed by an awareness drawn from experience (that our disposition is not always constant), and here again we find reason driven somehow to eliminate the contradiction in order to facilitate the moral life.

The critical question, of course, is whether it can do so. Does there in fact exist a tenable and satisfactory answer to the general question "How can I ever be morally worthy?" in view of what this question entails? In seeking an answer, the observed parallel to our earlier discussion may be useful. There we saw the problem eliminated by the qualification of one term in the apparent contradiction. In that case it was the second term, the one drawn from experience, which was rendered less than necessarily true by the addition of certain supra-empirical beliefs. Can a similar move be made in this case? Unfortunately it seems not, for the sheer fact of my past defections from duty seems to rule out forever any hope that I can *always* be moral. In other words, since the judgment I make upon myself cannot permit any dereliction from the moral law, my past acts represent a permanent obstacle to becoming worthy, and no beliefs I hold about my future behavior can wipe this fact away. If there is to be any relaxation of the dilemma, therefore, it must pertain to the first term of the contradiction. Somehow, the rational awareness that to be judged morally worthy we must always maintain an upright moral disposition must be shown to be not utterly and absolutely true; it must in some way be qualified. But how can that be? That judgment is a product of our own impartial reason and seems impervious to our efforts to relax it. Insofar as we regard ourselves, we must be convinced that each and every failure to will the absolute priority of the moral law is a sufficient ground for unsparing moral condemnation. Indeed, any effort on our part to compromise this judgment upon ourselves must become a further ground for self-condemnation. Is there, then, any way out of the dilemma?

I might say here that Kant's own effort to answer this question is of limited value. This is because here as elsewhere Kant moves too quickly from a detailed examination of the problem of pure reason to a specific theistic solution to that problem. That is, in order to resolve this problem, Kant moves precipitously and without any intervening steps to a solution employing concepts borrowed from the Western religious tradition. This move is understandable, since Kant's knowledge of alternative religious traditions was very limited and it naturally seemed to him that Western religious solutions to this problem were the only ones possible. But whatever the reasons for his moves here, the effect is to perplex the more critical reader who is not convinced by Kant's quick transition from the dilemma of reason to a specific theistic solution. The reader naturally asks, "Must I really believe that?" More serious is the fact that with this hasty transition, the bare form of reason's solution, the next step in the rational deduction, is lost and one is unable to determine precisely what reason calls for at this point. Be that as it may, Kant's solution is at least worth examining. In general, it amounts to the required belief that if I recognize fully my inadequacy but still resolve at every new moment of time to reorient my will firmly toward morality, then I can assume that God will accept that volition in lieu of my continued moral obedience and that God will assist me in maintaining the uprightness of my will in the future. By dint of a belief in a gracious God, in other words, that to which I morally have no claim will be accorded to me.[24]

Actually, Kant's theistic grace solution is slightly more detailed than this because it has an aspect corresponding to each of the three specific problems he has identified. Thus, to the problem posed by my awareness of the inconstancy of my disposition, Kant advances as necessary the belief that in the moment of sincere moral commitment, I may suppose as given to me from without a Comforter or Paraclete who will assist me to sustain that commitment in the future.[25] To my awareness that no single volition but only a completed life of virtue is an adequate basis for moral worth Kant responds with the required belief that God, who judges the heart directly, will accept the predominant orientation of the will for the deed (a perfect life).[26] And, finally, to the awareness that I must bear continued guilt for my past wrongdoings, Kant advances as a solution the belief that insofar as I change my will, the penitent suffering I undergo in the moment of change will somehow serve as an acceptable retribution for my past misdeeds.[27]

Kant's dependence here on the Jewish-Christian conception of a gracious God is clear, even down to the matter of terminology. And surely if one accepts belief in such a deity, this problem of reason may be solved. But all this indicates is that certain Judaeo-Christian beliefs may be among the class of adequate representations for reason's needs. What is not shown is whether reason is propelled to these and only these beliefs for its solution or whether that solution might not take a more basic form. Nevertheless, although Kant's answer here is not necessarily the next step in reason's deduction, it may help us to see what that next step might be. For if we regard what is important in this notion of a gracious God, it is the general idea of the existence of a supreme and perfectly moral causal agency *that is not neces-sitated always to judge and act morally as we ourselves must al-ways judge and act.* In other words, by unpacking Kant's notion of God and reducing it to the bare level of what reason strictly demands, we are led once again to the idea of a supreme and perfectly moral causal agency. Following the same procedure with the idea of God's grace leads to the idea that the supreme causal agency, though perfectly moral, is not strictly required always to act or judge as we must do. For what is a gracious God but a personal agency who refrains from punishing us when we know we deserve it, or, what is the same, when we must condemn and punish ourselves? Assuming this translation or reduction of Kant is correct, what remains to be seen is whether it really satisfies reason's needs. Two questions seem to be involved. First, is it even rationally possible to hold the idea of a causal agency that is strictly moral but that is not required always to judge or act as we must? Second, if this idea is thinkable, does it really provide an adequate and sufficient solution to reason's need, to the problem of despair caused by our deep awareness of moral inadequacy?

The first question is troubling. Can our reason really enter-tain the idea of a supreme and perfectly moral causal agency that is not, at the same time, always required to judge or act as our reason demands that we do? Can it do this, for example, without altering its normal means of judgment or without converting the "morality" of this supreme agency into something qualitatively different from what we conceive morality to be? Can our reason tolerate any such move if it means the abandonment of reason's customary grounds of judgment?

To help answer this question we might keep in mind the fact that every finite agent is called upon to act in two distinct but deeply related ways. One way is always to uphold the moral law by conforming to the principles it establishes. The other way is willingly to condemn and punish violations of that law, or at least those for which the self is responsible and to which it is susceptible.[28] Now, for a being who is prone to violate the moral law, these two ways of acting necessarily imply one another. A willingness to uphold the moral law requires a willingness to condemn and punish (at least the self, and sometimes others) for violations of that law. For in this case, where an unjustifiable violation of morality's requirements is involved, an unwillingness to punish must go hand in hand with the intention to violate the law at some future time or with the belief that the law can and should occasionally be violated. In other words, a willingness to punish is, for a finite being, the necessary confirmation of the purity of its moral intention. But for an agency that is, by definition, supremely and perfectly moral, the failure always to punish immorality in no way impugns its ability or willingness always to follow the moral law. Obviously such an agency cannot punish itself. But its reluctance to punish others can never, as in the case of imperfect agents, be construed as an effort to compromise the severity of the moral law or to escape its restraint. Thus, at least insofar as punishment is concerned, a perfect moral agency is not always required to act as we must act. Whether its perfection permits this kind of agency to defect from other aspects of the law normally incumbent upon us is not certain. Given the qualitatively different circumstances of its action, and given the fact that many aspects of the moral law respond to the special problems of finite and morally imperfect beings, the possibility cannot be denied. But for the moment, at least with regard to punishment, the idea of a supreme and perfectly moral causal agency not required always to act or judge as we are can be rationally sustained.

Our second question is whether such an agency, even if it can be admitted by reason, can provide an adequate and sufficient solution to the necessary perception of our moral unworthiness and our resulting despair. One way to begin to answer this is to look at the implications of the opposite belief than that proposed. If there existed, for example, a supreme and perfectly moral causal agency necessarily motivated by our own interior judgments of worth and, like us, compelled to punish, then our predicament would be seriously worsened. For then, to our interior grounds of self-condemnation and to our sense of deserved punishment would be added the objective possibility that we might suffer proportionate unhappiness for our unworthiness. If, in opposition to this, we allow that a supreme and perfectly moral causal agency is not in every sense required to act as we are, then the predicament is eased. For then we have the hope that when it comes to punishment that agency is not compelled to inflict upon us the unhappiness we know we deserve.

In itself, of course, this awareness cannot eliminate the severest problem generated by the sense of moral inadequacy. For the genuine moral agent is not so much troubled by his destiny as by his self-estimate. What does the prospect of possible happiness mean to such an agent, in other words, if he regards himself as undeserving of that state? The only way for the agent to escape this predicament is to be given some basis for believing that his own impartial self-estimate is not the only or even the ultimate one open to a moral being. But within the operations of his own impartial reason, no such basis for belief can be found. Indeed, the agent cannot even allow himself to appeal to impartial reason to qualify his self-estimate lest in doing so he actually increase his defection from the moral law. We return here, in other words, to the apparently insuperable first term of the contradiction which generates this dilemma in the first place. That term requires the individual always to maintain a morally upright disposition in order to be judged morally worthy. And certainly, insofar as the individual's impartial moral judgment is concerned, that requirement is absolute. But must the final judgment of moral worth always be made by our own impartial reason? Is every individual's impartial self-estimate necessarily the final one?

At just this point the "supreme" component in the idea of

a supreme and perfectly moral causal agency can perform a decisive role, for in its supremacy that agency may be thought of not only as the ground of nature but somehow of all reality as well. That suggests that we, with our morality and our moral judgments, are in some way a product of its activity. All of our judgments, in other words, including our most pressing moral judgments, may be thought of as not necessarily absolute but as one expression, possibly only a partial expression, of the supreme and perfect moral agency from which they derive. None of this allows us to qualify our reason, of course, or to consider its imperatives or judgments any less severe. In every moment of moral action we are necessarily called upon to respect our own impartial reason. But when that reason leads us to an impasse, and when it actually threatens to paralyze moral action, then we may be permitted to appeal to a higher and more perfect ground of judgment upon which ours may depend. And if it is the case that this ground of judgment need not always conform to our own self-judgment, then we at least have a minimal basis for believing that our own condemnatory self-judgment is neither the only nor even the ultimate and most important final estimate of our worth. In fact, by strictly condemning ourselves, by despairingly continuing our striving to be worthy, and by appealing to the possible actions of a supreme judgmental agency in order to render rational what we do, we may actually be conforming to that supreme agency's ultimate standard of worth. We cannot, of course, establish such worth for ourselves even if we ardently conjoin moral striving with our own self-condemnation, for we must always regard ourselves as interested parties in our case. But an agency which cannot, by definition, be accused of self-regard in this connection may afford us grounds for believing in our own ultimate acceptability. Admittedly this is once again an uncertain and very narrow exit out of reason's impasse. But, as in the case of our earlier dilemma, the pressure of untenable alternatives makes this one attractive.

This translation and reduction of Kant's theistic solution,

therefore, seems to satisfy reason's needs. By means of it we are able to resolve the second major dilemma of moral reason, and we can answer the question posed at the beginning of this chapter. That question, "How can I ever be morally worthy?" finds its answer, we now see, in the belief that there possibly exists a perfect moral causal agency, supreme over all reality, which is not strictly required always to act or judge morally as we are, and which, in its very supremacy, stands as the final objective ground and arbiter of moral worth. By means of this belief, the individual's necessary self-condemnation is relieved and he is given the possibility—however slight it may be—of rationally doing what his moral reason commands: renewing at every new moment of time his commitment to the strict priority of morality.

This answer is admittedly spare. It does not furnish us with an understanding of the precise nature of this agency. Nor does it tell us just why that agency should remit the condemnation we know we deserve. But reason does not absolutely require such knowledge, since the confidence that an agency with these attributes exists is sufficient to satisfy its most pressing needs. Indeed, because it recognizes that such an agency has an experience qualitatively different from its own, reason is even prepared to concede the difficulty of attaining perfect understanding.

With this belief, I suspect, we have come to the end of our exploration and elaboration of the structure of pure religious reason. I say this because we now seem in a position to answer all those questions that must be answered if morality is to be given an unequivocal rational justification. Thus, we can furnish a justification of morality itself, we can tell each individual why it is always rational for him to be moral, and we can affirm with confidence, if not certainty, that moral worthiness is within each person's reach. Reason's strictest needs, therefore, have been met. This does not mean that human beings do not have other than rational needs nor even that reason does not desire (but not require) more than these beliefs can furnish. In subsequent chapters we shall see what a rich series of edifices historical religious systems have erected upon the foundations of religious reason, frequently in the effort to satisfy other needs than those produced by reason. At the same time, however, we shall see how strictly the rational foundation rules the task of construction, for it is reason in its theoretical, moral, and religious employments that ultimately furnishes the objectives to these historical systems and that sets the limits upon how these objectives may be pursued.

5.

The requirements of pure religious reason

I have reached the point where I should consolidate and clarify the argument I have been developing. Up to now, I have been concerned with following the course traced by reason as it advances through its deliberative and moral employments. Occasionally the pace has been so rapid—with the need for the solution to some problem pushing me on—that I have neglected subsidiary issues or implicit ideas in an effort to keep up with the advancing argument. Now is the time, however, to gather all these matters together in a presentable and coherent form. The task is all the more important because of what lies ahead. In the next chapter and in the remaining chapters of Part II, I want to examine some major historical religious systems for their conformity to the requirements of religious reason. The aim will be to ascertain whether an understanding of the fundamental rational structures underlying religious belief can help us comprehend and explain important aspects of the belief and development of these major traditions. But for that purpose we must have the whole structure of religious reason clear in our minds at the outset, and the following table is meant to identify this basic structure:

THE REQUIREMENTS OF PURE RELIGIOUS REASON

To comply strictly with the demands of reason . . .

1. A religious system must advance and sustain beliefs which always conduce to full obedience to the moral law such that:
   a. moral obedience is always in fact rendered to that law above all else, and to that law in the same form as given to us by our impartial reason;
   b. obedience extends to all aspects of the moral law including its strict duties (whether interpersonal, institutional, or international), its standard of moral worth (virtue), and its rules of supererogation; and
   c. obedience on the part of the religious believer can be expected to be at least as rigorous as that of a non-religious moral agent and possibly even more rigorous.

2. A religious system must advance and sustain beliefs which solve the problem of moral obedience by postulating the possibly real existence of a causal agency (or form of causality)
   a. supreme over nature and history;
   b. actuated perfectly by morality;
   c. directly respondent to inner human volitions; and
   d. capable of bestowing happiness, not just self-contentment (the personal satisfaction produced by virtue), in proportion to an agent's moral worth.

3. A religious system must advance and sustain beliefs which resolve the problem of human moral inadequacy by affirming that the supreme moral causal agency need not always act or judge as we must and, therefore, need not necessarily determine the fate or worth of moral agents in keeping with their own moral judgments.

4. A religious system must advance and sustain belief supporting a valid moral anthropology which recognizes that
   a. human beings are able to exercise moral freedom, are morally responsible, and can be judged as morally blameworthy; and that
   b. human beings are prone to the wrongful assertion of their particular ends over those required by morality.

5. A religious system must advance and sustain beliefs which do not contradict theoretical reason in either its natural-scientific or historical knowledge.

6. A religious system must advance and sustain belief which when going beyond knowledge grounded in experience do so minimally.

7. A religious system must advance and sustain all the beliefs required by reason, whatever the tensions between them, with no effort made to suppress necessary beliefs in order to eliminate these tensions.

Instead of reviewing all the arguments we have explored, I want to proceed directly to an examination of each of the requirements of religious reason contained in this summary table. If this table seems surprisingly long, given the limited set of required beliefs we have discussed, it must be kept in mind that in its religious employment, reason assumes those aspects of its other employments, whether theoretical, prudential, or moral, that bear upon the religious enterprise.

One other preliminary point. As we have seen, the beliefs pertaining to religious reason are, in fact, beliefs required by reason. This means that a table of religious reason's program is also a statement of those beliefs which each individual must hold if he wishes to be fully rational. Since our task in the chapters ahead, however, is not primarily to explore the implications of these beliefs for the rational individual but to examine actual historical religious systems for their conformity to the fundamental requirements of religious reason, this table presents these requirements in a form suited to the concrete task of formulating a system of religious belief. It goes without saying that this framework for examining and testing traditional religious speculation also contains those fundamental beliefs which each rational agent must hold and elaborate if he wishes to be both moral and fully rational.

To one who has followed the argument up to now, the stipulations of the first broad section of this table (requirement 1) may seem entirely new. But, in fact, they express nothing not already contained in the moral law out of which religious reason develops. The first sub-requirement, for example, merely expresses the fact that each moral agent must always be led to make the moral law itself, in the form given him by his impartial reason, the supreme determining ground of his will. Absolutely forbidden by this requirement is the placing of any merely particular or private incentive above the moral law, or the positing of any beliefs which must have this effect. This requirement, as we know, follows from the demand of impartial reason that its directives take priority over all others. As such, this requirement expresses the essential idea of the Kantian notion of moral autonomy, although the use of this term may have some misleading connotations in this context. Thus, there are two things that this requirement—and the idea of autonomy—does not require and it is important for our understanding of religious reason to point these out. First, this requirement does not require the elimination of all other motives for moral behavior. In keeping a promise, for example, I am certainly permitted by impartial reason to have many motives for doing so apart from the consideration that this behavior is right: I can like the person I have made the promise to, fear reproach, or whatever. All that moral reason requires is that none of these other motives ever establish supremacy over duty itself and threaten to supplant it as the final determining ground of the will. In the last analysis, I must always do what duty requires, whether I have additional reasons for doing so or not.[1]

In the second place, the idea of autonomy as expressed in this sub-requirement does not necessarily imply (as the term may unfortunately suggest) that the moral law must be acknowledged to be a product of moral reason. It is fully permissible, for example, for an individual to obey the moral law without ever acknowledging that the law itself is a product of reason. And it is even possible for the law's authority to be grounded in beliefs, needs, or desires that have nothing to do with a respect for reason. All that is ever required is that whatever reason an individual has for obeying the moral law, and whatever he believes the source of the law's authority to be, these beliefs can never in any way conduce to disobedience to the moral law.[2]

An example may make this difficult point clearer. If an individual has the improbable passion of intensely loving the impartial will of each and every rational being, and if, as a result, he is committed to never doing anything which could not be impartially agreed upon by every other rational being, then he would never be led to violate the moral law and he would have a reason for being moral that is fully acceptable to reason. This is true despite the fact that he does not acknowledge the authority of the moral law, despite the fact that he insists that his behavior has nothing to do with his acting rationally, and despite the fact that his reasons for acting are very personal, if not peculiar. Reason, in other words, does not demand that one acknowledge its authority but only that one *always* do what it requires, whatever one's own reasons for acting may be.

When we turn to historical religious systems, we shall see how important this understanding can be, for it is the common tendency of most of these systems to provide ultimate reasons for acting—love of a moral God is a leading example—which, though ostensibly having nothing to do with human reason and sometimes even disparaging of reason, nevertheless are of a character that they necessarily and without possible exception motivate compliance with reason's commands. Nor should this be surprising. We are well aware by now of the difficulties produced by the acknowledgment of the merely human and rational basis of morality. It is these very difficulties, we saw, that finally force reason to establish a supra-empirical support for the moral life. Small wonder, then, that religious systems which begin by positing this kind of support for morality invariably seek to obscure the rational basis of morality as well. In doing so, however, they must be careful—if they wish to conform to reason—never to allow whatever new bases for the moral life they introduce to undermine the constant priority of the moral law. Hence the curious but common phenomenon of systems denying the authority of reason, whose belief structure in every way actually leads one to conform to reason's demands.

The remaining stipulations of this first general requirement need very little explanation. They largely express the demands of moral reason. If we recall that reason is forced into a religious employment in order to facilitate moral obedience, it is natural that reason should require whatever religious beliefs it advances not to erode moral responsibility and, if possible, even to enhance moral compliance. Ideally, the religious believer should not only be moral without reservation, but among the beliefs that make this possible, he should find additional reasons and motivations for adopting a rigorously moral life. Such a life should include full compliance with the moral law as it bears on personal, social, political (institutional), and international relations. It should reflect the fullest development of the dispositional basis of morality (virtue), and it should be characterized by the performance of supererogatory acts, those not strictly required but encouraged by reason.[3]

The second and third general requirements of the table also pose few difficulties. Each expresses the conclusions I have tried to develop over the course of the preceding chapters. Some points are emphasized here, however, that were passed over too quickly earlier. Thus, the perfectly moral agency postulated by reason is here described as directly respondent to interior dispositions of the self rather than to externally observable moral performance. This focus on disposition and volition has its basis in a fact known to each moral agent—that ultimately it is for the direction of his will and not the consequences of his acts that he is held morally responsible. No moral agent, after all, can normally be held responsible for what lies beyond his control. It is a reflection of the limits of our nature that our will to bring a state of affairs about does not guarantee that our objectives will be realized. Thus, we know, and our moral reason knows, that we can be held strictly responsible only for what we will. This does not mean that we can ignore the consequences of our actions. I am not speaking here of an attitude that contents itself with the disposition and lets the consequences be damned. Our reason knows that each of our wills must contain the most exacting and scrupulous regard for the real consequences of our actions.[4] But still, it is only for this willing that the agent is held responsible. In view of the centrality of the will for judgments of moral worth, therefore, it is to be expected that a perfectly moral agency whose task is to mete out happiness in proportion to virtue should be thought of as being motivated by what transpires at the very core of each personality. Just how such a supreme agency can penetrate each person's conscience is something reason does not strictly require to know. Indeed, it may even not be necessary for this agency to enter from without (it having some permanent basis within the self). However, it is also true that in his own command and surveillance of his will, every individual (who also knows himself from without) has the experience of a judgmental agency which can transcend the ordinary barriers to personal knowledge. This experience of regarding himself from without and within at least suggests the possibility of another, more perfect agency doing the same to all persons.

Reason's willingness to remain uninformed about all the conditions of its demands extends, as well, to several other items in these second and third sections. I have already observed, for example, that reason does not require knowledge of why a supreme moral agency should remit the punishment that each agent knows he deserves. Also not demanded by reason is the knowledge of just how a supreme moral causality can mediate happiness to the virtuous. Happiness, we know, is that state in which the real desires of an agent are satisfied. It is quite different from self-contentment, for which the satisfactions arise from the will's ability to suppress or control the force of desire. Now, in view of our experience that moral agents are not always happy, how can a supreme causal agency make them so, especially if in doing so it may operate in a realm beyond our experience? What kind of happiness can such an agency mediate? All these questions are naturally raised by a rational individual with understandable urgency. But this individual also knows that these questions do not necessarily have to be answered. The very supremacy of the posited causal agency sufficiently justifies reason's confidence that what it requires may be forthcoming. No possibility, except self-contentment and that which is absolutely contradictory, is closed to such a supreme agency.

Even beyond this, however, if a rational agent seeks some understanding of how happiness can be expected outside the ordinary bounds of sense experience, he can once again regard his very special experience as a rational and moral being. Here he can perceive genuine satisfactions generated by reason itself, by the love of moral persons or by forms of knowledge. This experience suggests that the prospect for happiness, perhaps even a consummate happiness, beyond the range of sense experience is not impossible, and this provides further support for reason's confidence. In proceeding this way, religious reason displays one of its more characteristic moves and one in which, as we shall see, religious speculation commonly engages with great success. This involves using aspects of our rational and moral experience as a basis for elaborating elements of the supra-empirical beliefs required by reason. Although such elaboration is not rationally required, it seems to be a constant feature of actual religious systems.

The fourth requirement of the table merely specifies some of the estimates of human nature which religious reason assumes. We have seen how the specific features of this anthropology grow out of reason's own self-scrutiny. What the table emphasizes here is not merely that these beliefs about human nature are correct, but that they ought to be effectively respected by any religious system seeking strictly to obey the requirements of religious reason. This does not mean that a religious system must actively affirm these beliefs, for it can always remain silent about the whole matter. In the final analysis, religious reason is most concerned with the practice of the moral life, and this means that the presupposition of freedom and human moral inadequacy must be evidenced in the total structure of a faith, not necessarily in explicit teachings.

Since requirements five and six of this table offer nothing new, I want to move quickly to the final, and in some ways, the most important requirement of religious reason. This requirement has heretofore been only implicit in what I have said, and because this is the first time we encounter it as an explicit requirement of reason, I will take some time to explain and justify its presence in the table. I might begin by saying that it is the nature of moral reason that it culminates its deductive process with a series of rather striking paradoxes. Two, in particular, deserve attention. First, there is the fact that moral reason requires each individual to be prepared to suppress his happiness at the same time as it permits each individual to hold his happiness as his end. Second, moral reason demands an unwavering constancy of moral disposition at the same time as it requires each individual to confess his own inability to maintain such a disposition. These beliefs are properly termed paradoxes rather than outright contradictions, we know, because reason, with the assistance of certain supra-empirical beliefs, is able to render these opposing awarenesses coherent and harmonious. But within the realm of moral experience these beliefs seem to be sharply opposed.

Now, since religious reason aims at a final and supra-empirical resolution of these contradictions, and since it is not led to its proper solutions to them unless the contradictions are openly recognized, it must clearly refuse to allow their premature resolution by any effort to compromise one side or the other of the contradiction. In the face of these awarenesses, in other words, it must affirm the truth of each, however incoherent that may make the ensemble appear. Thus, religious reason rejects efforts to soften the first contradiction by claiming that human beings do not really need to be happy. Similarly, it rejects efforts to remove the second contradiction by holding that since human beings cannot be unwaveringly moral they need not strive to be so.

All these seemingly contradictory ideas are correspondingly imported into religious reason. But here, too, reason does not permit the contradictions simply to be effaced. Since each term of each contradiction represents a permanent and important demand of reason, it must be preserved even as the contradictory character of the whole is eliminated. Typically this is done within religious reason by bringing together all the terms of a contradiction within the description of some supra-empirical object or state. Thus, the causal agency postulated by reason is declared to be perfectly moral and perfectly powerful, despite the obvious presence of suffering righteousness in the world. Or again, it is declared to be perfectly moral even as it is said to be unmoved by the moral inadequacies or failures of ordinary moral agents. On the surface some of this may seem like nonsense. But looked at carefully, these kinds of assertions represent a very subtle and important rational activity. Refusing to relinquish its various contradictory insistences, reason succeeds in preserving them by joining all opposing terms in a domain where they cannot, by definition, be said to contradict. That is, it is just the nature of objects, agencies, or realms beyond our experience that they can have qualities not permissible within our experience, and reason precisely employs this fact to affirm what it cannot ordinarily affirm without contradiction.[5]

We should not be surprised, therefore, to find religious traditions frequently making claims about the objects of their concern which appear to contradict ordinary experience. In doing so, these traditions are in fact obeying an important requirement of religious reason which, in turn, derives from moral reason. This is the requirement that they not eliminate fundamental truths of moral experience simply to ease the apparent contradictions they create. Indeed, we have here an important way of understanding and characterizing the whole religious enterprise. We can think of religion as the effort to utilize a possible but unknowable domain beyond our experience as a way of rationally harmonizing, while always retaining in their integrity, those demands of our reason which must be affirmed but which, within our ordinary experience, remain contradictory.[6]

In view of this we are also in a better position to understand the frequently paradoxical and enigmatic nature of religious discourse. If religious systems commonly make reference to states or objects with qualities not capable of being brought together within our experience, this is not because such objects or states really exist or have been experienced *but rather and primarily because they must be affirmed as existing.* I can perhaps make this point clearer by indicating what I think religious belief and discourse are not. Occasionally, in view of the enigmatic nature of certain religious utterances or claims, it is maintained that religious discourse has its basis in certain extraordinary experiences. Typical is Otto's view that there is an experience of the "numinous" at the heart of all religion and that this numinous transcends all the normal categories of our experience.[7] Because of this, Otto maintains, religious discourse is unique and often incomprehensible—it is an effort to put into ordinary terms and categories the experience of objects or states that defy these categories or terms. But if what I have been saying is correct, Otto has the matter turned around. In fact, it is not in the first place a real experience that gives rise to the affirmation of an enigmatic object with opposing qualities. Rather, it is reason's own requirements that give rise to the need to affirm the existence or experience of an enigmatic object. Thus, if I affirm the existence of an agency or state that is consummately moral and yet in some ways "beyond morality," it is not necessarily because I have experienced such an agency or state but because I must affirm its existence. I do not want to deny, of course, that many religious believers have reported—and possibly have had—enigmatic experiences of the numinous such as Otto describes. But even if this is so it remains unclear whether these experiences are everywhere at the heart of religious experience (as against being isolated aberrations) or even whether these experiences do not themselves proceed from the needs and activities of reason. Thus, it may be that reason appropriates diverse and idiosyncratic experiences for its own use. Whatever is the case, all we can responsibly speak about is that aspect of such discourse we can comprehend, the aspect that proceeds from reason's needs.[8]

It is worth noting in this connection that the analytic tradition of philosophy has been right in maintaining that religious discourse has a logic of its own, that it involves a "language game" (or "form of life") quite different from that encountered in ordinary discourse or in science. Observing the way religious believers stubbornly resist evidence that seems to imperil their beliefs, analytic philosophers have also rightly identified an important "commissive" dimension to religious discourse—its role in expressing commitments rather than merely stating facts.[9] But what analytic philosophers have usually failed to provide is any insight into the underlying moral logic of religious discourse or the way it works to satisfy the requirements of practical reason.

This gap in the analytic program is not, I think, accidental. It reflects an assumption, already present in Wittgenstein's writings, that it is not really possible to understand or make sense of religious claims in any propositional way at all. Just as moral philosophers in the analytic tradition have sought to find a place for moral utterances by denying them cognitive status and reducing their significance to the subjective and unchallengeable expression of feelings or commitments, so analytic philosophers of religion have made room for religious belief by placing it, in principle, beyond the reach of rational justification or criticism. But this approach, I would argue, is as inadequate for the understanding of religious discourse as it has been for the understanding of moral discourse.[10] Both moral and religious statements have their basis in justifiable practical rational arguments and it is this basis that explains their common persuasive force.[11] Thus, despite some superficial similarities, the approach to religion I am offering here, with its stress on the underlying rationality of even the most perplexing religious utterances, differs substantially from the approach taken by the analytic tradition.

All these considerations should be kept in mind as we begin in the next chapter the task of examining historical religious traditions for their conformity to these requirements of pure religious reason. This task is made difficult because of the contradictory and confusing nature of so much religious discourse. Despite the rational and moral basis of religion according to this understanding, for example, religious traditions seem frequently to want to disparage both reason and morality. In itself this tendency is no ground for denying these traditions' conformity to the requirements of religious reason, and it may even be a reason for affirming such conformity since religious reason can help explain remarks of this kind. But this does point up something we must always keep in mind as we look at the various traditions. It is never sufficient to hold up one or another isolated belief of a religion as a ground for affirming or denying that tradition's conformity to reason. To test an understanding of this sort, one must take all aspects of the tradition together. One must ask "Does the whole religious system actually conform to the demands of reason?" or "Does the system in its entirety produce the kind of moral life that reason demands, and does the total structure of belief actually contribute to that end?"

A further problem we will encounter in testing a theory of this sort is that human beings are not always fully rational, so that some of their religious traditions may not be fully rational. That is, in the history of the great religious traditions, we shall sometimes encounter failures to conform to the requirements of our table.

Does this mean that our understanding of religion is inadequate? Not necessarily. It must be kept in mind that the complicated structure demanded by religious reason is difficult both to comprehend and to respect. Errors in judgment are natural. Nevertheless, it is a test of the essential validity and pertinence of this rational structure that when errors are made they have significant and perceivable consequences. In time, these consequences must stimulate efforts at reform or lead to the demise of the system that has refused to correct itself. An analogy to the area of physical construction may help explain what I mean. No one, I think, would say that it is a refutation of the laws of physics that houses occasionally fall down. Indeed, collapse or strenuous efforts at repair indicate the very pertinence of these laws. The same is true of religious systems and the demands of religious reason. We should not expect perfect conformity to the requirements of religious reason. But whenever we encounter marked disconformity we should also expect to see within a reasonable space of time characteristic corrective maneuvers. These can take the form of sharp dispute and discussion over the pertinent matter within a religious community, schismatic movements that distance themselves from the original community over the disputed point, or even complete religious collapse. In other words, our test of a tradition's conformity to the requirements of pure religious reason must to some degree be diachronic; we must look at religious traditions not as static achievements but as ongoing efforts to conform to reason's exacting demands.

II.

Applied religious reason

6.

Judaism: the justice and mercy of God

To the observer schooled in the ordinary canons of logical discourse, historical religious traditions characteristically present a confusing picture. Because of their basis in the operations of religious reason, these traditions frequently defy the usual requirements of clarity and consistency in expression and belief. Among the historical religions, probably no tradition illustrates this tendency better than Judaism. The Rabbis who shaped the normative Talmudic tradition of classical Judaism drew upon the rich moral experience of centuries of Jewish national life as they sought to address the diversity of problems raised by morality. In this task they were unencumbered either by the demands of logic that beset later Christian theologians (who worked in a Hellenistic philosophical milieu) or by the pressures for coherence of thought sometimes associated with centralized religious authority. As a result, the Rabbis had free rein to respect, express, and emphasize the many seemingly opposed beliefs required by religious reason. As Solomon Schechter remarks, "Whatever the faults of the Rabbis were, consistency was not one of them."[1]

To say that the system of faith and ethics elaborated by the Rabbis has its basis in the operations of human reason would certainly have appeared to the Rabbis themselves as blasphemous. In their eyes, both faith and morals proceeded directly from the revealed will of God. It was Torah, by which they meant the teachings of the Bible, the associated oral tradition and the commentary on both, that made known to men the course of life they should follow. In the process of interpreting Torah, to be sure, human reason had a role, and it was even held possible for unassisted reason to arrive at the most fundamental precepts of morality and religion. But in the final analysis all knowledge of right and wrong, and the very distinction itself, had a basis not in man's reason but God's will.[2]

None of this should surprise us. The derivation of morality from a transcendent source is a characteristic feature of religious ethics. It is a feature that does not so much contradict as support the claim that reason is operative within a tradition, since reason in its religious employment naturally seeks to develop an objective and authoritative basis for its imperatives. Moreover, as I have already pointed out, no religion is actually required by reason to confess its rational basis. All that is required is that the final conduct of believers, or the beliefs upon which that conduct necessarily depends, be such as could receive rational approval. Specifically, in order to display its conformity to the requirements of religious reason, a system of faith must in no way promote immoral actions and must positively encourage the moral life.

As far as Judaism is concerned, therefore, the fundamental question is not whether its code of behavior is or is not represented as being enjoined by God, but whether the substance of that code conforms to the pattern required by reason. The answer to this latter question, I think, must be strongly affirmative. Indeed, it is an indication of this tradition's pervasive adherence to the program of religious reason that, without its authority ever being questioned, the revealed ethic and faith system is constantly being brought under the control of rational and moral considerations. Nowhere is this fact made clearer than in the divine command issued to the nation Israel and its individual members to model their behavior on the ways of God (Leviticus 19:2). As many commentators have noted, this kind of *imitatio Dei* is the Jewish moral and religious principle of widest scope, the foundation of all specific behavior demanded of the pious Jew. Such a command does not in itself demonstrate Judaism's conformity to reason, for everything depends on the nature of the divine model which men are called to imitate. But it is just here that the pervasive rationalism of Judaism displays itself. For in Jewish piety, the God whose holiness men are called upon to imitate is in fact the archetype of a perfected human moral life. In his attributes and his behavior, the God of the Rabbis represents the fullest expression of the kind of person which reason compels each of us to become. Thus, in following this command it is impossible for an individual to err from the course prescribed by reason. Moritz Lazarus puts the matter correctly, I think, when he observes that in Judaism the command to imitate God as much "divinizes" morality as it moralizes the divine.[3]

A cursory review of the descriptions of God offered by the Rabbis will make this clearer. Of first importance is the fact that the Rabbis repeatedly affirmed that our knowledge of God's nature is limited to his moral attributes. They unequivocally rejected efforts to speculate on those aspects of God's nature that have nothing to do with his role as just ruler of the universe. Nor was this reluctance based on a general reverence for the divine or on a philosophical appreciation of the gap between the divine and the human, for, as is almost embarrassingly evident to any modern reader of the Talmud and Midrashic literature, the Rabbis did not refrain from the most graphic anthropomorphism when it suited their purpose of shedding light on God's moral character and his activity. Thus, they depict God as acting as the best man at the wedding of Adam and Eve, as mourning over the world like a father over the death of a son when the sins of the ten generations force its destruction by flood, as visiting Abraham on his deathbed, or even as keeping school in heaven for those who died in their infancy. Many similar anthropomorphisms could also be cited.[4]

In actually describing God, the Rabbis drew principally upon a series of scriptural passages, especially upon Exodus 34:6, Deuteronomy 10:17-18, and, by inference, Psalm 15.[5] On the basis of these and other passages, they summed up God's nature in terms of two moral qualities: perfect justice and perfect mercy. To the former attach the host of specifically moral attributes: God's universal concern, his impartiality, his fairness, his faithfulness, and his hatred of all evildoing, treachery, and malevolence. To the latter attach his forbearance from promptly punishing wrongdoing, his patient awaiting of repentance and his willingness to forgive the sins of those who turn away from evil. The Rabbis were very conscious of the tensions that exist between these two aspects of the divine nature, of course. Later I shall note some of the means they employed to bring God's firm justice and his hatred of evil together with his willingness to overlook and forgive sin. But the important point for now is that in their descriptions of God, the Rabbis held forth a complete, if necessarily difficult standard for the moral life. Framed between the extremes of perfect mercy and perfect justice was a single ideal code comprising the full range of acts and attitudes demanded by impartial moral reason. Indeed, it is an indication of the Rabbis' firm grasp of the tensions within moral and religious reason that they refused to compromise their moral description of the divine nature merely to render that description more immediately coherent and comprehensible. In the unity of God's moral nature, as Hermann Cohen has observed, the Rabbis held tenaciously to the unity and entirety of morality.[6]

The Rabbis' implicit commitment to the program of moral reason is further evidenced by what they omitted from the moral description of God. The God of the Hebrew Bible, especially as he is described in the earliest literary strata, is not always a perfect moral exemplar. Despite their general insistence on the imitation of God, therefore, the Rabbis were quick to point out exceptions to this rule. Thus, they taught that man should not imitate God in the four instruments mentioned in Scripture which he alone can use: his jealousy, revenge, exaltation, and devious ways.[7]

Two further aspects of this portrait of God deserve mention as an indication of the fullness and richness of the moral example the Rabbis sought to advance. One is God's deep and abiding concern with the moral quality of communal and social life, his "justice" in the social and institutional sense of the term. In subsequent chapters we shall see how pervasive is the tendency of religious systems to understress this portion of the total program of moral responsibility demanded by reason. Perhaps because of the priority they place on the shaping of individual character as manifested most intensely in interpersonal relations, and perhaps, also, because common religious doctrines of ultimate reward frequently minimize the importance of social and economic circumstances in this world, religious systems tend characteristically to give less attention to this side of moral responsibility. Though they were not untouched by this tendency, the Rabbis were relatively forceful in their social and economic teachings. With their roots in the prophetic heritage, they took pains to emphasize God's concern with social justice and especially with equitable and compassionate treatment of the poor and disadvantaged. Constantly referring back to the Biblical affirmations of God's love for the poor, the orphan, the widow, the visiting alien, and the bondsman, the Rabbis condemned in all their forms judicial favoritism, commercial chicanery, and the failure of a community to support those in perilous economic or social circumstances. Resort to false measures or usurious practices, they maintained, is even equivalent to denying the Exodus from Egypt: it is a denial of God's special preoccupation with this moral area as evidenced by his historical relationship with the bonds-nation Israel.[8]

A second aspect of the divine nature emphasized by the

Rabbis and indicative of their moral concern is God's humility. Probably no virtue has a more central place in the moral life than this one. As the voluntary renunciation of the special advantages or "merit" provided by the accidents of birth or fate, and as a recognition of the contingency of all one's accomplishments, humility has a fundamental role in prompting the individual to adopt the moral point of view in the first place. This point of view, as we know, grows out of a decision to adjudicate social conflicts not by pressing one's claim or exploiting one's powers, but by divesting oneself of attachment to these particular advantages and willingly assuming the standpoint of impartial, equal reason. On the other side of morality, morever, once actions have been performed and reward and punishment are in order, it is humility that prevents dangerous self-glorification or excessively harsh treatment of those who have succeeded less well than the self in living up to reason's demands. In many ways, therefore, humility is the characteristic moral virtue with a vital role in motivating the moral life and in guiding moral judgment through its most difficult and demanding moments. In this respect, the Rabbinic ascription of humility to God should not be surprising. In view of their location of the full pattern of man's moral life in the divine exemplar, such a move is to be expected. Still, it is rather astonishing testimony to their persistence in perceiving God in moral terms that hand in hand with the glorification of God in his power and might (glorifications which, as we shall see, also have a rational basis) the Rabbis did not shrink from declaring God to be humble and condescending. Texts to this effect abound in the Talmudic literature. Some are primarily imaginative and merely pedagogical in intent, as when God's choice of a lowly thornbush as the instrument of his revelation to Moses is adduced as proof of his humility. But other texts drive the moral point forcefully home. Thus, God is frequently contrasted with human rulers. These pridefully look down upon their inferiors and are harshly punitive when their subjects rebel. This is not true of God, however. He dwells especially with the poor and lowly. He puts up with men's sins and hastens, on the slightest display of repentance, to forgive.[9]

In view of this highly moralized depiction of the divine nature, therefore, Rabbinic teaching, despite its appeal to revelation, in no way furnishes a ground of moral obedience antithetical to moral reason. The Jew who always seeks to model his behavior on the ways of God, although he recognizes no rational basis to his endeavor, would necessarily always conform to the moral dictates of impartial reason. Moreover, a review of other Rabbinic efforts to furnish general guides or principles to the moral life supports this conclusion. Two such guides, in addition to the command to imitate God, stand out. One is the famous Golden Rule of Leviticus 19:18, "You shall love your neighbor as yourself," a version of which the venerated teacher Hillel advanced as the cardinal principle of Jewish law.[10] As has been frequently noted, this kind of generalization principle, whether in its positive or negative form ("What is hateful to you do not to your fellow"), is not a complete guide to valid moral reasoning since permissible actions then become a function of the needs or volitions of particular persons. Hence, the troubling case of the fanatic who, in his hatred of a race or group, would be prepared to suffer persecution should he or his loved ones by chance be members of that group; or of the sadomasochist who would gladly generalize his aberrant desires. The point is that valid moral reasoning depends not merely upon the willingness to generalize principles but equally upon an impartial standpoint and, from that standpoint, a rational weighting of all the differing needs and desires involved in instances of social conflict. But this is a technical criticism. The Golden Rule certainly suggests this total methodology and it has perhaps rightly earned its place in popular esteem. Thus, its very assertion further expresses the rational thrust of Jewish ethics.

Against this background, however, the Golden Rule's leading contender as a guide to conduct in Jewish thought must be mentioned. This, according to the opinion of Rabbi Ben Azai recorded at several places in the Talmud, is "the Book of the Generations of Adam," that is, the Genesis account of man's earliest history which Ben Azai maintains teaches an even greater principle than Leviticus 19.[11] The basis of this claim seems to be that, in this portion of Scripture, man is properly instructed in his common descent from a single individual made in the image of God. Many interpretations can be given within the context of Rabbinic thought for the preference for this text. It is striking, nevertheless, that in terms of contemporary moral analysis the Genesis account does perhaps provide a firmer guide to moral reasoning than does the Golden Rule of Leviticus. By stressing the importance of man's generic nature and by endowing this with a sacred quality, this text effectively recommends the precise moral point of view. As I have already suggested, the fundamental principles of morality are those general rules of behavior that could be agreed upon by impartial rational agents. Where the human community alone is concerned, these rules are those that serve the interests, not of one or another particular person, but of men generally, that is, of individuals deprived of all the knowledge that distinguishes them from one another and limited to the knowledge of their basic generic qualities. Reason, from this generic—or simply "human"—standpoint, must provide a sound guide to the formulation of the general moral rules. Thus, Ben Azai's choice of a text lies as close to the sources of moral reasoning as he maintained, and to the degree that Rabbinic thought recognized the force of his view, not in response to his claims alone, of course, but as a way of approaching a host of moral and religious questions, it further evidences the rationality of its foundation.

So far I have emphasized the conformity of Rabbinic thought to the initial moral requirements of the program of religious reason. I have suggested that the religious character of Rabbinic moral teaching in no way weakens the overall rationality of this teaching and, indeed, even serves—as in the case of the command to imitate God—to reinforce the moral life. Lest it appear, however, that I am merely retracing the much criticized path of nineteenth-century Reform Judaism which sought to reduce all of Torah to moral instruction and eliminated all non-moral teaching, I want to give some attention to the vast bulk of ritual and religious law which the Talmud contains and which has always assumed an important place in Jewish life. That these ritual and religious commandments form a major aspect of Judaism is suggested, if nothing else, by the fact that a majority of the six hundred thirteen commandments discovered by the Rabbis in Scripture concern themselves with aspects of the ritual, sacramental, or worship life of the Jewish community. To rationalists these commandments have always been a source of embarrassment. Critics of Judaism have presented them as evidence of the fundamentally irrational and immoral nature of this faith. And Jewish rationalists, in response, have sought to relate every particular commandment to the service of the moral life or some other rationally defensible purpose.[12]

In view of both of these responses, however, it is important to assert here that religious reason does not require each and every component of a faith system, nor even the bulk of its contents, directly to serve the moral life. Religions, like many other human creations, are complex organic unities with features developing out of historical circumstances, special internal needs of the system, or the labor of gifted individual contributors. Just as the history of architecture reveals not merely adherence to physical laws but also a rich heritage of not strictly functional decoration and artistry, so does the history of religion reveal many excursions into speculation, piety, and worship that serve purposes beyond or supplemental to those of strict religious reason. From the point of view of religious reason, of course, the elaborations a religion may undergo should ideally serve the basic moral purposes at which the system aims. But even this is not strictly required. All that religious reason finally demands is that the additional overlays of tradition and piety not undercut the moral life. It is a mistake, therefore, to look for a rational and moral explanation of every facet of a religion. More pertinent is the question of whether particular non-moral features endanger the moral life, although it is also in order to ask whether the total fabric of piety enhances, rather than erodes, moral obedience.

With regard to Judaism, this understanding prompts two questions: First, do the ritual and religious teachings of Torah encourage the commission of immoral acts or the development of immoral dispositions? Second, does this ritual and religious law in any way work generally to stimulate, rather than enervate, the moral life? The first of these questions, I think, must be answered strongly in the negative. Not only did the Rabbis constantly maintain a clear understanding of the difference between the moral and the specifically sacramental requirements of Torah, but they repeatedly affirmed, in cases of conflict between the two, the priority of the moral requirements. As might be expected, however, when conflict did not force choice, the Rabbis insisted upon the unity of Torah and the equal importance of performance of all the commandments, but this position was readily abandoned in the face of conflict between commandments.[13] Unfortunately, the Christian polemic has tended to misrepresent Judaism seriously on this matter, not least in those Gospel episodes where Pharisees are depicted as placing the requirement of Sabbath observance over the responsibility to succor human beings in distress. Nevertheless, on this issue alone the genuine Rabbinic position reveals its strict sense of priorities. Thus, it is an axiom of Rabbinic teaching that the Sabbath might be broken to assist someone dangerously ill. Indeed, a rabbi living in a town where this is not understood commonly by the Jewish community is held to be seriously derelict in his duty.[14] Many similar instances of the separation of sacramental observances from moral requirements in order to lay stress on the latter could be cited. No less important, for example, is the Rabbinic insistence that the entire elaborate structure of Temple worship, with its means for the sacrificial expiation of sin, served only to restore relations between man and God but were of no use by themselves in recti-fying wrongs committed between men. For these, concrete acts of restitution and reparation were required.[15]

There is no evidence, therefore, that the specific sacramental and ritual observances of Jewish law necessitated or promoted violations of the moral rules.[16] Of course, it might be objected that the mere observance of these purely religious command-ments drains time and energy away from moral concerns and tends over-all to enervate the moral life. Those who would argue in this way, in other words, would want to give a negative answer to the second of the two questions posed above. Jewish ritual and sacramental law, they would claim, does not work over-all to stimulate the moral life. In fairness to the Rabbinic tradition, however, this answer does not seem justified for several impor-tant reasons. First because many of the presumably sacramental observances have moral implications or a morally supportive ef-fect—as the Jewish rationalists frequently sought to point out. Indeed, it is sometimes difficult even to distinguish between what is a sacramental and a moral commandment. How, for example, does one classify the host of Sabbath requirements, some of them frighteningly detailed and apparently removed from any direct moral purpose, when they nevertheless function to preserve a complex institution providing a day of rest for man and beast? Are these detailed ordinances sacramental or moral? The point is that the interweaving of sacramental and moral commandments is so dense in Torah that it becomes extremely difficult to sepa-rate these two domains from one another. In saying this, by the way, it is not necessary to maintain, as some Jewish rationalists have done, that all of the commandments have an original moral intent. Whatever their source or original basis, it is enough to observe that over the centuries the Rabbis repeatedly brought the moral and sacramental ordinances into close connection with one another.

Beyond this matter of single commandments, however, there remains the question of the moral effect of the religious system as a whole. Here it is important to record the opinion of knowledgeable interpreters of Jewish law that the effect of the commandments is not to drain away energies better spent on moral concerns, but rather to fabricate a system of life in which restraint, self-discipline, and the tendency to relate every facet of human existence, however apparently inconsequential, to the will of God become a matter of instinct. If the moral life has, as one of its vital preconditions, an integrated, disciplined and attentive self, then one important effect of Jewish law, both in its moral and religious dimensions, was to create this kind of ordered and sensitive personality.[17] The very abundance of the commandments illustrates this fact. According to early tradition, the total number of affirmative and prohibitive commandments was fixed at six hundred thirteen. Rabbinic piety explained this number as corresponding to the number of days in the year plus the number of "limbs" or parts of the body identified by their physiology.[18] The lesson of these numbers, Schechter observes, is "that the whole man stands in the service of God, each limb or member of the body being entrusted with the exercise of its respective functions." The law was thus conceived, he adds, "as submitting all the faculties and passions of man to the control of the divine."[19] The actual number of these commandments should perhaps not be taken too seriously. Many of the commandments governed vestigial aspects of Jewish life—such as the Temple rites—or were pertinent to specialized legal questions and of interest only to Rabbinic scholars and judges. It is not merely specific commandments but the whole fabric of life created by these commandments that is of greatest importance. Thus, it is common for Talmudic contributors to suggest distillations of the law that express its essential spirit. Invariably, these distillations reduce the corpus of the law to one or another of its guiding moral principles and, hand in hand with this, a principle enjoining faith in God.[20] This indicates that the Rabbis themselves were keenly aware of the religious-ethical function of the whole enterprise of Torah.

The organic unity and ultimate moral thrust of Jewish religious law could be illustrated in other ways, as well. One could point, for example, to those aspects of Torah that stimulate the performance of morally supererogatory acts such as the injunctions to *Chasiduth* (saintliness). This was understood as the constant willingness to assume a free initiative and go beyond the letter of the law.[21] By presenting this and other ideals side by side with ordinary moral prohibitions, Talmudic teaching was able to motivate a richer pattern of moral life. We shall see, by the way, that this special stimulus to supererogatory acts is not unique to Judaism but forms a common characteristic of religious ethical systems. It seems that the powerful motivational resources of a religion frequently serve not only to support the moral life but to propel it beyond the minimal levels required by reason. Judaism accomplishes this, however, by weaving requirements and supererogations together in a unified moral teaching.

Related to this tendency to promote supererogatory acts, and a further illustration of the over-all moral intensity of Torah, is the emphasis placed on scrupulous performance of the law's every demand. So central a place did Torah have in human destiny for the Rabbis, that they sometimes insist that the fate of a generation or even of the whole world might rest on the performance of a single pious or wicked action. "He committed one sin," it is said, "woe is unto him, for he may by this have inclined the scales both with regard to himself and with regard to the whole world to the side of guilt." Similarly, a single pious act performed with utter purity of intention may have the effect of ushering in the Messianic age.[22] It may be that in this insistence Rabbinic thought sometimes drew the bow of moral concern too taut for it to withstand the tensions generated. In the next chapter I shall suggest that Christianity, or at least the thinking of St. Paul, may partly be understood as a rationally defensible effort to release some of the pressure within the moral life built up by Judaism's all-embracing sacramental-ethical system. But if that is so, Judaism's difficulty here, if it is a difficulty, is not a religious displacement of the moral or a "pharasaical" hardening of the moral life, but an extreme intensification of the sense of moral and religious obligation. With this point I hope that enough has been said to place Judaism's conformity to the first general requirement of religious reason sufficiently beyond question for our purposes. Many more chapters, and possibly volumes, could be written on the sensitive conformity of Jewish law to the demands of moral reason, and the Talmudic heritage remains a resource for those concerned with many complex moral issues, both traditional or contemporary. But I want now to turn to the second general requirement of religious reason, a requirement that emerges, as we know, from the fundamental dilemma of moral obedience.

The broad outlines of the Jewish response to reason's second general requirement are very familiar. Judaism's radical monotheism, its conception of a god who is at once Creator and Judge of the universe and its rich eschatological speculation have, in fact, established the model for theistic solutions to this basic problem of moral retribution. But details of those aspects of the Jewish understanding of God that bear on this matter are sufficiently important to deserve closer attention. So far, our review of the Jewish description of God has shown him to be an agency fully and completely motivated by moral concerns. To this aspect of the divine nature, Judaism adds four other major attributes: omnipotence, omnipresence, omniscience, and justice (not now in the sense of God's moral quality but as a description of his function as Judge of the world). Taken together with the specifically moral attributes, these qualities render God precisely the kind of morally retributive causal agency that religious reason requires.

The affirmation of God's omnipotence lies very much at the heart of Hebrew monotheism. From its beginning this was far less a philosophical than a moral monotheism—concerned not with the logical unification of reality so much as with the supreme and unchallenged power of righteousness.[23] For the Rabbis the link between God's omnipotence and his existence was absolute. To deny God's ability to control destiny as he willed was for them a form of atheism.[24] Polytheism and idolatry were correspondingly unacceptable because they sought to locate power and authority elsewhere than in the single righteous will. It was in his role as eternal and pre-existing Creator of the world, of course, that the omnipotence of God was most characteristically perceived by the Rabbis. In their view, the constitution of nature and all its subsequent development, whether ordinary or extraordinary, proceeded from the will of God. With respect to nature, God's power was limitless and the claim that "God's strength and might fill the earth," is common in the Talmud.[25] This emphasis on God's majesty, however, should not be interpreted as a glorification of sheer power since, for the Rabbis, God's might is always perfectly fused with his righteousness. Thus, in describing God's creative activity, the Rabbis sometimes liken him to a king who proceeded to his enormous tasks of construction with an architect's plan in his hand. This plan is Torah, so that God's mighty acts of creation were guided from the first by a pattern of the moral and religious law.[26] As we look at other traditions, we shall see similar efforts to relate the constitution of the universe to a primordial moral plan. All these efforts, including Judaism's are, of course, responses to religious reason's demand that the obdurate natural order be thought of as somehow finally ruled by a supreme moral intentionality.

The two divine attributes of omniscience and omnipresence can partly be thought of as serving a purpose similar to omnipotence since they ensure God's supervision of every event in history and nature so that nothing escapes his control. More importantly, however, these attributes are required if God is to perform the task of judging the good and evil that men do. Since it is easy for human beings to conceal acts of wickedness, a supreme judgmental power must be thought of as carrying its gaze simultaneously to all corners of the world, even the most remote and hidden. And since it is finally on the basis of their consciences and wills that men must be morally judged, this power must be able to penetrate the deepest recesses of the human heart. As we might expect by now, the Rabbis strongly affirmed God's possession of these abilities. In contrast to a human king who cannot be in the reception room and the bedchamber at the same time, God is said to fill both at the same moment. Or, he is likened to the sea which can completely fill a cave on the coast and yet be everywhere undiminished.[27] His knowledge is also complete. No sinner can hide his misdeeds before him and the very effort to do so amounts to a wicked denial of God's power.[28] For this reason, some Rabbis maintained that the sin of adultery, since it is typically committed in secret, involves the additional sin of heresy.[29]

God's knowledge also penetrates to the inner forum of conscience and will. "You know the secrets of the world and the hidden mysteries of all the living. You search into the inmost recesses, and try passions and heart," reads the solemn prayer on the Day of Atonement.[30] That "God desires the heart" and that he judges the motive over the deed are axioms of Rabbinic teaching.[31] Interestingly, an exception to this rule is made where evil intentions are concerned. Though a good intention is taken for the deed, an evil intention must be successfully carried into effect before God renders a definitive judgment on it. Thus, while they rightly brought intention under divine judgment,[32] the Rabbis also seemed to comprehend that the relationship between volition and deed, ordinarily too fragile to render deeds a valid basis for the judgment of persons, is strong enough and can be used to moderate the hateful process of condemnation. The underlying rationality of the Rabbinic description of God's activity is evidenced here.

One final aspect of God's omniscience as understood by the Rabbis must be mentioned: his foreknowledge. "Everything is foreseen" and "God knows what is to be in the future" are basic

Rabbinic convictions illustrated by numerous discussions and anecdotes in the Talmud. This foreknowledge also extends to human volitions and intentions: "Before even a creature is formed in his mother's womb his thought is already revealed to God," or again, "Before even a thought is created in man's heart it is already revealed to God" are typical expressions of this view.[33] Very shortly we shall see the difficulties generated by this kind of affirmation, and we shall see how the Rabbis tried to handle them. But for now it is sufficient to view the idea of foreknowledge in its natural context as an implication and extension of the attributes of omnipotence and omniscience.

God's capacity as supreme Judge, the conviction that he will certainly punish the wicked and reward the righteous, is the final major aspect of God's nature emphasized by the Rabbis that deserves mention here. This characteristic of God is, in fact, the focal point of all his other attributes and its central importance is properly recognized by the Rabbis. "Know what is above thee,— a seeing eye, a hearing ear and all thy deeds written in a book," declares an oft-quoted passage in the tractate *Aboth,* and another equally well-known passage in this morally important tractate presses the point home: "Keep far from the evil neighbour, and consort not with the wicked, and be not doubtful of retribution."[34] To doubt retribution, to maintain that "there is no judgement and no Judge" is for the Rabbis a form of atheism.[35] Thus, it is maintained that the besetting sin of the Generation of the Flood for which they were destroyed was to declare the world "an automaton" lacking a Judge.[36]

The Rabbinic portrait of God sketched to this point is, in its broadest outlines if not in its details, relatively familiar. So familiar, perhaps, that it is hard for the Western reader to appreciate its actual complexity and the way its features have been subtly molded to fit a rational agenda. That this process may be operative becomes clearer, however, when we look at the way rational difficulties generated by this portrait itself are handled. For in seeking to correct the problems generated by their own fundamental religious propositions, the Rabbis betray how much reason is in command of the total religious enterprise. In this connection, for example, an immediate problem is posed by the attribute of omniscience as it extends to God's foreknowledge.[37] We have seen the rational basis for this in the wish to ensure God's supreme control of every event in nature and history. Nevertheless, as generations of introductory philosophy students have realized, divine foreknowledge appears strongly to conflict with the idea of human freedom of the will. Assuming that no kind of philosophical resolution of this problem is fully acceptable, logical consistency might suggest abandonment of one or another of these ideas, foreknowledge or freedom. It is firm evidence of the priority the Rabbis gave to the requirements of religious reason, therefore, that they refused to relinquish either of these ideas. God's foreknowledge was too firmly a part of his nature as omnipotent, omniscient Judge to be sacrificed, and freedom of the will was an axiom (as it must be) of the Rabbis' whole moral viewpoint.[38] Their solution—if it can be called that—was determinedly to bypass the whole problem. A statement attributed to Rabbi Akiba recorded in the tractate *Aboth* has usually been interpreted as a refusal to accept any precipitous solution: "All is foreseen, and free will is given, and the world is judged by goodness, and all is according to the amount of work."[39] It is common to say that the Rabbis had little philosophical interest and if by this is meant a desire to present a patently coherent series of propositions, the statement is correct. But if it is extended to characterize their thinking as non-rational or irrational, it is certainly mistaken. In this instance and elsewhere, the Rabbis preferred to tolerate apparent and possible inconsistencies rather than sacrifice or compromise any of the key members in their faith's structure of religious reason. This does not mean that they refused to suggest ways of possibly reconciling the opposing doctrines they affirmed. Most frequently—and in a characteristic move of religious reason—they did this by locating the solution in a realm necessarily and understandably beyond man's comprehension: in the knowledge, activity, or nature of God. Thus, in the quotation from Rabbi Akiba we have just looked at, it is God's "goodness" that is intimated as a basis for possibly reconciling the contrary aspects associated with his nature and his demands. Such transcendent retreats are very important minimal bids to satisfy the requirements of logic. But they should not be taken more seriously than that. They are not so much an answer as an effort not to answer without at the same time appearing illogical. They are, in other words, efforts to avoid the kind of definitive resolution which logic superficially appears to require but which reason forbids.

A final major component in the Jewish understanding of God as it bears on the second general requirement of religious reason is the doctrine of ultimate reward and punishment. That God, the righteous, all-seeing, and all-powerful Judge will finally recompense the righteous for their suffering and will punish the wicked, whatever their respective present situations, is an article of Jewish faith. In its earliest Biblical expression, this confidence took the form of an imminent expectation of peace, prosperity, and Jewish national independence as effected by the hand of God.[40] Later, in response to the sustained hardships wrought by foreign domination, this teaching was transmuted into a Messianic expectation, by means of which the belief in a future recompense was placed beyond refutation by worldly reverses.[41] At the same time, the glory awaiting the righteous was correspondingly magnified. Thus, in the idea of the Kingdom of God the hope for a merely historical reign of national well-being was converted into a vision of blessedness so complete that for the just all the normal hardships and difficulties of life—even death itself—were forever banished.[42] Hand in hand with this went the doctrine of resurrection, by means of which the righteous who perished before the advent of the Kingdom were assured their enjoyment of God's reward. The importance of this resurrection doctrine in Rabbinic piety is evidenced by the fact that it was the center of a prolonged dispute between the Sadducean and Pharisaic parties in Palestine. With their victory, the Pharisees handed this doctrine on to their Rabbinic successors as a dogma of Jewish faith.[43]

The ideas of a Messianic reign, the resurrection, and the Kingdom of God in their Jewish or Christian expressions are once again so familiar to us that we take them for granted. It is worth noting, however, just how much this particular set of beliefs responds to the difficult demands imposed at this point by religious reason. A major problem is raised by the fact that reason requires the reward experienced by the righteous to be happiness, or the real satisfaction of their desires, and not merely contentment, the self-satisfaction produced by virtue. The question is "How can the righteous who perish hope to experience anything like happiness if, at death, they leave behind the bodies and senses whose needs and satisfactions are so intimately associated with most of what we ordinarily think of as happiness?" The resurrection doctrine seeks to answer this question, by assuring the righteous that they will regain their physical and sensuous natures. This idea has the incidental effect of rendering the wicked, who are also re-embodied, suitably subject to chastisement.

Rabbinic speculations on the nature of life in the World to Come (their general term for the Kingdom of God) run the gamut from popularly inspired and colorful descriptions of astonishing material abundance, to more modest disclaimers of the human ability to know what lies ahead.[44] Between these two extremes are spiritualized descriptions of the future life in which the supreme happiness awaiting the righteous is to dwell in the presence of God and to revel in the divine glory.[45] This spiritualized eschatology has special interest for us because it reflects a Rabbinic solution to another characteristic problem of religious reason, one that grows out of the tension that exists between the first and the second general requirements of religious reason. As we already know, it is a firm demand of both moral and religious reason that the moral rules be respected for their own sake and not in order to obtain some contingently related benefits. At the same time, while it cannot allow reward to become the motivating ground of behavior, reason must also hold out the hope that reward will be forthcoming. The first and second requirements of religious reason reflect these demands. The problem for a religious system, therefore, is to prevent the hope of reward generated by whatever solutions it offers to the second requirement from becoming the motivating reason its adherents are moral. Put another way, it must assure that whatever sure grounds for unswerving moral obedience it has established in connection with the first requirement always assumes a commanding place in the believer's attention, but it must do this without dismissing the hope of reward. Obviously, this is a difficult tightrope to walk and its success in doing so is one measure of a religious system. Over-all, the Rabbis face the problem squarely and handle it well.

We already know that the hope of reward was given a firm place in Jewish piety. It is noteworthy, therefore, that even as they strongly affirmed the fact of reward, the Rabbis took special pains to prevent the hope for reward from becoming a motivating consideration. A frequently quoted statement by Antigonos of Socho in the tractate *Aboth* expresses their general position: "Be not like servants who serve the master for condition of receiving a gift, but be like servants, who serve the master not on condition of receiving a gift. And let the fear of Heaven be upon you."[46] Not reward, then, but the fear of Heaven, the Rabbis' somewhat misleading term for the mixture of awed reverence and love for the righteous God, is to be the fundamental motivating ground of the moral life.[47] To further describe this kind of response, the Rabbis employed a special word, *Lishmah,* which can be defined as the performance of the law for its own sake, or what is the same thing in this context, for the sake of him who commanded it.[48] *Lishmah* was understood to exclude all worldly intentions as well as the hope for the future rewards promised in Scripture. The only satisfactions it allowed were the joy directly attaching to the performance of a commandment and the related sense of communion with God.[49]

For many Rabbinic commentators the sense of nearness to God produced by obedience to the law was a more than adequate reward. In the midst of torture Rabbi Akiba was said to have been filled with joy at the unique opportunity given him to serve God with all his heart and soul.[50] This kind of stress on communion with God is a sophisticated conception, since it has the effect of virtually eliminating the tension we have noted between the demand for a morally pure motivation and the hope of reward. Reward here becomes that complex set of satisfactions produced by communion and (relative) self-identification with the supreme source of righteousness and moral purity. In some respects, this satisfaction is similar to self-contentment or the personal satisfaction attendant upon virtue. Like contentment, it represents a form of approbation emanating from the highest faculty capable of judgment. Unlike self-contentment, however, the idea of communion with God is capable of fully satisfying reason's needs. Self-contentment cannot do this, we know, because it is finally unable to certify its authority to reason, it being reason's own product. But this is not true of the divine approval which facilitates communion with God. By definition, God is the real and supreme ground of judgment. The fact that he approves of an individual and draws him near to him, therefore, provides a confident basis for self-satisfaction in the way that self-contentment cannot. It is important to observe in saying this that it is the stipulated special characteristics of the divine agency (its supremacy and objective reality) which, when fused with the moral qualities, provide these qualities with an authority they would otherwise lack. We see here, therefore, a characteristic move by religious reason as it employs a religious postulate to ground what morality demands and to place those demands beyond reason's corrosive power.

I should add that much the same analysis can be applied to

any of the other specific satisfactions (beyond self-approval) contained within the complex idea of communion with God. One of these, perhaps, is the satisfaction taken in loving God, as opposed to what we have just looked at, God's loving or approving the agent. Since God is consummately righteous, this love and the satisfactions it produces is very much the same as the love for morality itself. But where reason can never permit the latter to be a solution to its needs for an answer to the question "Why should I be moral?" love for God can serve this purpose. Love for morality must always be suspect by reason, because reason knows this love partly at least to be a product of its own impartial activity and sees the dangers to the individual hidden within it. But God, whose conception includes an infinite solicitousness for the well-being of each of his creatures, is beyond. mistrust. Once again, in other words, the fusion of the special features of the divine with morality enables reason to do what it ordinarily cannot do, make morality an adequate satisfaction for happiness.

In stressing communion with God, therefore, the Rabbis were pressing toward a very advanced solution to the religious problem of reward, one which eliminated the need for a host of beliefs not supported in any way by experience. For, unlike the various eschatologies Judaism experimented with, this particular notion of reward does not require the hypothesis of future events radically different from those which had ever before come to pass. In place of these, all that is required is belief in a kind of experience, love of and by a moral person, which our own moral life everywhere suggests on the plane of social and personal relations. Very shortly I shall suggest at least one other Jewish belief as sophisticated as this. But in stressing ideas of this sort, ideas really at the cutting edge of Jewish religious speculation, I do not want to suggest that the Rabbis abandoned their traditional eschatological conceptions. Their role as popular religious teachers was too important to let them do that. Nor was the idea of an historical Kingdom of God totally without value, since its stress on the ultimate fate of life in this world worked against the immoral disconcern with history that frequently characterizes religious eschatologies. Nevertheless, it remains an indication of their sensitivity to the various possibilities in this area that the Rabbis, while always maintaining the hope for a future reward, progressively spiritualized their conception of this so that even in the future life communion with God came to be viewed as the principal satisfaction of the righteous.

Judaism's effort to respond to religious reason's second requirement has many other features of interest to our inquiry. Again and again solutions to reason's needs generate new problems which reason must resolve, and in many instances we can see the Rabbis involved in the process of acknowledging and meeting the challenge. Of these, however, one problem is of such importance to Jewish and religious thought generally that it demands our close attention. I refer to the problem of evil and the suffering of the innocent or the righteous. The matter of theodicy, of course, lies very close to the heart of religious reason, and it may seem odd to identify it as a problem *after* the existence of an all powerful, righteous, and recompensing Judge has been affirmed. For was it not the original purpose of that affirmation to overcome the difficulty posed by unjustifiable suffering? The answer to this is that although the description of God and his activity eliminates the problem in principle, the brute fact of suffering still remains and demands some explanation.[51] Indeed, in some respects the problem is accentuated, for in view of God's power and righteousness it is natural to want to know why there should be any unjustifiable suffering at all. Reason's very solution, in other words, sharpens the problem in a new way.

It is evidence of the Rabbis' keen sensitivity to the demands of religious reason that they generally rejected one of the most immediately attractive, popular, but ultimately dangerous solutions to this problem: the idea that all suffering is really morally deserved. This idea can never be accepted at the beginning of rational religious reflection, of course, because it is the fact of undeserved suffering that gives rise to that reflection in the first place. But once religious propositions have been advanced which resolve reason's deepest problem and which reveal unjustified suffering not to be genuinely indicative of the nature of the universe, the temptation to dismiss particular cases of apparently unjustified suffering as really deserved becomes very strong. There are several reasons for this. For one thing, as I have already said, the sheer scandal of unjustifiable suffering in a world ruled by righteousness is so great and such a threat to the received religious solution as to force efforts to overcome the difficulty in any way. For another thing, the empirical connection between vice and unhappiness is sufficiently strong to prompt the relationship of single cases of apparently undeserved suffering to real, although well-concealed sins. Finally, it seems to be typical that once a religious system with its consolations and its rewards has been worked out, the very affirmation of a transcendent support becomes easily transmuted (especially where social privilege and religious authority are closely connected) into the confidence that the righteous cannot really suffer. The superficially drawn conclusion is that, with the exception of special cases of martyrdom, those who suffer must not really be righteous. This conclusion, of course, represents a morally devastating reversal of the reflection which gives rise to religious belief in the first place, since it not only accepts but lends religious and moral sanction to injustice and to the arbitrary workings of fate. Still, this conclusion is understandable enough and it has frequently manifested itself in the history of religion (along with the corollary tendency to affirm that the prosperous are genuinely righteous).[52]

It is to the Rabbis' credit and it is an indication of their moral sensitivity, therefore, that they ultimately rejected this solution to the problem of evil. That Hebrew thought flirted with it is perhaps evidenced by the Book of Job, where just such a position is expressed by Job's comforters.[53] And, occasionally, similar views are found in the Rabbinic literature. Thus, at one point, the eminent Rabbi Joshua is quoted as explaining the suf-

fering of children—a particularly difficult theodicical problem—
by means of God's foreknowledge of their future sins.[54] But this
position is a minority view in the Talmud and it is not even representative of Rabbi Joshua's full teaching. In place of this, the
Rabbis advanced at least four different explanations of undeserved suffering.

One related it indirectly to the deserved suffering of the
wicked. The righteous or innocent, it is held, sometimes suffer
as a result of the punishment of the wicked just as a fire raging
through thorns must sometimes devastate the stacks of corn.[55]
Apart from its valid emphasis on the solidarity of human destiny, of course, this teaching can at best furnish only a partial
solution to the problem. A second Rabbinic response was reso-
lutely to bypass the whole question. "There is not in our hands
either the security of the wicked or the chastisements of the
righteous," R. Janna is quoted as saying.[56] By now we are in a
better position to appreciate the sense of this kind of response,
representing, as it does, an effort to place beyond further assault
the rationally required but in this case somewhat opposing insistences on divine justice and divine power. Characteristically,
as well, to acquit themselves of the accusation of sheer illogic,
the Rabbis wed this reluctance to inquire with the insistence on
God's incomprehensible, but ultimately righteous wisdom. A
third solution is more complex and, in some ways, more sophisticated. According to it, suffering is not to be understood as a sign
of God's indifference or scorn, but of his love. It is at once his
means of testing the righteous and evidencing his concern for
them. Thus, God is compared to the potter who knocks only on
the good pots, not the bad, or to the father who especially corrects the son in whom he most delights. The general lesson is expressed by R. Jose b. Judah: "Beloved are the sufferings before
God, for, through them the glory of God falls upon him who is
being chastised."[57]

A final Rabbinic solution to this problem carries us beyond
the second requirement of religious reason and into the domain

of those subsequent requirements having to do with human moral inadequacy. As we shall presently see, the Rabbis were fully aware of the frailty of the human will and of the propensity of even the best men to place self-serving ends above obedience to God's will. As a result, they were driven to a certainty of the blemished nature of all human moral achievements, and they eventually related this awareness to the problem of suffering. "When a man sees that suffering comes upon him," it is taught, "he has to examine his actions."[58] The meaning is that each individual, no matter how righteous, knows in his heart that his own suffering is deserved and merciful in comparison with the divine punishment that he might justifiably undergo. The further implication is that suffering is a means for the atonement of sins. "Man should welcome suffering more than happiness," it is said, "for if man is happy he cannot acquire forgiveness of sins; how does he acquire it? By suffering!" Or again, "Beloved is suffering, for as sacrifices are atoning, so is suffering atoning."[59] Thus, the appearance of leprosy on a man's body is declared to be the very altar of atonement.[60]

This teaching, of course, comes dangerously close to the idea that all suffering is deserved, an idea whose implications for our moral responsibility to others we know that moral reason cannot accept. The Rabbis worked to prevent this conclusion, however, by insisting that one is never entitled to interpret the sufferings of one's fellow men in this way, that this interpretation applies only to one's own suffering.[61] So applied and understood however, this teaching has remarkable value. It represents an important instance of a process whereby religious reason comes full circle upon itself. At the same time as an objectively perceived reality is taken for what it is and the claims of experience are fully respected, that reality is radically reinterpreted and revalued. Suffering remains suffering. The question which stimulated religious reflection in the first place, "Why if I am righteous am I not happy?" is not answered with assertions that my experience is false ("You really are happy") or only incomplete

("You will be happy"). Instead, the whole complex structure of religious reason is invoked to supply a justification of what, on the plane of experience, remains perceived as the evil that it is.[62] In looking at the structure of Jewish faith I have not made a separate point of the Rabbis' efforts generally to satisfy the fifth and sixth requirements of religious reason (those requiring minimal departure from the facts of experience). Certainly, by placing most of the objects of their belief (God, the World to Come) beyond the range of experiential refutation, the Rabbis exhibit their sensitivity to reason's requirements in this area. But in this instance we witness a special effort on their part minimally to depart from experience while rendering experience rationally and morally acceptable. If the measure of any religious belief, or of a whole religious system, is the degree to which it satisfies all of the requirements of religious reason, this particular effort to solve the problem of suffering righteousness must be considered an important rational achievement.

The Jewish awareness of human sin and the effort to speak to the serious moral problems sin involves are the last major aspect of the Jewish response to the requirements of religious reason I want to look at. The claim that Judaism denies the corruption of man's will or that it has no corresponding notion of divine grace is commonly made by non-Jewish (especially Christian) writers and it has sometimes been supported by Jewish writers as well.[63] If true, these claims would have serious implications for the integrity of Judaism as a religious system or possibly for our very understanding of religious reason. It would be odd to insist that a series of conceptions form part of pure religious reason if a major and viable historical system of faith ignored them. Fortunately, we do not have to confront this possibility because Judaism fully responds to religious reason's requirements in this area.

No one familiar with the Biblical basis of Jewish thought

can maintain that Judaism is without a profound awareness of the perversity of the human heart and of the egoism men display in the best and worst of circumstances.[64] Like the prophets before them, the Rabbis fully appreciated the extent of human sinfulness and, like the prophets, they interpreted sin as a form of persistent rebellion against the divine will, or what is the same, as an effort to assert the will of individuals or groups against that of the righteous and universal God.[65] To characterize this tendency, the Rabbis employed a term, *Yetzer Harah* (or "evil imagination") which was drawn from the Bible where it is used repeatedly to characterize that fundamental aspect of man's constitution that leads him to defy God's will and do evil. Rabbinic teaching on the nature or source of this *Yetzer* is not entirely clear. Sometimes, it is identified with man's physical passions or desires, and there is an undercurrent in Rabbinic teaching (one is tempted to call it a "Gnostic" motif) which links the evil *Yetzer* to sexuality. Thus, it is one Rabbinic position that the evil *Yetzer* arises with the sexual act and is passed on in that way to subsequent generations.[66] But over-all, the *Yetzer Harah* was not linked with any one human passion so much as with the whole range of impulses, both "spiritual" and physical, which underlie man's frequently inordinate search for security, comfort, pleasure, or esteem. Characteristically, therefore, the Rabbis located the evil *Yetzer* in the heart, which they believed to be the center of reason and emotion.[67] This does not mean, however, that these desires, closely tied up as they were with man's condition as a material and finite being, were considered evil in themselves. Though the Rabbis may sometimes have flirted with the idea that man's corporality or finitude is responsible for his persistent wickedness, they did not accept that idea in the end. For one thing, they asserted that the *Yetzer Harah,* for all the difficulties associated with it, was at least originally good. Like all aspects of God's creation, it received his approval at the outset, and still functions as part of his beneficent plan. Thus, according to one Rabbinic legend, the evil *Yetzer* was once banished from the world. As a result men did not marry, build houses, or engage in commerce. Even chickens failed to lay eggs.[68]

If the *Yetzer* was originally good, why has it become bad? The Rabbinic answer is forthright: man is responsible. In the final analysis, it is man's weak, foolish, and selfish uses of his will that have corrupted what God meant to be good. Man either abuses the passions that in themselves are necessary, or, through a failure of the will, he refuses to surmount those strong passions that can be an obstacle to righteousness. Thus, to the question "If God described the *Yetzer* as evil, who could make him good?" one Rabbinic commentator offers as God's answer: "Thou [man] hast made him bad." The proof offered is that little children commit no sin and it is only as man grows and cultivates the evil *Yetzer* that sin comes.[69] Though they were acutely aware that Man's total nature as a finite being furnishes the occasion for the most dangerous and self-directed exercises of the will,[70] therefore, the Rabbis seem equally to have recognized—as religious reason requires—that it is to the free exercise of that will that one must finally trace human wrongdoing.

Be that as it may, the Rabbis were also aware that the evil *Yetzer* remains an abiding feature of human existence. Its presence in man obstructs his obedience to God's will and even threatens the stability of the world. Seeing the world as man would make it, however, God has provided a remedy: Torah. Before we turn to the profound motifs of grace and forgiveness which the Rabbis, in response to man's wickedness, made part of their conception of God, one very important point must be made: for them, God's righteousness as revealed in Torah was the chief expression of his mercy and love. Without the additional guidance and restraint furnished by the revealed law, the creation itself could not endure.[71] This is a further reason why Torah is conceived by the Rabbis as being present with God at the moment of creation and why its revelation is part of his original plan. In conceiving the world and human nature, in other words, God in his foreknowledge took sin into account, and, in his mercy, he added the additional revelation of Torah as a corrective.[72] It is a misunderstanding of Judaism, therefore, to see reflected in Torah the face of a judgmental, punitive god. The very existence of Torah, according to the Rabbis, is evidence that God freely chose to suspend man's deserved punishment (that due Adam and his successors) in order to renew his relations with his beloved creatures.

Should the point be missed in connection with the gift of Torah, the Rabbis scarcely ever fail to elaborate upon God's grace and his long-suffering nature.[73] For example, the gap that stands between the best of human moral efforts and the requirement of perfect righteousness, according to the Rabbis, is closed when God freely completes the self-purification which man, in his sinfulness, can only begin. Thus, the Rabbis report an exchange in which Israel says, "Master of the world, Thou knowest the power of the evil *Yetzer,* which is very hard," whereupon God is said to have replied, "Move the stone a little in this world, and I will remove it from you in the next world . . ."[74] Beyond this assistance, God's grace also extends to the actual cancelation and forgiveness of sins. That God is long-suffering, that he patiently endures and overlooks many human sins is a constant theme in the Rabbinic literature. Indeed, so far was this teaching taken by Rabbinic commentators that it gave rise to the belief that God forgives all sins. "God is gracious and merciful, full of loving-kindness and forgiveness; then all the lines between righteousness and wickedness, sin and virtue, are wiped off."[75] Clearly, this idea of God's consummate mercy resides in a tense and uncomfortable, if necessary, relationship with his justice. Though mercy, in one sense, is a fulfillment of God's justice—for without it how could the world endure?—it also constantly threatens to weaken and compromise that attribute. This tension, of course, lies at the heart of moral reason where it is expressed as the perpetual conflict between the principles of punishment and forgiveness, and it naturally finds expression in religious reason where it sets the moral conception of a supreme causal agency in opposition to the requirement that such an agency be thought of, finally, as not strictly necessitated by the moral restraints that bear upon us.

Against this background, it is to the Rabbis' credit that while remaining fully sensitive to the tension between these two attributes of God, they refused to eliminate that tension. Thus, repeated Rabbinic accounts testify to God's own internal struggle in connection with his attributes of justice and mercy. These are likened in some passages to each of God's two arms and it is only by a supreme effort of the stronger right hand of mercy that God is able to subdue his left hand of justice.[76] Another passage, commenting upon the text Isaiah 56:7 in which God appears to refer to "My house of prayer," provokes the question "Does God, then, pray?" One Rabbi replies that he does indeed and the content of his prayer is "May it be My will that My mercy may suppress My anger, and that My mercy may prevail over My other attributes, so that I may deal with My children in the attribute of mercy and, on their behalf, stop short of the limit of strict justice."[77] In view of this tension, it should be noted that the Rabbis did their best to reduce the difficulties that God's grace must always present to moral reason. They insisted, for example, that God's forgiveness of sin was not absolute but depended upon man's prior act of repentance. Thus, while God's power of forgiveness was unaccountable and mighty, it had always to be preceded by the human effort—however small—at a changed disposition. In one passage, God's activity is likened to a king who sends a message to his rebellious and distant son, "Travel as much as it is in thy power, and I will come unto you for the rest of the way."[78] Human cooperation might be slight—elsewhere it is compared to the pinpoint opening of a door which God will swing wide—but cooperation is still required.

This stress on repentance and man's cooperation reduces but does not eliminate the scandal to justice and to the sense of moral responsibility which mercy inevitably represents. Evidence of this is the ongoing debate within the Rabbinic literature over the question of whether the sins of some individuals are so great as to be beyond the atoning power of repentance. Thus, according to one ancient tradition, because of his grievous sins and despite his repentance Manasseh was excluded from the World to Come. But some Rabbis protested against this tradition as "weakening the hand of penitence." One colorful passage even depicts the Angels as seeking to bar Manasseh's plea from entering Heaven and God as circumventing their efforts by digging a special passage beneath his Throne of Glory through which to hear the king's supplication.[79] The point is that repentance, though it is partly a concession to reason's insistence upon moral responsibility, to some degree also represents an annulment of responsibility in that it compromises the demand that the wicked must fully pay for the evil they do. In the final analysis, the Rabbis could not resist the belief that God's freedom from the strict requirements of the moral law was no less important, and possibly more important than his justice.[80] In this, I suggest, they reveal their profoundest sensitivity to reason's complex moral and religious requirements.

The detailed attention I have given to Judaism here will prove its worth in the pages ahead by focusing and, in some instances, shortening our inquiry. Thus, the next tradition we will be looking at, Christianity, clearly owes so much to Judaism that we can direct most of our attention to the important innovations and complexities which it brings to the rational basis Judaism established. Further on, as well, I hope this attention to Judaism will show its value. For in looking carefully at this tradition we have seen in operation some of the characteristic moves of religious reason: the reliance upon revelation or other non-rational grounds of authority; the simultaneous affirmation of apparently incompatible propositions with the concomitant effort to resolve contradictions by reference to their ultimate reconciliation in a mind or a realm of experience necessarily beyond our comprehension or limitations; and, finally, the important effort to bring religious reason full circle upon itself so that reality is at once untouched and transcended by a total moral transformation of experience. In the pages ahead, in different forms and with sometimes quite different conceptions, we shall see these moves frequently repeated in new ways.

That the Rabbis should have been able to work their way so faithfully through reason's difficult program is a testimony to their good sense and to the vitality of the tradition they served. It is no less an indication of the rich and sometimes tragic historical experience undergone by the Jewish people. As a result of this experience, Judaism was able to avoid precipitous, incomplete, and ultimately unacceptable answers to reason's difficult questions. That Judaism perceived history as the locus of divine revelation, therefore, is perhaps the final important testimony to this faith's moral and religious consciousness. In a complex involution of reason upon itself, and in an intense effort to remain faithful to experience while transforming its meaning, Jewish thinkers came to interpret the very events which steered them through reason's difficult course as experiential proof of the existence and activity of the supreme and righteous God.

7.

Christ as moral symbol

Many things can contribute to the rise of schismatic movements within religious communities, including such relatively trivial matters as personality differences among leaders or struggles for personal power. But when a schism shatters the peace of an important faith tradition with dramatic consequences for that tradition's future course, it is wise to seek an explanation for these developments within the operations of religious reason. At such moments, an effort may be underway to correct errors that have appeared in the tradition's earlier efforts to meet reason's requirements, or nuances within reason's complex program may be demanding more vigorous attention. These considerations should perhaps be borne in mind as we approach the major schismatic movement within Judaism that is Christianity. To understand fully the development of Christianity we must ask which features of the Jewish effort to meet the demands of reason were likely, at the time of Christianity's appearance, to pose rational difficulties serious enough to provoke a schism of this magnitude. In response to this question, and with the genius of retrospect, we can identify three major areas of predictable discord.

A first area involves the problem raised by the particularistic and nationalistic motifs of Jewish faith. In identifying this difficulty, however, we must be extremely careful not to confuse it with the false, polemical, and sometimes anti-Semitic accusation that Judaism is an immoral religion of Jewish national self-glorification. A preoccupation with the destiny of the Jewish nation is, of course, a major feature of Jewish faith. It is to Israel, first of all, that God has revealed the full content of his will, and it is from Israel, above all, that God demands obedience. The election of this one nation is thus a central affirmation and motivating consideration of Jewish faith.[1] Nevertheless, in Jewish thought this election is not conceived of as being separate from or inimical to God's universal moral purposes. Indeed, it is precisely through his election of one nation that God is believed to manifest his larger design. Thus, by singling out a despised slave community as recipients of his special regard, God is considered to have made known his particular concern for all those who are oppressed and outcast among men—a fact which undergirds God's subsequent commandment to Israel to respect the stranger, the poor, or the bondsmen in their midst. Similarly, it is through his covenanted pledge to sustain against all adversity the righteous nation—and only when it is a righteous nation—that God is seen to reveal his universal power and justice. Jewish religious nationalism, therefore, rests most fundamentally on the idea of election, not to glory, but to service. In the first place, this is service to God's moral will. But ultimately, it is service to the universal revelation of God himself, so that the understanding of Israel as a "light to the nations" which emerged in later prophetic thought really captures the animating spirit of the whole Jewish national self-preoccupation.[2]

In view of this, the claim that these nationalistic and particularistic motifs should constitute a rational problem for Judaism may seem strange. And yet, this claim gains force when we consider that Judaism's essentially universal religious and moral message is likely to be perceived as such only from within the confines of the Jewish national community. That is, the universal message is clearest only from within this particular standpoint. From within this community, for example, the truth of the claim that God is truly impartial and universal in his concern is pointed up every time he shows himself willing to scourge his beloved nation for its violations of his moral will. Similarly, from within this community the claim that God is gracious regardless of human merit is evidenced by his continuing regard for this worthless and recalcitrant nation. Yet God's very attention to Israel, which from the inside must magnify and exalt his justice and impartiality, may well appear to those outside the orbit of Jewish national experience as a scandal to that same justice and impartiality. To those not singled out for God's special kind of concern—and who cannot therefore clearly see it as a call to service only—the very selection of one nation must appear to be unjust. Certainly, as well, this interpretation has been reinforced by the egoistic distortions of God's intent which occasionally arose within the Jewish community itself.

That Judaism perceived the difficulty caused by this difference in perspectives is evidenced by the vigorous proselytizing it undertook during the decades immediately preceding the appearance of Christianity.[3] This proselytism was clearly an effort to dissolve the misunderstanding of Jewish purpose caused by being outside the realm of Jewish national experience. If God's universal message is fully clear only to the Jew, it follows that everyone has to become a Jew. The Pharasaic proselytizer of Matthew 23:15 and the extensive network of Jewish "God-fearing" semi-proselytes who later swelled the ranks of Christianity testify to the zeal of Jewish efforts in this direction. Those who accuse Judaism of a form of religious egoism and nationalism must naturally neglect to consider this proselytizing energy since such proselytism, although it preserves the national framework of Jewish experience, is the very opposite of any self-centered, exclusive, or prideful religious nationalism.

Be this as it may, it is also clear that the Jewish position here is a difficult one. Though proselytism was a possible instrument for bringing outsiders within the reach of Judaism's universal message, it was an unwieldy instrument at best. To become a full participant in the Jewish national destiny—and therefore in the Jewish understanding of God—required not merely the adoption of certain beliefs but of a whole national religious culture, and one largely opposed to that of potential proselyte communities. Here is the issue of the "law" in its sacramental sense and of such difficult specific commandments as circumcision which, by itself, prevented many gentile Jewish sympathizers from taking the final step into Judaism. Thus, if Judaism's universal message was to reveal itself and cast aside the misconceptions it characteristically generated, something had to be done to facilitate the outsider's entry into and perception of the realm of experience which Judaism carried with it. This problem of reason—really an internal problem for a system with Judaism's universal expectations and ambitions—is the first major one we can identify in Judaism in the years before the emergence of Christianity.

A second problem is far more subtle and takes us into some of the deepest recesses of the operations of religious reason. This problem has its origin in religious reason's third requirement, that which demands that the supreme moral causal agency be thought of as not required always to act or judge as we must. In the preceding chapter I traced some of the specifics of the Jewish response to this demand: the idea of a gracious God quick to assist efforts at moral reform, eager to accept repentance and to blot out the record of past wrongdoing. In all of this, Judaism was prepared, as reason demands, partly to annul moral responsibility in order to relieve the self-condemning despair which paralyzes further moral striving. Nevertheless, as it stands, the Jewish solution may not have been sufficiently radical. Motivated by the understandable desire finally to preserve a modicum of responsibility, the Rabbis continued to insist upon the necessary first step, however small, of honest and open repentance. But it can be asked whether, in view of their own profound comprehension and description of sin, the Rabbis' solution could bear all the weight placed upon it.

There are at least two ways of regarding what I am trying to say here, one from within the context of religious reason and the other from within the Rabbinic expressions of reason's demands. Taking the first of these we can see immediately why repentance is not a fully adequate response to reason's needs. Recalling the various forms of self-condemnation to which a rational being is led, we can see that repentance at best handles only the problem of prior evil acts. Assuming repentance to involve a profound suffering for one's past wrongs, it may be represented to the self as a valid punishment for these wrongs. But even here it is only partially satisfactory. For every rational individual must always ask whether any voluntarily accepted suffering is really adequate to compensate for his prior evil.[4] And even if an affirmative answer can be given to this, there remains the serious problem of the worth of one's present dispositions and the constancy of one's resolve. Since even the most fervent will to mend one's ways is no guarantee that will can be counted on to remain firm in the future, individual acts of repentance cannot by themselves entirely relieve the crippling sense of moral despair produced by profound self-analysis.

Within the Jewish religious system itself, the same conclusion results from the insistence that repentance, in order to be regarded as genuine, must be accompanied by a firm resolve never again to commit the sin in question.[5] Quite rightly, Judaism recognized that a repentance undergone with mental reservation is no repentance at all. But since any honest moral self-examination cannot yield the assurance of such a firm intention, it may be seriously asked whether, even within the framework of Jewish thought, the stress on repentance was as liberating as it was meant to be.

What these considerations point to is the conclusion that the Jewish position with its effort not to relinquish the final toehold on moral responsibility was untenable. If it is true that an honest self-examination must drive each rational individual to the conclusion that his every moral effort (including his efforts at reform) is ultimately morally worthless, and if this conviction must generate a despair which paralyzes further moral striving, then the conclusion is inescapable that the final judgment upon the individual must be thought of as radically separated and freed from any efforts—however small—he may make to be moral. Without this conclusion further moral striving is pointless. Put in terms of the requirements of religious reason, this conclusion means that the supreme judgmental ground or agency must be conceived of as totally unnecessitated by the individual's own moral achievements. Neither the individual's presumed worth nor, what is more important, his real unworthiness must be the determinative considerations in the ultimate judgment made upon him.

This conclusion, of course, is offensive to reason in almost every way. It radically undercuts the moral awareness that what I do morally matters, or at least should matter. By itself it annihilates moral responsibility, and within the total framework of religious reason it leads to the seemingly preposterous affirmation that there is a supreme agency of judgment that is at once perfectly motivated by morality but in no way called upon to conform its actions or judgments to our own. And yet, for all its difficulties and for all its potentially devastating implications, this conclusion is inexorably demanded by reason. Had reason some other way out of this dilemma, were there some other way of relieving the morally paralyzing self-condemnation to which it leads, reason would undoubtedly seize upon it. But since no other solution is forthcoming, this one, offensive as it may be, is demanded.

In fairness to Judaism, it must be said that the Rabbis were not unaware of the necessity of this conclusion. Some of their teachings clearly pointed in this direction. There is, for example, their morally understandable insistence that to be truly worthy, an act of obedience to the law has to be performed with joy. Recognizing, however, that virtually every moral or sacramental performance is attended by a measure of perceived obligation that works against unfettered joyfulness, the Rabbis naturally asked how any commandment can really be joyfully fulfilled as is demanded. The answer, according to one Rabbinic commentator, is that God supplies the joy.[6] What is this, however, but a confession, emerging from a different side of this same problem, that God's judgments are not finally based on human striving but proceed freely from his own will? He who really fulfills the law, in other words, does not do so because of any effort on his own part but because of God's prior decision that he shall do so (or be considered as having done so). Other illustrations of Judaism's sensing this problem and of its tentative efforts to respond to it could be given.[7] But the fact that all these efforts are only tentative points up the potential rational problem facing the tradition. Once this issue is brought fully to the surface and faced in all its troubling implications, it demands attention. It would perhaps be hasty to say that the circumstances prevailing at the moment when Christianity emerged forced such attention. In matters of historical development one can never sufficiently credit chance factors—in this case, perhaps, the appearance of a particular religious genius for whom this problem was experientially significant. Nevertheless, it can be said that from within Judaism this problem was on the agenda of religious reason. In retrospect, it is a second important factor contributing to the emergence of Christianity.

We have already met the third and final problem of reason reverberating within Jewish thought which can help explain Christianity's sudden emergence and eventual schism with Judaism. This is the problem of the relationship between the second and the third requirements of religious reason, or what is the same thing in a theistic context, the relationship between the justice and mercy of God. Specifically, since every suspension of judgment or deserved punishment for wrongdoers undercuts moral responsibility and brings into question the ultimate reliability of any supreme justice, the question is How is it possible to conceive of God as both just and merciful? If God were only just, of course, there would be no problem, although Jewish thought rightly recognized that God's mercy has to be affirmed. But if God is merciful what becomes of his justice, and with it, the human sense of moral responsibility? Thus, very specifically, the constant problem facing Judaism or any religious system as far advanced is how God can be merciful without at the same time annulling his justice.

That Judaism had not worked out a fully satisfactory answer to this question is indicated by the ongoing debate within the Rabbinic literature over whether there are kinds of sins for which God will not accept repentance.[8] This reflects uncertainty over whether God's power to forgive can really be thought of as absolute. In a different way, this same basic difficulty was expressed in terms of the continuing struggle between justice and mercy within God himself, some of the more colorful descriptions of which we saw in the preceding chapter. These descriptions, to be sure, have the value of openly and honestly presenting this tension as existing at the highest level. But since they afford no hope of an understandable resolution of the problem, because even God is presented as not being able fully to master it, these efforts were only tentative. In addition, the difficulty of the whole problem could only be exacerbated if Jewish thought were to come to grips with the radical annulment of responsibility implicit in the full program of religious reason. For then the question of how God can be thought of as just at the same time that his behavior seems to defy the strongest ordinary requirements of morality would demand an answer. Thus, these last two "soft spots" in the Jewish effort to conform to reason, the not fully acknowledged pressure toward an accentuation of God's radical freedom from moral restraint and the question of how this freedom can cohere with affirmations of his justice, are related to one another. If the first were to be directly addressed, the second would press itself on more urgently.

To sum up, then, from the point of view of religious reason at least three important problems were resident in Rabbinic thought as it developed during the opening years of the common era. One was the problem of how the scandal of particularity could be eliminated in order to render apparent Judaism's universal message. The second was how it was possible to affirm anything less than the most radical mercy of God and his freedom from moral restraint. And the third was how such radical mercy could abide with the continued insistence on God's perfect justice. It would be wrong, I think, to insist here that these problems urgently demanded a solution during the period we are talking about. The judgment I made in the preceding chapter that Judaism represents a remarkably effective effort to satisfy reason's demands remains correct. Nevertheless, the pressure of historical events and the particular needs of individual personalities can sometimes greatly magnify the importance of small and finely nuanced matters of doctrine and belief until, it seems, major historical developments are made to rest upon the way they are handled. Not just religion, but the history of political life shows this to be true. What is important is that from the point of view of religious reason these difficulties in Jewish thought were real ones, and all the more so because of the intensity with which Jewish thinkers approached such issues. Sooner or later these problems would be addressed, and we can think of Christianity as the movement within Judaism which, whatever its other impetuses, sought to do so.

In dealing with Judaism, I treated the Rabbinic tradition—especially the main lines of that tradition—as representative of Jewish religious thought as a whole. The central place given obedience to the law in Judaism has tended to dampen ideological or creedal dispute and has limited the spread of eccentric theological positions. In Christianity, however, where, for complex reasons, a greater emphasis has been placed on creedal matters, there has been a corresponding proliferation of conflicting theological positions. This makes the identification of a representative Christian position more problematical. Even so, in this chapter I want to focus primarily on the writings of St. Paul. I do so because I think the essential lines of the Christian position and of its characteristic response to the rational problems I have identified are most readily found in Paul's letters.[9] I make this statement recognizing that Paul's teachings are not the only ones to present themselves as normative within the Christian community. Paul's own letters are proof that his interpretation of Christ's life and death was contested even in his own day by other members of the Christian community (Rom. 16:17-18; I Cor. 1:10-13; 3:3-7; II Cor. 11:1-13; Gal. 1:6-9). Nevertheless, there are several considerations that prompt the identification of Pauline thought with Christianity. These include the canonical position given to Paul's writings, the persuasive evidence that other major portions of the Christian canon were colored from the first by Paul's teaching, and, finally, the crucial fact that Paul's own reflection arose directly from the proclamation or "kerygma" that animated the Christian community from the outset: the proclamation of Jesus Christ, Son of God, dead and resurrected to glory for the forgiveness of sins (I Cor. 15:3-8; Gal. 1:1-5; also, I Cor. 1:23; II Cor. 1:19). The further question of whether Paul's thought corresponds to that of Jesus is, I hope, one that we can bypass here.[10] This is so most fundamentally because no record of Jesus' teaching exists that has not already been colored by post-Easter interpretations, not least of all Paul's own.

Like any great system of thought, Paul's position forms a complex organic whole with every major component significantly related to every other. This means that the necessary task of singling out individual ideas runs the constant danger of distortion by isolating ideas from their attendant implications and qualifications. If this difficulty presents itself in interpreting any profound thinker, however, it is doubly serious where Paul is concerned. At the very center of his thought stands a conception of Christ which functions less as an idea than as a symbol. Captured within the rather simple lines of Christ's description—and these lines are essentially those of the kerygmatic proclamation I just mentioned—are a galaxy of meanings and ideas running in divergent directions. By themselves, some of these ideas are inadequate or contradictory. Yet when united in the Christ symbol and brought into inseparable connection so that one idea cannot be considered without leading to another which corrects or complements it, the array of conceptions makes sense. Indeed, I shall eventually suggest that the genius of Paul's thought lies precisely in his employment of Christ as a symbol to unify equally necessary but opposing ideas. Nevertheless, as far as the task of making sense of Paul is concerned, the very density and unity of his thought makes an orderly and systematic presentation very difficult.

This being so, I am not being especially bold if I suggest that we approach Paul by means of one of his more difficult teachings, the doctrine of justification by faith alone. As knotty as this doctrine may be, it has the advantage of offering direct entry into the whole realm of his thought. Paul himself gives expression to this teaching in various letters, but nowhere more forcefully than in the Letter to the Romans, especially Romans 3:20-26 (but also Rom. 1:16, 17; Gal. 2:16-21). Here one finds all the essential ideas: no human being will be justified in the sight of God by "works of the law" (v. 20); justification derives only from God's grace "as a gift" through the redemption in Jesus Christ "whom God put forward as an expiation of his blood, to be received by faith" (vv. 24, 25); in this, God reveals his righteousness by passing over former sins (v. 25). This Pauline teaching, then, has two major thrusts: a negative one in which the possibility of justification by "works of the law" is denied to all, and a positive one in which justification is offered by

God freely to all who have faith in his grace as given in the sacrificial death of Christ.

If we want to try to make sense of what Paul is saying here, we must first of all keep in mind that the negative side of his doctrine, the condemnation of "works of the law," is far more than a rejection of the sacramental components of Jewish religious law. That Paul would finally relax the restraints of the sacramental law for both Jew and Gentile is evident (I Cor. 7:19; Gal. 5:1-6). This followed from his more fundamental opposition to law of any sort as an instrument for eliciting divine approval. That he was a critic of the sacramental law in the traditional prophetic manner because of its tendency to usurp the priority due moral responsibility is also true (Rom. 2:25-29). But his fundamental objection was not to the sacramental law as such nor even to that law as it obstructed moral obedience, and nothing makes this clearer than his extension of blame and universal guilt to the Gentiles. Since they are capable of "doing by nature what the law requires" (Rom. 2:14-16) they are rightly condemned for having failed to do so, and they share in the condemnation of all those who seek justification through works of the law. Certainly Paul is not speaking here of law in its sacramental sense, for that would imply that the Gentiles, without even having received a specific revelation, are called upon to comply with all the commandments of Torah. Such a view, besides being nonsense, is something no pious Jew would hold. Rather, Paul seems clearly to be referring here to the general moral obligations known to all by the light of reason.[11] Thus, although Paul's condemnation of law frequently extends indiscriminately to law in either its sacramental or moral sense, it was to law in both of these senses, either together or separately, that the condemnation was meant to apply. In this refusal clearly to distinguish between the moral and religious law, by the way, Paul reveals his own deep rootage in the Rabbinic tradition.[12]

But if "law" is understood to mean the moral law, either as this is known independently by reason or as it has been revealed as a part of Jewish religious law, why are "works of law" condemned and why is law itself so closely associated with sin as to demand replacement by a new instrumentality for mediating divine acceptance? Paul's efforts to answer this question are by no means always fully clear or understandable. Thus, his frequent statements to the effect that law "makes sin known" will hardly serve by themselves to answer the question (Rom. 3:20; 4:15; 7:7-8). It is true that knowledge of morality's requirements—whether this knowledge is mediated by natural reason or by a morally valid published code—must highlight the nature and possibility of wrongdoing. But it would hardly seem to follow from this that efforts to obey the law are wrong or that matters would be better if the law were never known. The fact that medical science diagnoses sickness and recommends steps to combat it, for example, would not justify accusing a physician of fomenting disease. If the moral law has as its purpose a salutary human condition, in other words, why should its illumination of morality and immorality not be welcomed?

The comparison with medicine has some use, however, and can help us understand the real object of Paul's concern. For while the illumination afforded by medical science is ordinarily to be welcomed, this is only so when such knowledge holds out a genuine hope of prevention or cure. But what if this were not true? If our physicians possessed brilliant diagnostic skills, for example, but were utterly and necessarily incapable of preventing or alleviating illness in any way, would we really cherish their knowledge? Indeed, if such were the case might our health not even be worsened as new and intensified anxieties about our well-being were added to the normal burden of illness? By following out this analogy we come up directly against the real object of Paul's concern. For medical science and efforts at treatment to be offensive, they must be useless in facilitating their desired objective, health. For the moral law and "works of the law" to be offensive, they must be useless in facilitating their objective, righteousness. But for this to be true, human beings must be fundamentally incapable of complying with the law's demands. We must primarily perceive the law not as something which traces the salutary path to righteousness, but as something which highlights and accentuates our own iniquity. Only thus could a full knowledge of the law be seen as grounds for lamentation or dread.

That all men are unrighteous, that none, not even those who are ostensibly among the best, are capable of complying with morality's demands—or the demands of the law—is, in fact, the central conviction that animates Paul's polemic against the law. Again and again throughout his letters this conviction is voiced (Rom. 2:1; 3:10-20; 5:12; 11:32; Gal. 3:10-11).[13] In addition, it provides the vitriol in his specific attacks upon the Jews. These attacks are misunderstood if Paul is taken simply to view the pious Jew as a religious hypocrite or a moral fraud, although in the most heated moments of polemic he does offer this picture (Rom. 2:21-24). As a Jew himself, Paul well knew that in many ways the observing Jew was morally among the best of men (Rom. 10:2-3; Phil. 3:4-6). His standard of conduct was not only lofty for the day, but he even maintained an inner moral life or relative purity and humility. Yet, because of Paul's overpowering conviction that no man can ever really fulfill the holy demands of the moral or religious law, he could not but regard any special claims to moral righteousness made or implied by his coreligionists as either misguided or wicked. Indeed, given his belief in the corruption of all human efforts, he was compelled to regard any claims of moral superiority as prideful boasting, worthy, because of the presumed moral pre-eminence of those who make them, of a special measure of scorn. Paul's attacks against his fellow Jews, therefore, are a direct reflection of his certainty that no man, not even the best, is free from the ravages of sin.

Why did Paul believe this to be so? One answer might be

found in his frequent castigations of the "flesh" (*sarx*) and in the constant motif of anxiety about sexuality that appears in his writings. To sin, for Paul, is to engage in "works of the flesh" and when these works are enumerated, sexual transgressions figure importantly among them (Gal. 5:19; Rom. 13:13-14). Paul's own impassioned confession of personal struggle in Romans 7, whether it is real or rhetorical, culminating in the plea to be delivered from "this body of death" only points up the theme.[14] Certainly, if "flesh" for Paul were understood to mean man's material, physical, and sexual desires, his claims about the universality of sin might make sense, for what human being is not in some way touched by these aspects of our finitude? Nevertheless, although Paul's position was later to be interpreted this way by some heretical (and perhaps a few orthodox) thinkers, this is not the real sense of Paul's view. Paul was too much of a Jew to trace sin to physicality per se, and a careful reading of those texts where he excoriates the "flesh" and "living after the flesh" shows this to be true. Thus, in Galatians 5:16-24, Paul lists among the "works of the flesh" not merely impurity and licentiousness but idolatry, jealousy, anger, selfishness, factionalism, and enmity. Similar characterizations of the life of the flesh are found elsewhere in his writings (Rom. 13:13-14; Col. 2:11; 3:5-17). These and other passages make clear that what Paul meant by "living after flesh" or according to one's "earthly" nature was not primarily a life dedicated to physical gratification, but one dominated by selfishness and egoism, by the willingness to place the self's desires, whether these are physical or, in our terms, "spiritual," before the interests of the larger community and, of course, before God (Rom. 8:3-8). In this respect, Paul once again reveals himself to be profoundly rooted in the prophetic and Rabbinic tradition. Indeed, some of his very castigations of the "flesh" parallel prophetic employments of this term as a general symbol for the selfish and egoistic dimensions of human life.

Thus, it was egoism and not physicality that troubled Paul and it was the universal prevalence of such egoism that underlay his conviction that all men are condemned to sin. In this respect, Paul shows himself to share in the awareness to which, I have argued, impartial reason finds itself finally driven. That awareness, we recall, is that no human action can ever be certified as free from some measure of morally condemnable self-regard. As free as each agent is to purge his acts and volitions of egoism, and as much as he is able before and after each act to take the measure of the wrong he has done, no agent is ever able fully to acquit himself of having allowed purely self-regarding considerations to enter into and corrupt his moral performance. In the well-known and moving passage in Romans 7, Paul gives vivid expression to this whole problem: "I do not understand my own actions. For I do not what I want, but I do the very thing I hate. . . . I can will what is right, but I cannot do it. For I do not do the good I want, but the evil I do not want is what I do." Despite the seeming presentation of this conflict elsewhere in this passage as a struggle of the mind and the will against the recalcitrant body, Paul's profound sense that this evil is imputable and worthy of moral condemnation indicates that, in the last analysis, he traced it to a self-serving and vicious exercise of the will, for no one can be held responsible for actions caused by uncontrollable impulse. The real problem, therefore, is not that I cannot control my body, but that I do not always want to, or more generally, that my will to righteousness in all its forms (and sexual purity, for Paul, is certainly one of these) is never firm.

Paul's appreciation of the seriousness of this problem is further indicated by his description of the situation of each human being as a state of bondage or slavery to sin (Rom. 6:17; 7:6, 23; Gal. 3:23). Taken literally, this idea seems virtually a contradiction in terms, since one cannot be held guilty of sin, for which the possession of freedom is assumed, at the same time as one is held strictly bound to do wrong. This apparent contradiction will continue to draw attention in the later Christian tradition as thinkers seek either to qualify Paul's claims or, in reaction against these qualifications, to reaffirm this position even more strongly.[15] Nevertheless, we are by now sufficiently familiar with the deeper logic of Paul's view to understand its rational basis: this conviction of responsible slavery to sin derives from the awareness that wrongdoing, though inevitable, is also culpable because reason can never excuse actions that have their final basis in freedom. That Paul should describe the state of man confronted by the law in these terms reveals the completeness with which he has recognized the problem. Thus, we can see here that Paul is driven by his own appreciation of the radicality of sin to the conclusion that no human effort is capable of extricating the self from the snares of wrongdoing. Each person is a slave to evil. In this respect, Paul's thinking represents the logical end point of the prophetic and Rabbinic analyses of the human condition.[16]

A radical problem requires a radical solution. Paul reveals his deep sensitivity to the full requirements of religious reason by setting forth as a remedy to man's predicament the total annulment of responsibility represented by Christ. Since no human effort to accomplish the moral law can accomplish its purpose and since, in religious terms, every such effort must finally elicit condemnation by the supreme Judge, God, man's only hope must lie in God's free and unnecessitated acceptance. If man cannot become righteous by himself, God must make or declare him to be righteous. This declaration, moreover, must not be conceived as merely a future possibility, for that would tend to make it appear to depend once again upon each individual's doomed moral striving. Rather, it must be something which has already come to pass, by means of which God has canceled sin in the past, the present, and the future. This, of course, is precisely the meaning of the positive side of the doctrine of justification by faith alone. To have faith in Christ, for Paul, is above all to accept the fact that God has already freely passed over man's sins and has declared sinners just, not because of what they have done but because of what he has done in his mercy. Since no man can adequately acquit himself before the bar of God's justice, God has chosen freely to accept the suffering death of one man as an expiation for all, and to have faith in Christ is to confess that truth about God.[17] This, of course, does not fully illuminate the meaning for Paul of Christ's life and death. We will have to look at this more closely when we examine the relationship between God's justice and mercy. But for the moment we can pass over the network of relations in which God involves himself in acquitting man. The important point for Paul and for our understanding of him in this context is that Christ's death is first of all evidence that God has chosen to withhold the punishment that all men justly deserve and to declare them acceptable for reasons that have nothing to do with their presumed achievements or real failures.

The radicality of this annulment of responsibility is evidenced in at least two important ways in Paul's thought. First, because it is understood to free each individual not only from responsibility for past actions but for future actions as well. Earlier in this chapter we saw that the full burden of moral self-condemnation is not relieved so long as God's mercy is extended only to the acceptance of repentance and the forgiveness of past sins. For then, in full self-awareness, the individual can still question his ability to maintain rectitude in the future (an uncertainty which finally even jeopardizes the quality of acts of repentance). Radically conceived, God's assistance must be understood not only as canceling past sins but as extending into the future as well to sustain the self against all future repetitions of evil. Moreover, it follows from this that any future moral achievements, if they are to be held up for approval, can never be presented as the work of the individual—since everything the self does alone it knows to be reprehensible—but as proceeding from their true author, God. Now, although Paul does once suggest that God's grace applies only to former sins (Rom. 3:25), it seems to be the predominant direction of his thinking to see God's grace as relieving the self of responsibility for future acts as well. His assertions that "it is no longer I who live, but Christ" who lives in me" and his frequent insistences that all moral sufficiency is from God merely point up a conviction reflected on almost every page of his writings (Gal. 2:20; II Cor. 3:5; Phil. 2:12-13).

This teaching undoubtedly poses further problems for moral and religious reason. What becomes, for example, of future moral effort? In view of his reception of God's grace, need the individual even continue to strive to be moral? Or is it possible to lose God's grace? Can the certainty of acceptance by God cohere with the possibility that misconduct can render that certainty false? In response to this latter type of question, and in view of the primary aim of relieving moral self-condemnation, it clearly cannot be permitted for grace to be thought of as dependent upon future achievements or failures. At the same time, continued moral responsibility must be affirmed. Paul himself barely deals with this matter, both because he believed the gift of grace naturally flowers in a life of righteousness and because the problem of backsliding—which forces a discussion of the permanence of grace—had probably not become as serious a concern in his lifetime as it was to become in the later Christian community. However, there emerged a host of positions, stimulated by real difficulties in the community, uniting grace with continued responsibility. Generally, the tendency was to insist that the reception of grace must be evidenced by a sustained course of upright conduct, that "justification" must be followed by "sanctification" (Rom. 6:19, 22).[18] Complementing these insistences were the rationally expectable efforts to explain differing successes among Christians in holding to this course by means of the prior mystery of grace. Though this is certainly the general shape of a solution to this knotty problem, there always remains, of course, much room for disagreement and for ongoing dispute over the precise relationship between grace and responsibility. As a result, the history of Christian thought reveals various specific resolutions of this continuing struggle between equally necessary ideas. Sometimes an amoral quietism is based on a supreme confidence in the permanence of grace. (Lutheranism in some of its moods may be an example.) At other times the high ground will be taken by a moralistic activism, and, indeed, this will sometimes even be fueled, paradoxically, by the conviction that the smallest transgression reveals not just a momentary turning from God but a state of total perdition. Weber's famous study of the relationship between Calvinism and capitalism rests upon the presumed discovery of this logic at the roots of later Calvinistic moralism.[19] In any case, the whole problem of the permanence of grace and its relation to future moral striving is part of Christianity's debt to Paul and to the seriousness with which he understood man's need for a freedom from his own moral efforts.

But if the self is freed from responsibility for its past and future, if God is thought of as the bestower of worth, then on what basis does he determine who will be accepted and who will not be? This is a further and extremely difficult question raised by reason's need radically to deny the importance of individual responsibility, and Paul's own handling of it is a second important indication of his willingness fully to satisfy reason's needs. The problem arises from the fact that if the supreme moral judge is not necessitated to judge us and to morally empower us on the basis of our actions, he must eventually be thought of as motivated by considerations which assault our sense of justice. Either that judge must eventually accept all—worthy or unworthy—taking no consideration of merit or he must arbitrarily accept some and reject others. In either case, our sense of justice is affronted. Nor can we retreat to the idea that the faith which seizes upon God's mercy is a responsible act, so that those who have faith and are redeemed somehow "merit" their redemption by having, in their freedom, accepted what God has offered.[20] For any vestigial role given to responsibility in the economy of this problem must only exacerbate self-condemnation.

To understand what I mean by this, we need only realize

that no fully honest individual can ever declare his own grateful response to divine mercy to be genuine or sincere so long as that response is seen freely to proceed from the self. This is because in order to turn to God's grace, an individual must confess his own final inability to do right and his genuine need for assistance, but no one in his freedom can ever allow himself to make such a confession. Indeed, the very attempt to do so must be condemned by his morally judgmental reason as an insincere and self-deceptive effort to secure quick release from responsibility. Alternatively, should an individual courageously refuse to confess his final moral inability, he must relinquish any hope of divine assistance.[21] Thus, just as the only human beings who are righteous are those who confess themselves not to be, so the only persons worthy of God's mercy are those who honestly declare themselves unworthy of it. This "Catch-22" or "damned if you do, damned if you don't" situation has its basis in the general fact that human beings, in their freedom, are uncompromisingly called upon to do what they know they cannot do. Here as elsewhere, however, the solution is to believe that the supreme agency—in this case God—can do what the self cannot. Concretely, this means that in order to be regarded as genuine, ardent confessions of moral inadequacy and appeals to God's mercy can never be conceived as arising from a responsible act of the self. The self must be regarded as "helpless" before such confessions and appeals and they must be seen as resulting from a prior, merciful act of God, one in no way determined by the self's efforts or achievements.[22] But this necessary transference of initiative to God brings us directly back again to the question: on what basis—if not the individual's efforts—can God be thought of as apportioning his redeeming judgment and assistance?

There may be some evidence in Paul's writings that he entertained a universalist solution to this question, one according to which all would eventually be redeemed (Rom. 11:32; 5:18; I Cor. 5:5).[23] But this position poses considerable difficulty since it seems to set the righteous and the wicked on an equal footing. On the other side there is a problem of arbitrariness if a harsh period of interim punishment is allotted to some and not others. In any case, if all distinctions between good and evil are not to be effaced, the problem of God's arbitrariness in this context must finally be considered, and this seems to be precisely the significance of Paul's apparent final retreat to a doctrine of divine predestination (Rom. 8:29-30; Gal. 1:15; Eph. 2:10). Whether God's primordial and preordained designation of the wicked and righteous was meant by Paul to culminate in total perdition for some, or whether it applied only to their interim punishment before some kind of universal redemption is not clear (cf. I Cor. 3:13-15 and Rom. 2:6-10). But, whichever is true, Paul was ultimately prepared to confess the arbitrariness of God's actions by our standards of judgment. Thus, although he suggests the defense that since all have sinned, none have a claim to acceptance (Rom. 9:14-15)—a defense not free of moral criticism since grave questions of justice can be raised about the arbitrary bestowal of even unmerited reward—he finally yields freely to a confession of the arbitrariness of God's ways from our point of view. To our objections, Paul replies that as the clay pot cannot question what the potter does with it, so can man neither question nor comprehend the wisdom of his creator (Rom. 9:19-21). By now, of course, we are familiar with the deeper logic of such a position. Driven by the most pressing needs of reason to affirm the sheer arbitrariness of God's bestowal of grace, but recognizing the claims of justice which oppose this, Paul acts finally to put the entire matter beyond further rational assault by suggesting, but not offering, a solution in a just wisdom beyond human wisdom. Centuries later, Calvin was perhaps more forthright in calling predestination a necessary but "horrible" truth of Christian faith.[24] In either case, however, the doctrine of predestination is fully understandable only when set in the context of reason's total program. Paul's retreat to this doctrine is concrete proof that he appreciated fully the dilemma of moral self-condemnation and responded to it with a radical, if difficult, solution.

The fact that Paul's presentation of the doctrine of justification by faith alone grows out of attention to the requirements of religious reason and is not the isolated fruit of some kind of irrational obscurantism becomes even clearer when we regard his efforts to fend off some of the more unfortunate but predictable consequences of his teaching. Offhand, it would be perfectly natural to interpret this teaching as an effort to shift morality from the center of the religious stage and to replace it, perhaps, with some kind of new method of relation to a transcendent reality. Thus, forms of mystical exuberance or dramatic disavowals of moral restraint are equally to be expected and, as Paul's letters make clear, both phenomena flourished in the wake of his teaching and writing (I Cor. 6:12; 10:23, 13:1; 14:6-33). Nevertheless, from the point of view of religious reason, both kinds of response, especially antinomian immoralism, are offensive. The whole purpose of the annulment of responsibility, we must remember, is to alleviate the paralysis of self-condemnation and despair in order to facilitate an enthusiastic return to moral striving. It is true that by themselves the propositions effecting this are neither logically related to nor even necessarily suggestive of a moral purpose. But within the total framework of religious reason, they are designed to have just that end.

We should not be surprised, therefore, that Paul should vehemently respond to some of the non-moral or immoral interpretations his teaching inspired. Castigations of antinomianism or amoral spiritualism are everywhere in his letters. In some instances, moreover, he directs his teaching to this whole problem and seeks to anticipate and correct possible misinterpretations of his views. Thus, in Romans 6 his exposition of the replacement of law by grace prompts the rhetorical question, "What then? Are we to sin because we are not under the law but under grace?" and this is followed immediately by a resounding "By no means!" or "God forbid!" Several verses earlier a more outrageous rhetorical question is posed: "What shall we say then? Are we to continue in sin that grace may abound?" and again the fervent response, "By no means!" (Rom. 6:15; 1-2). Paul's seriousness in this regard is reflected, of course, in the detailed moral prescriptions for the Christian life which fill his letters. Anyone looking to Paul for a freedom from moral restraint or even for the reduction of morality to only some flexible general principles must be taken aback by the lengthy and detailed lists of Christian virtues and vices he advances. This plethora of norms—perhaps a part of the "law of Christ" to which he sometimes alludes (I Cor. 9:21; Gal. 6:2)—is not an afterthought for Paul. Full obedience to such norms is, in fact, the whole object of his teaching and nothing makes this clearer than the way in which, at the end of almost every letter, after pages of tortuous and sometimes pained doctrinal argumentation, Paul turns enthusiastically to these descriptions of the Christian moral life (Rom. 12-13; Gal. 5-6; Eph. 4-6; Col. 3-4).

To students of Paul this completion of a brilliant diatribe against "works of the law" by an impassioned moral legislation has often seemed irrational and illogical, even if it has been esteemed as a kind of glorious irrationality.[25] Nevertheless, despite the superficial appearance of logical inconsistency, Paul's teaching here reveals its genuine rational basis and coherence in the light of a full appreciation of religious reason's demands.[26] This does not mean, however, that it is necessary openly to trace the course of reason to appreciate Paul's position. Paul himself was convinced that a full comprehension of Christ and of the meaning of his life and death reveals the foolishness of any selfish or immoral interpretations of God's grace. Not reason, but Christ condemns these interpretations.

We shall begin to look more closely at why he maintained this and why he believed the information imparted by Christ suffices to eliminate immoralism. Nevertheless, his claims should not surprise us. These claims, too, have their basis in reason and they reflect the fact that the beliefs or symbols with which a re-

ligion seeks to conform to the demands of reason need not ever
contain a confession of debt to reason itself.

We have just seen that Paul vigorously rejects any effort to draw
immoral conclusions from his teaching. Although we know from
our vantage point within religious reason why he does this, it is
important now to turn directly to what, for Paul, is the source of
this conviction: the figure of Jesus Christ. In three important
ways, Christ functions for Paul as the supreme revelation of
God's moral will. First, because in the death of Christ, God does
not compromise but reasserts his stringent moral standard. Second, because Christ himself, in the pattern of his life and death,
displays and encourages obedience to God's highest moral will.
And, finally, because through his death Christ facilitates similar
obedience by all those who would follow him. Altogether, Christ
not only vindicates the moral law, but he re-reveals its essential
content and he empowers those who would fulfill it. These implications of the Christ figure for Paul are intimately related to
one another. They are separable, however, and I want to look at
them in order.

We already know that the need to vindicate God's justice
arises whenever his mercy is affirmed. It is the nature of mercy
that it annuls justice because the morally demanded punishment
of the wicked is compromised or withheld. How, then, can God's
mercy be affirmed without abandoning the insistence on his strict
justice and righteousness? If this question is a troubling one for
Rabbinic thought, it is doubly so for Christianity, in which God's
forgiveness in Christ is so radically asserted. Nevertheless, for
Paul, Christ is the solution to this problem as well. In his death,
Christ not only consummately displays God's mercy, but he also
supremely upholds God's inflexible standard of justice.

The key to Paul's position is the conception of Christ as a
vicarious and expiatory sacrifice, the "paschal lamb" who atones
for human sins (I Cor. 5:7; also, Rom. 3:25; 5:9-10; Eph. 5:2).

This idea is not new to Christianity. Judaism provided the religious matrix in which vicarious sacrifice as a means of atonement was common, and later prophetic thought, upon which Christianity built, had even extended this idea to a human agent or national community whose suffering is meant to redeem others (Isaiah 53). In addition, the Hellenistic environment was filled with religious movements in which redemption was mediated by sacrificial saviour figures. Nevertheless, it is in Christianity that these various strands are most powerfully woven together to serve reason's pressing needs. Specifically, it is the nature of Christ's atoning death that it highlights sin even as it cancels it.

We can understand this better if we ask why forgiveness—especially God's forgiveness—constitutes a scandal for moral and religious reason. Certainly it is not just because some wrongdoers go unpunished. Reason can tolerate occasional lapses of punishment—it may even encourage them—so long as there are no further implications of the forgiving act. What is most troubling about unrequited wickedness is, first, that it tends to efface the very difference between right and wrong, and, second, that it thereby also encourages future wrongdoing. Where God's forgiveness is concerned, this second aspect is naturally of lesser concern since the burning question, in view of the perception of the depth of human sin, is not whether wrongdoers will be encouraged but whether those who wish to be righteous can carry on at all in the face of despair. But the first aspect is a serious problem: how can God, whose righteousness for the believer maintains the line between right and wrong, forgive without at the same time blurring that line and minimizing sin's destructive and lethal significance? Christ's sacrificial death answers this question. In that death, moral evil works itself out to the full: it reveals its basis, its nature, and its consequences to the highest degree. Yet, at the same time, the full penalty of wickedness is withheld and no wicked person is made to suffer.[27]

The basis of evil is revealed in the needless punishment and death of Christ. He is sinless and his suffering is in no way deserved. As a result, the usual moral defenses of apparent wrong-doing are inadmissible. No one dares argue that Christ's death was a just punishment for wrongdoing. Thus, evil is deprived of all reason and is shown to have its basis in a radical, if corrupt, employment of freedom. Similarly, the nature of evil is dramatically highlighted as it works itself out in all its forms: pride, dishonesty, disloyalty, injustice, cowardice, mercilessness, and wanton cruelty. Moreover, in Christ's death these various faces of evil reveal their deep relationship to one another so that the tight and self-multiplying relationship between evils is underscored. As the Gospel record of Christ's betrayal, trial, and sufferings comes into form, the details of this picture will be filled in. But the bare facts of Christ's death were known to the early Christian community, and in holding up this death, Paul must certainly have known the evils he was condemning. Finally, in Christ's death the full consequences of wickedness are revealed as it culminates in the tortured death of a righteous man. In our own day, it is true, we have come to measure evil by its quantity: so many tortures, so many millions of deaths. But from the strict point of view of reason, it is not the quantity of suffering that is most immediately offensive as is its moral quality. Worse than the suffering of the vicious is the suffering of the innocent or righteous. Such suffering, in fact, is the reverse of what reason most desperately requires: if the Highest Good is the full happiness of all the righteous, then the misery of even one righteous person must be evil. And, indeed, if there is only one truly righteous person and if he is plunged into the depths of suffering— not merely physical torture but shame and despair—then this is the Highest Evil and the ultimate fruit of human wickedness.[28] Once again, when the Gospel record comes into form, these awarenesses will be given full expression. But the implications of Christ's death were sensed in the earliest Christian community and were known by Paul. The Deuteronomic injunction "Cursed be everyone who hangs on a tree" (21:23) is quoted by him, and though Paul was convinced that Christ has transcended this curse, he was not unaware that to do so he had to submit to the cruelest abasement (Gal. 3:13).

So in Christ's death, the basis, nature, and consequences of evil are dramatically highlighted. The inexorable destruction that evil entails works itself out. But the equally necessary punishment is withheld. If all those who contributed to Christ's death suffered evil—and in the strictest sense no one, not even the members of Christ's entourage, is free from the charge of having willingly contributed to that death—then their sufferings would be just. If the moral rot and corruption their behavior evidenced were eventually to fall back destructively upon them, no one could declare that destruction unmerited. And yet, this does not happen. The power and destructiveness of evil is confined to one man. And since that man is conceived of as united with God—from this point of view it makes no difference whether Christ is the beloved son of God or God himself—in the last analysis it is God who genuinely suffers and who takes all the consequences of evil on himself. Thus, all of reason's most pressing needs are met. God is seen to prove himself merciful in forebearing to punish and in cutting the necessary connections he is held to have established between wrongdoing and eventual destruction. At the same time, this mercy does not abrogate his justice. The line between right and wrong is not effaced but underscored and the full consequences of sin—even if these are turned away from men—are revealed. To be sure all this is effected by means of a cosmic drama which initially seems bizarre. The standard objections to later Christian atonement theory point this up. Is God so wrathful that he cannot acquit without demanding some punishment? Is he so powerless that he is prevented from forgiving in some more expeditious way? These kinds of questions and objections, however, grow out of a fundamental failure to appreciate the importance of justice and the way in which God himself must be conceived of as subject to the standard arising from his own moral will. In other words, an atonement is required, and God himself must suffer precisely because of the importance of

God's own justice. Reinhold Niebuhr states this well: "The fact that God cannot overcome evil without displaying in history His purpose to take the effects of evil upon Himself, means that the divine mercy cannot be effective until the seriousness of sin is fully known. The knowledge that sin causes suffering to God is an indication of the seriousness of sin."[29]

Of course, Judaism also understood that sin causes God to suffer, as evidenced by the struggle within God before his mercy or his justice triumphed. Judaism also knew that mercy was never merely an abrogation of justice.[30] But what Christianity adds to this is the vivid revelation of this truth in the life and death of Christ. Just as a symbol can capture within itself a mass of divergent meanings, so the idea of Christ gathers together all these contradictory demands and awarenesses of reason, and, in bringing these demands into the closest possible connection, this idea effects a dramatic transformation of their relationship to one another. Heretofore, reason's opposing requirements could be affirmed only separately or in succession: "Yes God is just, but he is also merciful . . ." To consider God's justice was to ignore his mercy and to affirm his mercy was to neglect his justice, so that however quickly the transition was made from one conception of God to its necessary qualification, only one aspect of his nature could be comprehended at a time. In contrast, the symbol of Christ unifies God's different qualities in such a way that one cannot think one quality without holding fast to its qualification. To regard Christ is to see both God's consummate hatred of evil and his limitless mercy to the wicked. Indeed, this compression and unification of reason's demands is so striking as to support the claim that Christianity, while employing nothing more than the fundamental insights of Judaism, effects a qualitative change in those insights and in our understanding of them.

But we have still not exhausted the central moral implications of Christ's life and death, for as I indicated earlier, Christ also serves dramatically to re-reveal the content of the moral law and to furnish the knowledge needed to facilitate moral obedience. The first function is fulfilled by Christ as the very embodiment or incarnation of God's moral will. The second is met as Christ removes the principal obstacles to moral obedience. Once again these aspects of the Christ symbol are distinguished only with difficulty, but it is important to try to consider them separately and in order.

For Paul, Christ re-reveals God's moral will by becoming its physical embodiment. In the events of Christ's life and death, in other words, the Christian is presented with both a summarization and personal exemplification of the standard he is called upon to follow. Neither the effort to summarize the law nor the imperative to imitate the behavior of God are novel. Both ideas are borrowed from Judaism. But in joining the summarization of the law to the behavior of God in and through a flesh and blood exemplar, Christianity again forges something new. As far as the content of this exemplification is concerned, at least four central moral virtues are repeatedly emphasized in the course of Paul's writings: humility, selflessness, forgiveness, and love. Of these four, love is sometimes presented as the supreme summarization of the other three, and therefore of the law in its entirety.[31]

Humility and selflessness, we know, are at the very center of the moral life. As the free relinquishment of special claims and advantages, humility underlies the adoption of the moral point of view, while a degree of selflessness is always required for any fulfillment of morality's demands. It is true that extreme selflessness can also support supererogatory behavior, but a measure of selflessness also attends the most ordinary performances of duty.[32] Forgiveness, in turn, draws heavily upon both of these virtues and it also presupposes a precise understanding of morality's objective requirements in each new situation. Rightly to forgive, in fact, requires many things: a keen awareness of morality's sterner demands, a sensitivity to when these demands can and should be set aside, a humble sense of shared weakness with the wrongdoer, and finally, perhaps, a sufficient freedom from the narrow concerns of one's ego to be willing to "risk" exposing oneself to the future evil that a forebearance from punishment can occasion. Genuine forgiveness is the fulfillment of a perfected moral life and it naturally flourishes only in an environment of moral maturity. Next to these three, the Christian virtue of love (*agape*) assumes a special place. As a principle of universalization—the Golden Rule—it can function, as it frequently does in Judaism, to characterize the impartial moral point of view—an injunction to set the other's interests on an equal footing with your own. More forcefully, however, it can be fused with a profound emotional concern for the other, on the model of family love, so that a moral life based on this virtue must culminate not only in a strict regard for the moral rules, but where morally permissible, in genuine acts and attitudes of supererogation. Paul's own writings present *agape* in both these senses although it seems that the latter sense, at least so far as relations among Christians are concerned, predominates (Rom. 13:8-10; I Cor. 13; Gal. 5:14; Philemon). In this respect, *agape* may be thought of as both the summarization and perfection of the whole content of the moral law.

Against this general background, Paul's emphasis on the exemplification of these virtues in the life and death of Christ and his repeated injunctions to imitate Christ—or God through him—assume great moral significance. Whether Paul knew anything specific about Christ's moral teaching is uncertain. But there is no question that he drew the fullest moral implications out of the austere message of Christ's suffering death.[33] Thus, he maintains, as Christ humbled himself by relinquishing "the form of God" in order to become a servant "born in the likeness of men," so should Christians humble themselves and count others as better than they themselves (Phil. 2:5-8; II Cor. 8:9). As Christ, for man's sake, selflessly obeyed God's will, becoming "obedient unto death, even death on a cross" so must Christians obey God and set the interests of others before their own (Phil.

2:4-8). As God, in Christ, has freely forgiven them, Christians should forgive and be forebearing of the wrongs of others (Rom. 15:1-3; Eph. 4:32; Col. 3:13). Finally, and supremely, as Christ's death on the cross witnesses his and God's overarching love even for a sinful mankind, so should the Christian love his neighbor, including the neighbor who has wronged him (Rom. 5:8; 8:32; Eph. 2:5; 5:2, 25).

Emphasis on the moral significance of Christ's life and death is not the only way Paul employs the figure of Christ to delineate the pattern of Christian moral responsibility. Very commonly, as well, he makes use of a metaphor according to which the Christian community is presented as the very body of Christ in the world. Thus, just as each Christian individually dwells "in Christ" in the sense that Christ's spirit is his own, so does Christ dwell in the community of faith whose different members compose his "body" (I. Cor. 12:12-31).[34] This idea has many sources both in Hellenistic and Jewish thought, but, in this context, it is the moral implications that are important. They include the awareness of a strong community of purpose: Christians are to cooperate with one another without friction, just as the members of a body always work together. Also, just as the differing strengths and abilities possessed by different members of the body exist only for the benefit of the organism as a whole, so the various gifts of ability, position, or wealth within the community of faith must always serve the commonweal, especially the needs of its weaker members (I Cor. 12:22-26). This latter implication of the body metaphor will continue well after Paul to have controversial social and moral consequences. Either it will be interpreted, as during the medieval period, to sustain permanent religious and social inequality, or, more radically—and, I think, more correctly—it will become the basis of an explosive critique of any privilege that does not directly serve the needs of the most humble members of the community.[35] Either way, the body metaphor reveals its powerful moral implications, although this is especially true when this very general and not particularly Christian idea is interpreted in light of the cruciform pattern of Christ's life and death.

I could mention other features of Paul's understanding and employment of Christ as a full disclosure of the moral law, but I think the main outlines of his view are clear. Christ for Paul is the supreme and final revelation of God's moral will. He is the culmination of a process begun by God with the general revelation of his will in creation, renewed in the special bestowal of Torah to the Jews, and now brought to enduring conclusion in the embodiment of all the law in one man (Rom. 1:19-22; Gal. 3:19-24; Col. 2:9, 1:15-17). Not unlike the Rabbis, Paul would even locate this new revelation of the moral law at the center of God's eternal will, and Christ is presented as forming the plan of the creation. These are certainly grand claims, and they seem almost to dwarf the fragile figure on whom they are based. But they make sense from the point of view of moral and religious reason since, as described, Christ's life and death have the moral value given them. Humility, selflessness, forgiveness, and love are among the central virtues of the moral life. Paul's understanding of Christ as the final and complete revelation of God's moral will, therefore, reflects the perfected moral life that Christ represents.

To complete our understanding of the moral implications of the Christ symbol for Paul, we should observe that for him, Christ supplies not only knowledge of the full content of the moral law, but also the power needed to fulfill that law. This is accomplished principally by Christ's victory over death, suffering, and sin. In terms of reason, we can see the Christ symbol as thus eliminating the principal rational obstacles to moral obedience. We already know, of course, the problem which death poses to moral reason, and we have looked at Judaism's efforts to overcome this through the doctrine of resurrection. It is important, therefore, that a major significance of Christ for Paul lies in the demonstration of the truth of this doctrine (I Cor. 15:12-26).[36] Through Christ, Paul maintains, death, "the last enemy," is destroyed, the righteous are comforted in their present afflictions and the immoral retreat into brief comforts and enjoyments is shown decisively to be foolishness. Nor is this any longer merely a hope. In the death and resurrection of Christ, what had been an article of faith, the resurrection, becomes a matter of factual certainty (I Cor. 15:19-20), and the Christian can evidence this for himself by reliving Christ's death and resurrection in the rite of baptism (Rom. 6:4f.; Col. 2:12).[37]

In similar fashion, Christ's life, death, and resurrection overcome the obstacle suffering poses to both moral obedience and religious faith. In discussing Judaism we saw that it is not enough for reason to know that the suffering of the righteous will eventually be transcended. Reason must also know why, if God is as powerful as he is conceived to be, suffering is necessary in the first place. For Rabbinic thought suffering at its best was regarded as an act of atonement or as a token of personal favor with God. Implicit in this is the suggestion that God himself suffers with the suffering. In the figure of Christ this line of thought is carried to its logical conclusion: God's love of those who suffer in righteousness is evidenced by the fate of his beloved son; in that fate God reveals his nearness to all who suffer and his participation in their suffering. Henceforth, it is not power or glory that display God's presence, but the reverse: powerlessness and abnegation. God's own power and love are displayed in weakness, and the Christian is invited to rejoice in his sufferings because every instance of innocent or righteous suffering is a sharing with Christ and with God (II Cor. 12:9; Rom. 5:3-5; Phil. 1:29; 3:10).[38] Through this idea, the suffering of the innocent or righteous is morally transcended even as the real occurrence of suffering is accepted. Nowhere is this acceptance of and triumph over suffering better expressed, I think, than in the lyrical passage in II Corinthians 6: "We are treated as imposters, and yet are true; as unknown, and yet well known; as dying, and behold we live; as punished, and yet not killed; as sorrowful, yet always rejoicing; as poor, yet making many rich; as having nothing, and yet possessing everything." Unmerited suffering must always pose a profound rational problem for a religious tradition in which the source of supreme power is declared to be just. It can be argued, however, that Christianity removes the deepest moral and religious objections to such suffering when it not only associates it with God's highest purposes but also when it presents God as sharing consummately in that suffering himself.[39]

A final rational obstacle to moral obedience is sin. Here Paul's understanding of Christ comes into sharpest focus: in Christ's death and resurrection, the Christian has died to sin and has been raised to newness of life (Rom. 6:1-12; Eph. 2:1-6). To specify all the ways in which Christ works to vanquish sin as an obstacle to righteousness would be to review the contents of this chapter. But a brief summary of the ways in which wrongdoing impedes righteousness, and Christ's bearing on each, can be suggested. Most directly, of course, it is one's own temptation to sin, the illegitimate force of one's own ego, which hinders righteousness. Here, the selfless example of Christ, his transcendence of suffering, and his conquest of death (for himself and for others) provide the crucial and morally facilitating information. In the second place, it is the sin of others that presents an obstacle to morality, as it furnishes constant encouragement to violate the moral rules by means of self-regarding exceptions. Here, Christ's sacrificial example and his victory over death serve to empower the willingness to risk which every defense of the higher moral ideals requires. And, finally, it is the sense of one's own inevitable sin, despite a will to righteousness, that either corrupts or paralyzes moral action. For those who have refused to make themselves fully aware of this problem, and whose moral striving is consequently tainted by callousness or by self-deceptive and fanatical efforts at perfection, the figure of Christ first points up the universality of sin. Strictly speaking, no one can acquit himself of all the moral wrongs that culminate in the death of this righteous man. Observing Christ, the individual is thus driven to repentance, or what Paul calls "godly grief" (II Cor.

7:10; Rom. 2:4). But for those who have already advanced to this point and have found themselves confronted by the morally crippling problem of self-condemnation and despair, for which even the will to repent is not an adequate remedy, Christ's death and resurrection offer relief. As proof of God's free forgiveness, Christ prevents the very repentance he induces from turning into a hardened despair, and he thus facilitates a humbled, but nevertheless, committed return to moral striving, a return made all the more enthusiastic by a sense of gratitude for God's mercy.[40]

This, of course, brings us full circle back to the doctrine of justification by faith alone. To have faith in Christ, to believe, as Paul puts it, that "God's promises are not in vain" and that Christ is really the promised deliverer from sin and death, is to remove all of the major obstacles to enthusiastic moral commitment. In rational terms, genuine acceptance of the proclaimed significance of Christ dissolves all those reasons why one may be drawn to immorality and replaces them with positive reasons for dedicated moral striving. This is certainly one sense in which we can interpret Paul's claim that Christ is both the "wisdom and the power" of God (I Cor. 1:24). The proclamation of Christ conveys information sufficient to motivate any rational being, so that it is a knowledge which leads to action. Whether Paul himself would accept this interpretation of his claim that Christ is both wisdom and power is another matter. It seems clear that for him, the power of Christ in the believer is perceived in terms of a miraculously transformed will, an almost mystical indwelling of Christ in the believer and the believer in Christ. Nevertheless, we can also see that this transformation, whatever its particular psychological manifestations, has its foundation in reason, as the rational person is mediated knowledge in Christ, which, when appropriated, must effect a transformation of the will.[41]

We are now able to appreciate the moral richness and significance of the Christ symbol. Fully comprehended, we can see this symbol as representing the effort to bring to fruition the program of religious reason begun by Judaism. In the understanding of Christ as mediator of God's forgiving grace, we see a solution to the radical problem of moral inadequacy. By taking sin upon himself, God is conceived as freeing each individual from the necessary self-condemnation his self-knowledge must otherwise require. At the same time, because that freedom is effected through Christ, it becomes a vivid reaffirmation of the moral law and not, as it threatens to become, an annulment of God's justice. This is so because, through Christ, not only forgiveness but a resolute condemnation of iniquity is offered, because Christ's life and death establish a supreme moral pattern for all who see in him the revealed will of God, and because the proclaimed facts of that life and death, if accepted, must induce the most fervent moral striving. Since the affirmation of God's radical mercy and the strict relation of this to his justice were problems on Judaism's agenda, the Christ symbol can be seen as their direct solution.

The same can be said of this symbol's relationship to the third major problem before Judaism: the particularity of its universal religious message, or the fact that fully to know God's moral will seemed to require a sharing in the destiny and experience of the Jewish nation. From within the Jewish community, we know, this posed a moral and religious problem, especially when election was misperceived as a sign of favor rather than as a call to suffering service. From without, it was also this misperception of God's partiality that obscured the universal religious message. With the justice and mercy of God worked out in the life and death of one man, however, these problems are eliminated. In Christ, the new Adam, God's revelation is given an experiential basis not confined to a national community but open to all who are human. Potentially, anyone who can appropriate into his life Christ's suffering and death has access to the comprehension of God's nature and will. In this respect, Christ represents the full universalization of Israel's experience. Against the background of misconceptions of Israel's election, Paul is not wrong, therefore, when he presents Christ as abolishing the barrier of hostility which separated Jew and Gentile from one another and both from God (Gal. 3:28, 29; Eph. 2:14-16; Col. 3:11). Of course, it is also true that in its very universality and personalization this symbol offers new grounds for misinterpretation. Once God's moral will is severed from its rootage in national life, for example, it can easily be stripped of its important social and political implications until nothing remains but a code of personal moral behavior which, however lofty, is morally deficient.[42] Equally devastating is the tendency to interpret the wrongs which eventuate in Christ's death as peculiarly those of a morally condemnable pariah nation. This interpretation not only has tragic moral consequences in its encouragement to religious persecution, but it also generates a form of religious and moral self-righteousness which entirely obscures the central message of universal condemnation and grace which the Christ symbol bears. Unfortunately, history reveals how frequently Christianity was subjected to these and other misinterpretations. Perhaps this is the price paid for sundering Judaism's powerful religious message from its rootage in the concrete life of the Jewish nation. But from the point of view of reason, this process of universalization was almost inevitable, and it is at least the strength of the Christ symbol to contain within itself the resources needed to help correct its own misinterpretations.

In historical perspective, therefore, the idea of Christ carries to a new level the theistic religious program outlined by Judaism. Measured against the requirements of religious reason, Christianity strains toward a maximum fulfillment of each requirement at the same time as it seeks to minimize, without effacing, the tension between reason's separate requirements. This is especially true in the difficult case of the second and third requirements, where the perfect morality and freedom from morality of the supreme causal agency must both be affirmed. Like Judaism, of course, Christianity must have problems with religious reason's sixth requirement, that which demands a minimal departure from the facts of experience. For in transcending suffering, death, and sin, Christianity must advance beliefs whose truth lies beyond the range of verification by our experience. These include, above all, the belief that Jesus Christ was not merely another tragic victim of wrongdoing, but in fact the righteous, beloved Son of God, sent as a testimony to God's mercy and as a confirmation, through his resurrection, of the conquest of sin and death.

In some respects, it is true, this focus on Christ's life and death eases the tension with our ordinary experiential knowledge. For one thing, Christian belief in no way obscures the bitter fact of suffering. Just as the blunt reality of the Messiah's suffering and death is not denied, so the suffering of each Christian believer is taken for what it is: a hateful sign of human sin. Suffering and death are enobled and eventually transcended, but their reality on the plane of experience is accepted. In addition to this conformity to experience, there is the important claim that the event which fundamentally transmutes suffering and death has already occurred. In accepting the historical fact of Christ's death and resurrection, the hope that our condition might be other than it appears is replaced by the certainty that it is and will be. And since the death and resurrection is presented as a fact of experience, as something for which clear confirmatory evidence can be advanced, the whole structure of Christian faith is made to rest not simply on beliefs lying beyond experience but on those which experience itself is held to support. Paul's own claim that Christians have more than a hope grows out of this awareness (I Cor. 15:19). This does not mean, of course, that the focus on the resurrection does not present new problems for our experiential knowledge. For now, the whole truth of Christianity is made to rest upon the reality of an event unsupported by our ordinary experience and for which only the testimony of (by our standards) unreliable witnesses is advanced as proof. In one respect, therefore, Christianity increases the tension with experiential knowledge. But it does so—and this point is easily overlooked—precisely because it seeks to bring historical experience directly into the service of its whole structure of belief.

This rational concern with experience is further evidenced by Christianity's reliance upon the prophetic pronouncements and predictions of Hebrew Scripture. Again and again within the basic Christian proclamations of faith, Christ is declared to be the Messiah prophesied in Scripture, and the conformity between prophecy and Christ's own life and death is offered as further proof of the reality of his sonship with God and his resurrection. In terms of reason, we can understand some of these claims. As I observed at the conclusion of Chapter 6, the progressive unfolding of reason's full moral and religious program in the course of history is religiously expressed both in the Hebrew Bible and in Rabbinic thought in terms of the developing relationship between God and his people. Not surprisingly, within that rational development there is a sense of problems not fully mastered and of possible solutions to come. Chief among these problems are the continuing suffering of the righteous and, in a different direction, the developing recognition that power and glory are the fountainhead of sin, so that all simple hopes of messianic fulfillment are rendered suspect.[43] The solution to both these problems finds one of its most moving expressions in the prophetic predictions of future redemption, not to glory but to service. This is part of the meaning of the "suffering servant" motif of Second Isaiah. Within advanced prophetic thought, in other words, we can identify concrete religious representations, in the form of prophetic predictions, of solutions to reason's most pressing needs within this theistic framework. That Christianity should seize upon this crystallized record of prediction, therefore, and that it should see in Christ the personified fulfillment of prophecy, is not strange. To the degree that the understanding of Christ's life and death responds to the same needs that moved later prophetic and Rabbinic thought, the Christian confession that prophecy is fulfilled in Christ has a basis. Employment of the scriptural record to evidence the reality of disputed aspects of Christ's career, therefore, represents a complex effort to use reason's own most pressing needs, as expressed through prophetic prediction, to certify the truth of historical claims, Christ's divine sonship and his resurrection, made to satisfy those very same rational needs.

Lest we misjudge these moves as some kind of insidious religious sleight of hand, we must keep in mind that from the point of view of reason they are really nothing but a supplementary effort to minimize an almost unavoidable tension within Christianity's response to the demands of religious reason. If the Christian religious system commends itself to reason in the first place, it is not because certain historical events have transpired but because the total interpretation of those events represents a striking and compelling response to some of reason's deepest needs. This is perhaps especially true of the idea of an expiatory death which mediates forgiveness without annulling justice. But to give this and other important ideas their necessary force, and to further meet the demands of experiential knowledge, Christianity is led to base its beliefs not on future possibilities but on accomplished historical facts. Realizing, for example, the paralyzing significance of moral self-condemnation, and aware that the mere hope of justification is not adequate to relieve this paralysis, Christianity declares that the believer has already been made just. Similarly, it replaces the hope of relief from suffering and death with the certainty that suffering and death have been conquered. This means, however, that the principal historical events to which Christianity points—Christ's life, death, and resurrection—are not so much the source of belief as its consequence. One is a Christian, most fundamentally, not because Christ has risen, but because one believes that Christ has risen, and one believes that Christ has risen because one subscribes to the system of beliefs that point to that event. In this respect, a contemporary Christian theologian like Rudolf Bultmann is not altogether wrong when he maintains that Christian faith depends on the permanent existential significance of the resurrection and not on its historical veracity. Bultmann is mistaken, however, in believing that the matter of historical truth can therefore be set aside. For while it is faith—the complex of beliefs required by reason—which points to history, and not vice versa, that same faith demands belief in the reality of the events to which it points.[44] We see here, in other words, the same necessary blurring of the line between subjective and objective truth which we noted much earlier in connection with any of reason's supraempirical postulates. To derive certain beliefs solely from the interior needs of reason is not to declare them only subjectively true. For the very reason which postulates such beliefs knows that it must finally affirm the objective truth of that which it postulates.

This explains Christianity's peculiar relationship with history. On the one hand, the proclamation of Christ, Son of God, dead and risen to glory, can be seen as growing out of a pure rational faith. On the other hand, that very proclamation must always contain the insistence on the truth and reality of the events to which it points.[45] If Christians have sometimes adduced evidence or have employed exegetical techniques which are dubious by our standards, that is not simply because they have wanted to deceive. Rather, it is a consequence of their belief and a reflection of their certainty that in the manner of Christ's life and death something can be discerned to which all of history points and which necessarily has to be affirmed. We might ourselves translate this claim into the statement that in the Christian belief system, the theistic response to reason's demands is given powerful and virtually complete expression. Emphasis on the historical reality of the Christ event, therefore, though inevitably in tension with experience, is primarily an expression of the rational authority and persuasive force of Christian belief as a whole.

8.

The religions of India: *karma* and liberation

A view which places morality and moral reasoning at the basis of religious belief would seem to be seriously challenged by the religions of India. Not that these traditions neglect morality. On the contrary, the great religions which arose on Indian soil—Hinduism in its many forms, Jainism, and Buddhism—contain demanding moral codes. All support the common moral rules and all encourage the performance of supererogatory acts. The ideal of *ahimsā*, requiring abstention from injuring any sentient beings, is one example of a lofty Indian moral teaching. And yet, despite this, much can be said for the claim that morality seems not to be at the center of Indian religious thought. In all the Indian traditions, the ordinary demands of moral responsibility and the requirements of human moral relationships are typically subordinated to an individual quest for release from the world. Not righteousness for the self or the community, but "liberation" or "release" for the individual (*moksha* in Hinduism and Jainism; *nirvāna* in Buddhism) is the apparent goal of these faiths, and an important aspect of this liberation is always a freedom from the fetters of morality itself, the attainment of a state "beyond merit and demerit."

If the understanding of religion I have tried to develop up to now amounted to a simple reduction of religion to morality in the fashion of many Enlightenment rationalist views, or if, following Matthew Arnold, it presented religion as nothing but "morality touched by emotion" this drastic subordination of morality in Indian thought would pose a serious problem. We know, however, that the relationship between morality and religion is in fact very complex and that reason, as it advances into religious reflection in order to preserve the moral life, characteristically makes a series of complicated and paradoxical moves. One of these is precisely to subordinate morality to other concerns and to shift it from the center of religious attention. St. Paul's diatribe against the "law" and his emphasis on faith furnish an important illustration of this aspect of religious reason. In turning to the religions of India, therefore, and in disputing the fundamental place I have given morality in religious thought, it is not enough to point to these traditions' subordination of moral concern or their primary emphasis on individual redemption. What must be shown instead is that moral concerns have no basic role in the development of these traditions, that problems of the moral life neither significantly motivate them nor form a central object of their total religious concern.

What I would like to suggest is that a non-moral interpretation of Indian religion cannot be sustained. In fact, I hope to indicate that the basic dynamics of moral and religious reason furnish the key to understanding the most important and characteristic aspects of these traditions. I say this despite the wide diversity of the Indian religions themselves, for while it is true that the traditions and sub-traditions of India display a profusion of bewildering and sometimes opposing tendencies, there are certain important constants in all this diversity. These constants, moreover, are just those that moral and religious reason would lead us to expect. They include a firm insistence on strict moral retribution, the law or doctrine of *karma;* a deliberate effort to surmount the moral difficulties that strict retribution must entail, the emphasis on *moksha* or *nirvāna;* and finally, in one way or another, whether with reserve or enthusiasm, a determined return to insistence on the moral life. If my subsequent remarks tend to pass over the many particularities of the religions of India, especially differences within Hinduism and Buddhism and between these two faiths, it is because I want to bring out the presence and striking emphasis on these points in Indian religious thought.

Indian religious thinkers tend to pride themselves on the tolerance and openness of their traditions. They are typically puzzled by the emphasis on creedal uniformity and dogma in many of the Western religious groups. Nevertheless, Indian religion also has a dogma, not perhaps in the form of a belief supported by obligation or coercion, but as a postulate not seriously open to discussion.[1] That dogma, perhaps the only one in all Indian religious thought, is the teaching or doctrine of *karma.*

The term *karma* itself means literally "action" or "consequences of action" and the doctrine of *karma* describes a strict law of moral cause and effect: as each individual sows morally, so shall he reap. Just as in the realm of nature each event has its predictable effects, so do moral acts, whether good or evil, necessarily lead to predictable consequences for their producers. Part of this claim is not extraordinary. Human moral actions, like any phenomenal events, have results which, with adequate knowledge, can be predicted. What distinguishes the doctrine of *karma,* however, is the claim that the consequences of one's moral acts are impressed in keeping with strict justice not only on others but on the self, and not only in this life but in future lives as well. Linked to a belief in metempsychosis—the transmigration of the individual personality—the doctrine of *karma* holds that each individual inevitably receives the just recompense of his acts. Those who act virtuously find their conditions of life improved either immediately or in the future when they are reborn into more fortunate and prosperous worldly circumstances, perhaps into the womb of a princess or a goddess. Those who behave wickedly must face worsened circumstances, including possible rebirth into animal or insect existence.[2]

The teaching of karma, therefore, describes a perfect law of moral retribution. Without the intervention of any higher powers—there is no need for a god or recording angel—it distributes happiness to each individual in strict proportion to his moral worth. Universal in its operation—the Dhammapada tells us that one cannot hide from it even in "the clefts of the mountains"[3]—and keyed above all to the inward intentions and volitions of the individual, it scrupulously measures the worth of every one of us.[4] And to that worth, it apportions just reward, perhaps even a punishment that fits the crime. A habitual liar in this life, for example, is likely in some future existence to become the object of false accusations; one who gossips is not likely to be accepted at his word; the heavy drinker is likely to be reborn insane.[5] In this way, each one of us is linked to our actions and volitions in a tight chain of moral cause and effect. The Sanskrit word for this moral transmigratory process, samsāra, literally "passing through intensely," thus describes a world of absolute and uncompromising moral responsibility.

It is important to stress here that the idea of moral freedom is an implicit assumption in the Indian understanding of karma. This must be emphasized because the belief that each one of us is what we are because of what we have been has appreciable deterministic and fatalistic overtones. For example, if my conduct in this life is partly a result of my actions in the past, how can I be held responsible for what I do now? There is evidence that one or another Indian thinker or movement drew this conclusion from the idea of karma and consequently de-emphasized moral responsibility. But this position was always a minority view and it was characteristically treated with scorn and derision by the major Indian traditions.[6] For these major traditions, *karma* was interpreted to mean that although our choices here and now are *conditioned* by what we have done before, they are not *determined* by it. In every new moment of moral choice we retain an elements of freedom or "initiative" to shape our future. In this sense, life may be likened to a game of cards. Though we are dealt a limited hand—a hand, by the way, for which we are responsible—we always remain free to make the best play we can with what we are given. The *karma* doctrine is thus meant primarily to heighten moral responsibility by stressing that it is we who are responsible for the circumstances of our lives.

The origins of this doctrine are obscure. Most scholars are agreed that the idea of *karma* first clearly appears only in the Upanishads, although there are possibly suggestions of it in the earlier Brahmana literature.[7] This would date its appearance very roughly somewhere toward the middle of the first millennium B.C. It seems not to be present in the Vedic texts which represent the principal expression of the Indo-Iranian religion imported into central India in the middle of the second millennium B.C. by the Aryan conquerors. The Aryans possessed the more familiar retributive doctrine of worldly and heavenly rewards for the righteous and consignment to suffering in hell for the wicked. Nevertheless, certain aspects of Vedic religion and society perhaps contributed to the emergence of the idea of *karma*. One is the conception of a universal natural, moral, and ritual order, the Sanskrit term for which is *rita*. Like the Greek concepts *arta* and *dike,* to which it may be etymologically related, or the Chinese concept *tao,* and not unlike the Jewish conception of Torah or the Christian Christ-Logos, *rita* reflects the belief that the moral and religious orders are bound up with nature and with the very constitution of reality. Like these kindred concepts, *rita* also expresses the belief that there is an objective relationship between morality and nature so that the sustained neglect of morality must undermine the social and natural bases of well-being. And like its kindred concepts, *rita* was conjoined with a belief in a god or gods whose task was to punish and reward human actions in keeping with their conformity to this natural-moral standard. As such, the concept of *rita* may well have contributed to the emergence of the idea of *karma,* which, in one sense, represents only an accentuation of the claim that there is a relationship between the moral and natural environments, between moral performance and reward.

A closely related basis for the *karma* doctrine may also be found in the patterns of Vedic ritual activity which, by the late Vedic period, had developed to such a point that they had become virtually sundered from all notions of service to or propitiation of the gods of the Vedic pantheon. According to this conception, ritual activity itself, quite apart from its effect upon the gods, directly sustained and constantly re-created the cosmic order. Each ritual action or *karman* had its effect, whether rightly or wrongly performed. The translation of this idea to the moral realm is understandable if we keep in mind the fact that within the ritual and moral cosmos conceived by Vedic thought, no clear distinction can be drawn between a moral and a religious act. As the creative and sustaining role of ritual was elaborated, and as the gods with which it had been connected faded into the background, it was quite natural to assume that morality, too, had its natural and not divinely mediated consequences for the self.[8]

A final important source of the *karma* doctrine might be found in the social conditions of later Vedic society. This is no place to rehearse in detail the social history of early India, but I might briefly stress some of the important general developments: an initial period of conquest by Aryan invaders from the Northwest; a prolonged period of rule by these invaders during which they imposed their political and cultural hegemony over a darker-skinned (although already socially differentiated) native population; and a slow process of mutual accommodation during which the differing populations, cultures, and classes underwent significant intermixture but not without leaving, in the form of an hereditary caste society, a permanent residue of the earlier racial, cultural, economic, and religious hierarchies. Against this background, the doctrine of *karma,* with its dramatic implication that each individual is responsible for the circumstances of his life, might be thought of as having had enormous appeal. To those at the top of the social ladder, it could offer a nearly perfect method of social control, and to those at the bottom, it could hold out the prospect of escape from a seemingly hopeless situation. Does an individual unhappily find himself born into the poverty and lowly social status of the Shudra caste?[9] If so, he has no one to blame but himself, because his lowly birth merely displays the karmic consequences of his own vicious behavior in some earlier life. Ought he to resist accepting his social position, strive to elbow his way up the caste ladder or even, perhaps, participate in violent efforts to change society? Absolutely not. For within the cosmic justice effected by *karma,* each individual has earned his place, and his only hope for social advancement lies in the faithful performance of caste duties. These duties make up *dharma,* the later Hindu term for *rita,* or the total cosmic natural and moral order.[10] To fulfill *dharma* and one's own *dharma* one must accept one's place in the world as earned, and one must contribute to the overall justice and goodness of things through the performance of socially necessary caste duties. Thus, if the Shudra complies with his destiny, if he works off his punishment and contributes to the welfare of others from his lesser position, as *dharma* requires, he may anticipate being born in a higher social position, as a member of a Vaishya agricultural or trading caste, as a Kshatriya political or military leader, or even perhaps as a Brāhman, a member of the sacred priestly caste and order. Failing in the performance of his caste duties, however, the Shudra will be plunged down even below his present inferior status until he reaches the miserable sub-human realm of animals and insects and experiences rebirth, perhaps, "as a worm in the intestine of a dog."

No one can presently say with certainty that this caste use of the idea explains the emergence of *karma* on Indian soil. Religious and moral conceptions are rarely just the product of social needs.[11] But there is evidence that Indian religious leadership sometimes used the idea of *karma* in this socially conservative way. In numerous places in Hindu literature a karmic explanation is given to the relative caste status of individuals. Indeed, in one significant text in the great Hindu epic, the *Mahā-bhārata*, the very character and racial composition of the castes themselves (the Hindu word for caste, *varna*, means literally "color") is attributed to their primordial moral performances. The passage is worth quoting:

> . . . this world, having been at first created by Brahmā [the creator god or principle] entirely Brāmanic, became afterwards separated into castes in consequence of works. Those Brāhmans, who were fond of sensual pleasure, fiery, irascible, prone to violence, who had foresaken their duty, and were red-limbed, fell into the condition of Ksattriyas. Those Brāhmans, who derived their livelihood from kine, who were yellow, who subsisted by agriculture, and who neglected to practice their duties, entered into the state of Vaiśyas. Those Brāhmans, who were addicted to mischief and falsehood, who were covetous, who lived by all kinds of work, who were black and had fallen from purity, sank into the condition of Śūdras.[12]

In recent years it has become the fashion in modernist Hindu thought to interpret the ideas of *karma* and caste so as to avoid their employment as a justification for hereditary and hierarchical social distinctions. Characteristically, it is argued that the karmic relationship between virtue and birth into a caste is correct, but that the castes ought not to be thought of as hereditary social groups so much as ideal types of moral character and capacity.[13] According to this interpretation, a true Brāhman is not one born into the so-called Brāhman caste, but is rather a person, whether of Shudra or even outcaste birth, who throughout his life betrays a worthy, Brāhman-like character and disposition. Without doubt, some support for this interpretation can be found in important Hindu texts,[14] and it is also true that Jainism and Buddhism, as major religious reform movements, have—when they have not outrightly rejected the whole notion of caste—interpreted it in this way. Nevertheless, it is equally true that from a very early date, this has not been the dominant Hindu interpretation of caste. Instead, it has been consistently related to hereditary social status, and if we are to understand the appeal of *karma* and its implications within traditional Indian society, we must take into account its setting within this hereditary and hierarchical social system.

This is the background, I think, against which we must weigh Max Weber's forceful statement that the *karma* doctrine "transformed the world into a strictly rational, ethically-determined cosmos" and that it thus represents "the most consistent theodicy ever produced in history."[15] If we keep in mind the fact that the *karma* doctrine is not properly speaking a theodicy— its strict mechanical causality obviates the need for any god— Weber's statement has much to recommend it. As a rational effort to solve the problem of suffering righteousness and to satisfy the fundamental second requirement of religious reason with a belief guaranteeing the exceptionless and proportionate reward of virtue, the *karma* doctrine is a stroke of genius. Without any of the clumsy mechanisms or difficulties that burden theistic responses to this requirement, *karma* guarantees that each moral agent will incur the appropriate reward or punishment for his actions and intentions. It does so, moreover, as the fifth and sixth requirements of religious reason demand, with only slight departure from the facts of experience. True, it goes beyond experience by asking us to believe in our continuance beyond death as moral personalities. But it actually draws upon experience by emphasizing that moral actions have determinate and predictable effects for individuals and societies. In these respects, *karma* is what the philosopher or engineer might call an "elegant" idea: it performs its primary function with efficiency and a minimum of complexity.

Unfortunately, in philosophy, engineering, or religion, elegance is not the sole criterion of adequacy. On closer inspection, and especially in view of how it has been interpreted and applied in the Indian setting, the *karma* doctrine possesses at least one devastating flaw. Just as it furnishes an adequate rational justification for any disjunction between my present moral achievement and happiness by assuring me that in the future reward will be forthcoming, so does *karma* also give a full rational and moral justification for my present suffering. If I am poor, despised, unhappy, or ill, I have no one to blame for this but myself—it is the result of my own evil acts or dispositions in some prior existence.[16] Earlier, in the context of Judaism, we saw the effort made at the leading edge of Rabbinic thought to appreciate suffering as the deserved result of sin. In experimenting with this idea, the Rabbis knew that they were on morally dangerous ground since they were very close to justifying not only accidents of birth and existence, but even the suffering which men unjustly inflict on one another. Sensing this, they urged the qualification that such an interpretation may be applied by an individual only to his own suffering and never, by him, to the suffering of others. In India, this qualification was not forthcoming. In its place, the idea that one's fate is merited was applied not just to individuals but to whole social classes. Though there is no sure answer as to why this should have happened, I think we might find some explanation in the Indian social situation. For many hundreds of years it was perhaps in the interests of powerful classes and groups to maintain an idea of *karma* so interpreted. As time passed, it probably became in the interest of lower-class groups to do so as well, partly because in their rigid circumstances *karma* responded to deep personal needs and partly because there developed strong social reasons for adhering to this teaching. (Even today, sociologists note, the sense of caste is often strongest among the Indian lower castes where, for economic and socially defensive reasons, caste disciplinary procedures have been much developed.)[17] As a result, despite its potentially grave flaws as a rational religious idea, *karma* has become the point of departure for every important Indian religious tradition.

How central *karma* becomes for Indian religious thought

is suggested by the fact that it is one of the few major religious ideas for which Indian thinkers offer virtually no justification or defense. *Karma*, like the orderly course of the heavens, is not something that has to be justified; it is, as Zaehner says, "a self-evident fact of existence."[18] There are, to be sure, some suggestions of a "proof" of *karma* in Indian religious literature. The Buddha, for example, is said to have become able, on attaining enlightenment, to survey the full course of his preceding existences. And the same ability, inside and outside Buddhism, is sometimes attributed to those who have achieved exalted states of meditation and trance. In this sense, there is the implicit claim that the knowledge of *karma* is inductive. But this claim is rarely advanced since the truth of *karma* in Indian thought is not something seriously questioned. Even Buddhism, with its radical doctrine of non-self (*anatta*), which, taken strictly, eliminates the possibility of a continuing personality to experience karmic effects, felt compelled to insist upon some re-formation of the individual personality under the influence of karmic forces. And the sway of this doctrine is further underscored by the fate of the one tradition which rejected it: the Cārvāka or "materialist" school. Along with the rejection of *karma*, the Cārvākans were held to repudiate all ethical responsibility and to encourage a life of selfish hedonism. Their characteristic teaching was "while life remains let a man live happily, let him feed on ghee even though he runs in debt."[19] But Cārvāka did not survive. Theirs was a position which, in the words of Arthur Danto, enjoyed only "polemical longevity" as something to refute.[20] Thus, Cārvāka is the exception supporting the rule that *karma* for Indian thought is the unquestioned and shared premise of all significant religious speculation. This does not mean, however, as Danto seems to maintain, that *karma* must be accepted merely as an inexplicable factual belief, an oddity of the Indian way of seeing the world which infinitely distances their religious and moral thought from our own.[21] On the contrary, if what I have been saying is correct, the *karma* doctrine can be seen as an effort to fulfill one of the most urgent requirements of universal religious reason. If it has continued to dominate Indian thought, despite the fact that in its most objectionable but typical interpretation it is finally unacceptable to reason, this must be attributed to the special conditions of Indian history and not to some peculiarity of the Indian religious spirit.

Karma also furnishes the background for the second major common feature of the Indian religious traditions: their emphasis on liberation (*moksha* or *nirvāna*). Whatever the specific differences involved in their understanding and description of this goal, the major Indian religions are agreed that liberation is fundamentally a release from *samsāra,* from the endless course of rebirth conditioned by *karma.* For some reason, karmically determined transmigration becomes what Monier Williams has called "the terrible nightmare and daymare" of Indian religious thought.[22] As a result, the understanding of liberation as an escape from the wheel of rebirth becomes, in Weber's terms, "an absolute presupposition of Hindu philosophy after the full development of the *karma* and *samsara* doctrines."[23]

It is natural to ask why this should be so. Offhand, the prospect of an assured return to life does not seem so distressing. Moreover, if we keep in mind the fact that for Vedic religion life itself was deeply appreciated, with longevity and material prosperity being the principal goals, we are puzzled as to why, during the post-Vedic period, the prospect of future terrestrial existences should have become so loathsome. Perhaps it was not the prospect of successive future lives that became so fearsome but, as some have suggested, the possibility of repeated death, the infinite succession of future departures from loved ones and from life's satisfactions.[24] But why should this be so troubling if death bears the promise of new life? Or was the problem, finally, cosmic tedium? This is the interpretation of the Indian revulsion at *samsāra* that seems most to have captivated Western commentators. Facing the prospect of an infinity of repeated existences, we are told, Indian thinkers must have succumbed to a boredom that heightened the desire for a final escape from the sheer repetitiveness of existence.[25] But this explanation is not wholly persuasive. That life lived without end must eventually become tedious is probably true. But is this problem—one that no human being usually experiences—really serious enough to account for the horror which Indian thinkers display at the prospect of rebirth?

If we want a more persuasive explanation for this preoccupation with liberation from *samsāra,* we must seek it, I think, directly within the moral implications of the *karma* doctrine. We have seen that this teaching describes one of the strictest laws of moral retribution ever developed. Within a world governed by *karma,* no deed is without its effects. Each act properly performed, whether moral or ritual, contributes in some way to the agent's betterment in the future, and each evil deed makes itself felt in some form of future suffering. *Karma,* in its strict impartiality and necessity, is thus, in the objective sense of these terms, both pitiless and merciless. Because of *karma* I must bear the consequences of every wrong I intend or perform, and the hope that I may be "forgiven my trespasses" is as unfounded and foolish as the wish that the law of gravity might be temporarily suspended.

If we keep in mind the fact that no human moral action or intention can ever impartially be regarded as flawless or free from some measure of condemnable egoism, we can readily identify a first major moral implication of the *karma* doctrine bearing on the concern for liberation, an implication that is genuinely frightening: since everything I do violates the strictest standards of impartial moral judgment, even my best achievements in this life cannot prevent my experiencing justified suffering in some future existence. Perhaps my next life will be drastically marred by some deserved karmic fruition of my prior moral imperfection. Or perhaps, instead, my next few lives will be fortunate—characterized by higher rebirth, increased prosperity, and stature. But eventually, my prior evil deeds and volitions, however small, must ripen. I will, as some of the Indian texts say, eventually exhaust my good *karma* and become more and more the victim of my past wrongs. When this occurs, I will be pulled down from my privileged position and plunge again into a realm of increased suffering, a fate made all the worse by the relative respite from suffering I have enjoyed and by the knowledge that my suffering is my own fault. From one or another such destiny there is no escape. Within *samsāra* there is no possibility, for example, that I can ever achieve enduring well-being and permanent relief from suffering. That would require not only the liquidation of all my past wrongdoing, but the achievement within the world of moral responsibility of a state of perfect moral virtue. No finite individual can achieve such perfection, however, and *karma,* by visiting the penalty of one's past wrong deeds on the present, puts even relative virtue beyond many persons' reach. All these considerations must naturally prompt a fatalistic and despairing view of one's condition, and it is evidence of the fact that *karma* was perceived to have these implications that, despite the constant assertion of freedom of the will, determinisms and fatalisms of various sorts repeatedly cropped up on Indian soil.

I do not want to stress only the moral and rational dimensions of this problem. The specific ritual aspects of Vedic religion and the special social conditions of Indian society must certainly have contributed to this rationally based moral difficulty. Vedic religion, we know, had elaborated an enormously complex series of ritual performances whose initial purpose was to win favor with the gods and to expiate moral and religious sins. We should not be surprised, therefore, that the profound sense of inadequacy attaching to all moral activity should have had its counterpart, in the ritual and religious sphere, in an almost magical fear of ritual taint and pollution. Such a fear repeatedly shows itself in the numerous appeals for the forgiveness of sin that appear in the Vedic texts.[26] Certainly, the burden created by this vast religious edifice must have heightened anxiety and the sense of inadequacy so as to make the fear of karmic punishment even stronger.

On a slightly different plane, the peculiar Indian relationship between religion and caste might also have exacerbated this general problem. We in the West, during the modern period, have become disenchanted with the traditional eschatology of a transcendent realm ("Heaven," "The Kingdom of God") where the righteous are gathered to receive their reward of enduring bliss. But this eschatology, whatever its defects, has at least one useful feature: it removes the elect from our midst. The appealing but improbable vision of finite agents experiencing perfect happiness in conjunction with perfect virtue is removed from our careful scrutiny. Not so in India. There, the righteous, or at least the relatively righteous, are everywhere to be seen: they are the members of the higher castes, and especially the sacred Brāhmans. We do not have to go far to discern the implications of this awareness. The moral imperfections of elites are always obvious. Ruling groups tend to be characterized, if not by outright wickedness, at least by the sins of pride and arrogance. And, indeed, in Indian religious literature, the conceited and corrupt Brāhman has almost as standard a place as the prideful Pharisee or the venal Catholic priest in the West. Although the sight of such an elite might not prevent members of lower groups from aspiring to climb the karmic ladder, it must certainly give them pause and turn their ears toward those who preach the superior goal of *moksha* or *nirvāna*. Imagine what it means to struggle for eons upward, only to become a person whose characteristic disposition necessarily drives him once again down the karmic ladder.

From the point of view of the elites themselves, this problem is even more acute. In their honest moments, members of these elites must know how far they are from the ideal standard their caste position represents. Indeed, the very complexity of their social responsibilities must heighten their sense of moral inadequacy. And to their moral anxiety, they must add the sense of taint produced by frequent, and perhaps unintended, sacramental and ritual pollutions. All this must convince them of how perilous is their toehold on security and well-being in a society where both insecurity and misery predominate. It is perhaps not accidental that concern for the goal of liberation has most frequently emanated from thinkers or movements connected with the two highest castes. Buddhism is an important example. Lower caste individuals might be sufficiently attracted by the goal of higher birth to be content with a world dominated by *karma,* and even today it is the simple promise of higher birth that principally motivates the Hindu lower castes and the Buddhist laity. But high caste individuals, or those who otherwise have known high karmic privileges, must naturally be distressed by the prospect of continued rebirth. Not only does that prospect hold out, at best, only more of the same fragile and fleeting enjoyment (and within this context even birth in the *deva*-world, or the realm of the gods, is only a glorified Kshatriya or Brāhman status), but there is the ever-present possibility—indeed, almost the certainty—of rebirth downward.[27] Small wonder that in this context the principal goal should become liberation from rebirth itself, liberation to a state "beyond merit and demerit" where evil does not "stain" and where it departs from the self "even as water rolls off the smooth leaves of the lotus."[28]

We might, against the background of these insights, evaluate a common non-moral interpretation of Indian salvation striving. It is frequently maintained that the idea of salvation in India differs fundamentally from the same idea in the West. In Western religion, it is said, salvation is very much a redemption from sin, while in India it is above all release from the frustrations, dissatisfactions, and sufferings of life.[29] But surely, in the strict moral world created by the idea of *karma,* no simple distinction between sin, on the one hand, and dissatisfaction or suffering on the other, is tenable. In such a world, suffering is always the result of sin and sin must always express itself in suffering. Correspondingly, liberation from the endless cycle of existence with its hardships and its frustrations, is always a liberation not only from suffering but from sin. It is certainly true that classical Indian religious thought does not emphasize a notion of grace or of the divine forgiveness of sins. This follows from the fact that, within this setting, the gods have had their retributive function usurped by the inflexible operation of *karma*. But surely the concept of grace finds its analogue in *moksha* or *nirvāna*. Just as grace cancels sins and frees one from the penalties they must otherwise entail, so does liberation from *samsāra* free one from the constant burden of renewed misery and hardship which one's flawed moral efforts must necessarily and justly produce. In this respect, we can think of the preoccupation with *moksha* or *nirvāna* as an effort within the unique thought-world created by *karma* to respond to the third major requirement of religious reason: to locate within reality an objective basis or reason for subordinating and transcending the remorseless demands of moral reason.

In addition to this important matter of sin, there is perhaps one other major moral implication of the *karma* doctrine which may help explain why liberation from *samsāra* becomes the immense concern it does for Indian thought. This involves the problem of moral autonomy. We know that it is an important aspect of the first requirement of religious reason that the actions performed by a moral agent always be of the sort that could be approved by impartial reason. This does not mean that moral agents cannot have many motives for being moral, nor even that their supreme motive must make appeal to reason, but it does mean that the supreme motive cannot ever be of the sort that prompts violations of the dictates of impartial reason.[30] In the West the idea of obedience to the will of an absolutely moral God probably furnishes a motive that satisfies the requirement of autonomy in this sense.

Against this background, we can identify a permanent problem for religious ethics: in satisfying the second requirement of religious reason, religions tend to furnish purely prudential motives for being moral which can jeopardize this demand for autonomy. That is, by assuring the proportionate reward for virtue, systems of religious belief can tend to encourage an attitude to the performance of moral actions which is less concerned with whether these actions are objectively right or (speaking now in religious terms) whether they are required by some source of absolute righteousness than with whether they are in some way profitable to the self. As a result, morally dangerous motives can develop, and the prospect of wrongdoing can be enhanced. This is the reason why religious traditions, even as they promise rewards for virtue, constantly strive to prevent these rewards from moving to the center of moral concern. In theistic systems these efforts are characteristically directed against the tendency to make the hope of future reward, or even divine approval, the principal motivating ground for behavior.[31] In their place, morally purer motives such as love for the righteous God are commonly advanced. One way of reading Paul's elaborate theology of grace, for example, is to see it as an effort to purge moral motivation of all possible self-regarding considerations, not least of all of the hope for divine approval generated by the religious system itself.

But if this problem of moral autonomy is a persistent one for all religious traditions, it would seem to be significantly magnified in those traditions where *karma* is the fundamental principle of moral recompense, for it is the nature of *karma* that it necessarily connects every moral action with a concretely identifiable reward or punishment for the self. In this sense, *karma* is a perfect principle of retribution since it has the effect of converting every moral decision into a purely prudential one. This very perfection, however, aggravates the tension with the demand for autonomy by encouraging the habit of regarding actions not primarily in terms of whether they are right or wrong, but whether they are advantageous or disadvantageous to oneself. Indeed, where *karma* is accepted as an inescapable law and where one's fate is seen as utterly determined by its operation, it becomes virtually impossible to make a moral decision without insinuating into one's deliberations condemnable considerations of personal profit or loss. But of all the possible motives for moral action, this one is the most offensive to impartial moral reason, since self-regard is always the principal threat to moral responsibility. *Karma*'s assurance of the presence of this possible motive in each moment of moral decision, therefore, is potentially a serious source of moral concern.

Taking these considerations one step further, we can see that *karma* tends to place the scrupulous moral agent in a very difficult position. If he wishes to attain enduring well-being and a freedom from the possibility of rebirth to suffering, he must be morally perfect. Such perfection includes a fundamental heedlessness of his own self-interest and a concern only for what is right. But a belief in the necessity of *karma* can prevent one from ever achieving this state because this belief has the effect of alloying every moral choice with some measure of self-regard. To the normal burden of guilt, therefore, the belief in *karma* itself adds an additional condemnation of the improper inversion of motives, and the penalty for this, within the karmic framework, is rebirth to continued suffering. The curious conclusion to this series of ideas, in other words, is that a belief in the reality and necessity of *karma* can perpetuate one's very involvement in *samsāra,* the world of karmically determined suffering.

Is there any way out of this conceptual and moral trap? There is one, I think, that is quite obvious: an individual can believe and hold reasons for believing that *karma* does not absolutely dictate his fate. He can believe that in some fashion the self can be freed from karmic effects and be essentially untouched by the good or evil it performs. Such a belief can allow one thereafter to perform actions without considering their necessary consequences for the self and without thereby becoming guilty of a condemnable measure of self-regard. But this, of course, is precisely the direction that all Indian liberation speculation takes. *Moksha* or *nirvāna,* however precisely they are defined or understood, always involve an emphasis on the self's ultimate freedom from *samsāra*. As such, the knowledge that liberation is an attainable goal is a guarantee that the self can achieve moral purity, full moral autonomy, and with this, a justified freedom from rebirth to suffering. A belief in liberation, in the possibility of passing beyond merit and demerit, in other words, is itself a means to the goal of perfect happiness and perfect virtue. Although this goal initially stimulates the development of the idea of *karma, karma* itself must be overcome if the initial goal is to be reached. Thus, once again we do not have to look beyond the immediate moral implications of the *karma* doctrine to see why a liberation from the necessity of *karma* should become the central concern of Indian religious thought.

Whatever the bases of the Indian quest for liberation, there is no question that this quest becomes the dominant preoccupation of cultured Indian religious thought as well as the special focus of the Indian religious genius. Typically, this quest has its point of departure in a concrete technology of mystical ecstasy as represented by the classical Yoga technique which, if not unique to India, is developed there to an unprecedented degree and is moved to the very center of the religious life. The historical roots of this preoccupation with the technique of Yoga and with mystical experience are not easily identified. It may be that despite the dominant tradition of the Vedic religion, a constant pre-Vedic indigenous tradition of asceticism, breath control, and self-induced trance (*samādhi*) continued to live a subterranean existence, only gradually surfacing again when time, social turmoil, and the teaching of *karma* accentuated the desire for a flight from *samsāra*. Whatever the case, it is Yoga and mystical experience that nevertheless form the touchstone for virtually all efforts to describe the nature and significance of liberation. In the self-induced mystic trance, Indian religious virtuosi were able briefly to experience a state of undifferentiated unity with all of reality, a calm and rapture, and an intimation of the blissful immortality and freedom denied them by rebirth. They subsequently interpreted this experience as at least suggestive of the more enduring goal of liberation from *samsāra*.

The Indian concern with liberation is not confined to Yoga or the personal search for mystical ecstasy. On the basis of this experience, Indian thinkers also engaged in extensive metaphysical speculation as they sought rationally to explain and to establish the significance of the altered state of consciousness associated with trance.[32] In the course of time, this speculation produced virtually every major philosophical option among the possible explanations of the relationship between conditioned reality and the mystically experienced, timeless, unconditioned state. Monisms and dualisms in their various forms, theism, pantheism, and panentheism are all to be found. In one sense, this speculation is important: it represents an effort to understand the transcendent realm or state discerned in profound meditation and trance. If liberation is to be a real prospect and not merely a delusion, it requires some sort of grounding in the objective order of things. Buddhism, it is true, could initially dispense with metaphysics as it focused single-mindedly on the technique of liberation. But this was probably only a temporary possibility—one formed in reaction to the extensive metaphysical speculation, the "greed for views" of the Hindu schools—and even Buddhism in its dominant Mahayana form eventually succumbed to metaphysics.

But if metaphysics itself is important in this context, the precise formulations of metaphysical positions and the differences between them are less so. Indian metaphysics proceeds from a base of two unquestioned certainties: that the conditioned world is governed by *karma*, and that in mystical experience all the distinctions of conditioned reality, especially those created by *karma*, can be transcended. Against the background of these two certainties, the many different efforts to relate liberation and *samsāra* are not individually so important. Unlike Western metaphysics, where an inadequate conception can throw open to question the reality of the rationally postulated religious object, God, Indian thought always retains an undisputed experiential basis no matter where speculation leads. This may be an important reason why a surprising tolerance has reigned among the leading Indian metaphysical schools.

These same two certainties, *karma* and the mystical intimation of liberation from *karma,* also render history far less important in Indian religion than in Western theistic faiths. In the West, the possibility of a happiness not experienced in the present is sustained by the prospect of its bestowal in the future, and individual history, world history, or both, become important vehicles of redemption. But in India, history has almost no redemptive significance. Happiness, if it is to be experienced at all, is not found in the future but here and now in the self-authenticating and timeless mystical state.[33] Oddly enough, this devaluation of history is partly the result of one of the most rigorously historical interpretations of the human situation ever advanced; for what is the doctrine of *karma* but the insistence that everything I am or will be is the result of my own actions in time?[34] Nevertheless, if *karma* radically accentuates the importance of history, it also correspondingly devalues it. The endless course of *samsāra* holds out no promise of enduring happiness or of a final break with suffering. As a result, if happiness is to be a real prospect for human beings, it must be found not in the future but in an experience that transcends history and time.

This understanding of the mystical state as the touchstone and goal of liberation raises an important question. Is it in fact justifiable to term this state, and the goal of liberation which draws upon it, "happiness"? If we understand happiness to mean the satisfaction of desire, is the mystical goal one that can be described as maximally satisfying the desires of a rational agent? The answer to this, I think, is yes, although there are certain special problems that the mystical goal raises in this connection. A first and obvious problem has to do with the use of the term "rational" in connection with a psychic state, like mystical trance, which is characteristically said to involve a suspension of all ordinary rational and deliberative activity. Indeed, it is religious experiences like this that are commonly alluded to when religion is described as typically non-rational or irrational.

Without denying the peculiarly non-rational or super-rational quality of mystical experience or its important place in some religious traditions, I would reassert here a point made in the first chapter: that reason is a purely formal activity whose purpose is not to identify satisfactions but to organize their pursuit. But the satisfactions at which reason aims are not themselves either rational or irrational. They are merely the "stuff" with which reason works. As such, happiness for a rational being can include any of a variety of satisfactions, even those in which reason itself is temporarily and ecstatically suspended (so long as this suspension does not seriously interfere with the pursuit of other more important satisfactions and goals). On a rather mundane level, this point is illustrated by the fact that an occasional and harmless alcoholic or drug euphoria is considered a valid part of happiness by many persons.

Since religious traditions aim at facilitating happiness, it is not surprising that they commonly offer their adherents goals or states of satisfaction which are neither rational nor irrational. Indeed, since religious reason requires religions to proffer some kind of real (and non-moral) satisfactions as the reward for moral striving, it is natural that they should seek to meet this requirement by calling upon or elaborating particularly intense forms of satisfaction. Thus, in the Western traditions, the emotional joys of family life are typically borrowed by religious thought, and the believer is promised the ultimate happiness of a relationship with God not unlike that experienced between parent and child. In India, the central experience has been the less personal rapture and sense of wisdom found in mystical trance. These altered states of consciousness, desirable in their own right, have thus been cultivated and employed to meet reason's need for the possibility of a real happiness in connection with virtue.

I do not want to deny that the religious believer views the satisfactions and experiences mediated by his faith as the central and supreme object of his concern. For the Jew or Christian it is the love of God, while for the Hindu or Buddhist it is the mystical experience, that forms the touchstone of reality. To suggest that religious reason uses these satisfactions for its prosaic moral purposes would seem to be turning matters upside down. Experientially, of course, religious experiences and satisfactions must have just this commanding and ultimate character if they are always to elicit the sacrifices that morality requires. The fact that the peak experiences of religious traditions differ so from one another, however, suggests that it is not any one of these specific experiences that is fundamental to religious activity. Rather, what is fundamental and what is everywhere present is the rational effort to connect virtue with some form of sufficiently motivating satisfaction or goal.

A further problem involved in characterizing the mystical goal as a form of happiness has to do with the fact that this goal does not normally include the satisfaction of our more obvious physical or social desires. These desires and their attendant satisfactions might be given a place, as in later Hinduism, in the many-lived process of preparation for liberation, but they are not usually considered a part of liberation itself. This is not hard to understand. Satisfactions of this sort—sexual pleasures, food and drink, or the satisfactions attached to renown and success—are typically too contradictory to serve as the object of perfect well-being. But these desires are not the only ones human beings possess. Human beings are also capable of important intellectual gratifications which can serve as components of happiness. If these should become dominant even in Jewish or Christian conceptions of the afterlife, it is not surprising that in the mind-culture developed in India, liberation comes to be thought of largely in these terms. As such, liberation can still be regarded as involving happiness.

A final problem involved in characterizing the goal or state of liberation as happiness has to do with the inappropriateness of ordinary language for describing the state attained in mystical experience. As the *Kena* Upanishad oddly puts it, this is a state "Which cannot be expressed by speech but . . . which by speech is expressed."[35] Because this experience transcends virtually all the categories of thought or expression, those who seek to describe it commonly lapse into an extensive series of negations: *moksha* or *nirvāna* is not good, not evil, not concerned, not indifferent, not conscious, not unconscious, and so on.[36] Frequently, this process of negation suggests the interpretation of liberation as a state of non-being or non-experience. The occasional description of liberation in the Upanishads as a state beyond the deepest dreamless sleep is an example. Not too different is the Buddhist use of the term *nirvāna,* literally the "blowing out" or "cooling off" of a flame to characterize this same goal. Such use of negatives unfortunately suggests that liberation is not happiness but merely, like death, an end to unhappiness.

Indian conceptions of liberation certainly have a strong negative component. By enabling us to transcend our struggle for brief and deceptive gratifications whose pursuit, from a transcendent perspective, comes to seem foolish and irrational, liberation seeks to eliminate a major source of frustration and suffering. But this negative dimension is not all there is. Indian religious thought adds to this a major positive component: the understanding of liberation as a state of active, omniscient bliss. This understanding is clearly suggested in Hinduism by the classic formulation in later Vedānta of *Brāhman,* the mystically approached ground of reality, as Sac-cid-ānanda, literally, "Being, awareness-consciousness-knowledge, bliss." It is also strikingly suggested in the Upanishads by the use of the metaphor of the sexual act between husband and wife to describe the experience of liberation.[37] Like peak moments of sexual intercourse, liberation has its negative aspect: an obliviousness to ordinary stimuli, a loss of self, and an abandonment of the distinction between self as subject and the world or the other as object. But, as in the sexual experience, these negative dimensions form merely a part of the larger bliss of self-transcending union, and it is some such state of self-transcending rapture, although beyond the level of physical pleasure, that is the real object of Hindu salvation striving.[38]

Much the same can be said, I think, for the Buddhist conception of *nirvana*. Few topics have been more extensively debated than the meaning of this state, and the Buddha himself certainly did not illuminate later discussion by sometimes parrying requests for a positive description of *nirvāna* with the insistence that it is "incomprehensible, indescribable, inconceivable, unutterable." Negations of this sort and the very etymology of the term *nirvana* have contributed to a tradition of interpretation—especially in the West—which presents this goal as a state of self-annihilation, thus contributing to the characterization of Buddhism as life-denying and pessimistic. We cannot consider the long debate on this subject here.[39] Suffice it to say that for Buddhism, as for Hinduism, negative expressions do not convey the full meaning of liberation. That *nirvana* involves a negation of the self and its ordinary desires is certain. But this negation is once again merely part of a total positive experience which Buddhist texts repeatedly characterize as "happiness" and "bliss."[40] Indeed, Buddhist writers have even employed the term "pleasure" to describe this state, and *nirvana* has thus sometimes been lauded as "the most refined and sublimest form of pleasure."[41] This terminology should be regarded with caution, since all such use of language for a state of psychic transcendence is analogical. Nevertheless, in these various efforts at description, it becomes clear that the idea of *nirvana* involves some kind of positive state of well-being and fulfillment.

In the strictest employment of the term, therefore, I think it is correct to call the goal of the Indian quest for salvation happiness. We are obviously not dealing here with "self-contentment," any kind of self-satisfaction produced by virtue, but instead with some kind of independent satisfaction of rational desire. This does not mean that liberation necessarily involves the satisfaction of any actual desire I might possess, for it is the point of Indian thought to stress that, seen from the perspective of liberation, my ordinary physical or social desires are not really satisfying. None of them, in other words, forms the preferred object of a fully knowledgeable choice. Beyond these satisfactions, however, lies a state at once free from turmoil and frustration, blissful and rapturous, which is naturally favored by all those who have experienced it. In this sense, it is not only a state of happiness, but perhaps the supreme happiness.

Against the background of these general considerations, I think it can be said that *moksha* or *nirvāna,* in their varying expressions can be viewed as an effort to fulfill two important general requirements of religious reason. As a state beyond morality, "beyond merit and demerit," they transcend the operation of *karma* and mitigate the problems of moral inadequacy and heteronomy. Thus, they satisfy reason's demand in the third requirement of religious reason for a possibility of freedom from the moral causal process that governs nature and history. At the same time, in their positive content these ideas hold out the promise of real happiness, something, we know, which forms part of the goal of every rational agent. In meeting both of these requirements, moreover, the concepts of *moksha* and *nirvāna* depart very little from the terrain of experience. Indeed, it is one of the more important aspects of Indian thinking concerning a redemption from sin and unhappiness, that the possibility of this redemption is grounded in an experience which, if esoteric, is nevertheless potentially open to all those who seek it with determination.

Viewing the concepts of *moksha* and *nirvāna* against the total program of religious reason in this way brings up a serious question: what is the relationship between the liberating mystical experience and subsequent moral endeavor? We know that the full object of impartial reason is not just happiness, but happiness in direct proportion to virtue. We also know that within the total program of religious reason, the transcendence of strict moral causation is required for an ultimately moral purpose: without it moral striving is impaired. The object of this transcendence, in other words, is a rededicated and reinforced moral life. The precise question, therefore, is whether *moksha* or *nirvāna,* in guaranteeing both happiness and a freedom from self-condemnation, also work to unite these two with strict moral virtue. Is one who is liberated from *samsāra* also likely to be a morally virtuous individual? Compared with one who has not experienced this state, might he be even more scrupulous in his compliance with the moral rules and more dedicated to the development of moral dispositions?

Before attempting to answer this question, I should reemphasize the fact that the passage from a redemption from sin back to morality is always a difficult one for advanced religious traditions. Whenever the difficulties in the moral life are profoundly recognized and whenever steps are taken to relieve the distress this entails, it becomes difficult to reconstruct a basis for moral responsibility. The very effort to subordinate the moral life and to free the individual from the hopeless burden of self-condemnation involves, to some degree, a destruction of the ordinary reasons for self-restraint and is thus a kind of burning of bridges to moral responsibility. This is the reason why traditions which strongly emphasize a redemption from sin are frequently bothered by antinomian interpretations of their teaching. Christianity furnishes more than enough examples of this kind of development. Even so, however, Christianity always had one important asset in its struggle against antinomianism: its unification of moral demand and gracious redemptive activity in the person of a single God. The very moral character of God—as revealed in the midst of his redemptive act—furnishes a weapon against antinomianism, so that a thinker like Paul has relatively little difficulty in linking God's forgiveness to God's intensified moral demands. In classical Indian thought, however, this strong *personal* connection between morality and the transcendence of morality does not exist (except, perhaps, in some of the less central theistic movements). In general, *moksha-nirvāna* and *samsāra* tend to be more radically opposed, and even when efforts are made to connect them metaphysically, these efforts can have the effect of demeaning rather than affirming the world of moral cause and effect. The Śamkara-Vedānta interpretation of *samsāra* as an illusion (*māyā*) generated by *Brāhman* is an example.

In view of this, we should not be surprised if Indian thought were unable to validate moral striving at all. Even if Indian religion were fundamentally moved by the requirements of religious reason, it would not be astonishing if the very radicality of its effort to resolve the problem of moral inadequacy should have aborted the successful completion of reason's program. In that case, it would be ironical, but fully understandable, that a tradition which begins by affirming one of the strongest doctrines of moral retribution should culminate in moral indifference or even flagrant immorality. Nevertheless, this is not at all the dominant response of the Indian religious tradition to *moksha* or *nirvāna*'s promise of redemption from good and evil. Instead, we find in virtually all the specific Indian traditions a constant emphasis on moral responsibility as well as a complex series of conceptual moves designed to relate this responsibility to the very possibility of liberation. To be sure, not all of these moves were fully persuasive or fully successful, and, no less than in the West, moral indifference and antinomianism sometimes appeared. Hindu and Buddhist Tantrism reflect this impulse. But this was always a minority response and the striking fact remains that, even as they emphasized liberation from morality and *samsāra,* the major Indian religious traditions conformed to the requirements of religious reason and sought to rebuild and reinforce the moral life. This process is so complex, however, that we should look at it in some detail.

One of the more obvious ways in which the Indian religions have endeavored to combat the amoral interpretation of their teaching is by firmly tying the quest for liberation to a preparatory process of intense moral and personal discipline. It is noteworthy that the path to liberation for virtually all the major traditions involves strict obedience to a set of basic, and largely similar, moral rules. These include, among others, the "Five Great Vows" of Jainism, the "Five Restraints" of the Yoga philosophical system, and Buddhism's "Five Precepts."[42] All of these codes typically include a prohibition of killing or injury (of human beings in the first place, but, more radically, of any form of sentient life); insistence on truthfulness and fidelity in word and deed; the prohibition of theft and covetousness; the insistence on sexual chastity; and the avoidance of any form of disorderly behavior (for example, the Buddhist prohibition of the use of alcoholic beverages). The rationale for this set of moral demands is also very much the same: since liberation is a state of equanimity and calm, where all the restless strivings of the self are stilled, it is only natural that moral and personal discipline should figure in the preparation to pursue this goal. As the *Katha* Upanishad puts it, "Not he who has not ceased from bad conduct, not he who is not tranquil . . . can obtain him [*Ātman-Brāhman*] by intelligence" (II. 24).

Despite its prevalence, I do not want to overstress the importance of this insistence on a preparatory morality. Emphasis on such a morality might always be explained sociologically as a necessary means of maintaining order within a religious community, but as a means otherwise unrelated to the central goal of the religious life. Far more important for our understanding of the Indian traditions' perception of the relationship between liberation and morality, therefore, is the fact that obedience to the moral rules is seen by these traditions not just as a means to liberation, but as a necessary corollary of it. The key to this understanding is the insistence that liberation from *samsāra,* by effacing all of the ordinary discriminations we make and by transcending the very distinction between subject and object, also eliminates the distinction between myself and other selves. In the state of liberation there is no "I" or "mine" and all my ordinary self-preoccupation is replaced by a sense of participation in a unified reality comprising all selves. In the words of the *Brihad-Āranyaka* Upanishad, "one sees everything as the Self [*Ātman*]" (IV, ix. 23). This Self, myself, is in everything and everyone, and, at the same time, every "other" is in me. Thus, the ordinary boundaries separating my ego from other egos no longer really exist at all. I am freed, as a result, from my grasping concern for personal gratifications or self-perpetuation, and I am genuinely opened up to the interests and needs of others. Liberated selves, as the *Mahā-bhārata* says, are always "like-minded and friendly;" they "rejoice in the well-being of all creatures" (XII. 241. 11-14).

These ideas can be expressed in moral terms by saying that liberation represents a vivid attainment of the moral point of view. This viewpoint, we know, is always one of strict impartiality and universality. For the agent in the pure—and of course only ideal—moment of moral choice, there is no importance to the distinction between self and others: he must choose as though he might be any other person and he must endeavor actively to put himself in the position of any other individual. We can see, however, that the experience of liberation, as it is conceived in the major Indian traditions, conduces to just such a perspective. To this impartiality and universality it also adds something more: an ecstatic self-identification with others, a sense not just that I *must* regard their interests, but that their interests *are* my interests. In this respect, the Indian goal of liberation, like the morally equivalent (although not necessarily experientially equivalent) Western perception of all other human beings as "children of God" adds a profound positive dimension to the strict idea of impartiality.

This understanding of liberation as involving impartiality and universality of perspective, I think, also affords the appropriate background for interpreting the important Buddhist teaching of "non-self" (*anatta*).[43] Buddhism insists, and it is a fundamental aim of Buddhist meditation to support this insistence, that there is no such thing as the "self," if by that we mean an abiding ego in the midst of all ongoing moments of experience. That which I think to be myself is nothing more than the transient union of different lines of causally determined processes (*skandhas* or "aggregates") whose unity and distinctiveness are self-created as I—these processes—strive ignorantly to protect and preserve a meaningless personal identity. That identity, and the actions and volitions that serve it, are the source of all suffering (*duhkha*). When I once realize that there is no separate self behind all these processes of causation, "myself" ceases to exist, suffering ends, and the result is *nirvana*.

The difficulties in this teaching are obvious. Particularly important is the problem created for moral responsibility. If there is really no such thing as a "self," how can there be any significance to the moral rules that protect the welfare and interests of other selves? Whom do I injure if I steal or cheat from "others" who do not really exist? Accepting the objective truth of the teaching of "non-self" does probably eliminate most of the reasons I have for transgressing the rights of others. But the same teaching also seems to obliterate any barriers to my activity and makes possible, as a result, constant, if not particularly selfish, violations of others' interests. There seems, in other words, to be what Luis Gomez has called a "radical contradiction" between the doctrine of non-self and "any possible moral obligation."[44] But, in fact, this was not the practical conclusion drawn by Buddhism from this doctrine. Instead, only its morally edifying implications were stressed. *Anatta* within Buddhist thought comes not to mean primarily that there are no *other* selves, no other agents whose moral rights I must respect, but rather that there is no *myself*, no abiding ego I must protect. *Anattā*, then, has a moral objective. By denying any real existence to my ego, it aims at what Zaehner calls "unselfishness in the most literal sense of that word."[45] This moral purpose is even further emphasized by the fact that whenever *anattā* is actively applied to others than the self, it is so for expressly moral reasons. Thus, *anattā* is used to still resentment at wrongs done to ourselves by others, and to suppress the desire to retaliate or to punish: "If hurt is done to you by a foe . . . put your anger down," counsels one text. "Those aggregates by which was done the odious act, have ceased, so now what is it you are angry with?"[46] In other words, the urge to strike back against others is foolish, since that "other" with its volitions does not represent an abiding, responsible personality but only a non-responsible, always-changing process. It goes without saying that the same denial of responsibility is not stressed where my own actions are concerned.

This employment of the *anattā* doctrine illustrates why it is important to view religious doctrines not as essential factual beliefs shaping a view of the world so much as the conclusions of extended, and largely covert processes of moral reasoning. When the Buddhist teaching of *anattā* and analogous Hindu efforts to minimize the importance of the ego are taken at face value, they can seem to be life-denying or opposed to moral responsibility. If these implications are not stressed either in Hindu or Buddhist thought, it is because these specifically negative doctrines are perhaps only the visible expression of a deliberately unarticulated religious and moral position aimed at grounding moral obedience by chastening self-regard.

In an effort to stress the unexpected but persistent relationship between morality and liberation in Indian thought, I have so far purposely avoided a careful examination of the quality of moral life generated by these traditions. The rules associated with the preparatory morality, however, already indicate an important aspect of Indian religious ethics: its frequently negative character. In marked contrast to Christian ethical teaching, for example, there is a tendency within Indian ethics—a tendency particularly evident in the Sāmkhya-Yoga system and in Theravada Buddhism—not to stress active brotherly love so much as a rigorous restraint from committing evil. In keeping with this tendency, I am not asked to sacrifice myself on my neighbor's behalf or to enlist myself in the struggle against natural and moral evil. Instead, I am called upon to refrain from any action that might infringe my neighbor's rights or jeopardize his well-being. If the supreme image of the Christian ethic remains that of Christ succoring the outcaste or the suffering, the Indian exemplar is sometimes found in the homeless mendicant whose comportment is blameless but whose self-assertion in all domains is so reduced that he passes through the world like a shadow.

This negative strain in Indian ethics can partly be explained as a result of the overriding preoccupation with liberation. From the vantage point of *moksha* or *nirvāna,* the world with all its ephemeral satisfactions or dissatisfactions is rendered false, illusory, or merely unimportant. *Moksha-nirvāna* alone holds out the promise of enduring well-being, and this is attained by extricating oneself from attachment to the world. In view of these convictions, the urge to reach out and succor the suffering neighbor can come to make little sense. Why bother oneself with the world, after all, if it amounts to little more than a distracting illusion? Why descend from the lofty heights of knowledge and bliss to eliminate a suffering which, when properly understood, has no enduring importance?

Clearly, this is a terrain filled with moral dangers. It is one of the constant perils of religious thought that in advancing ideas to meet deep moral needs, it can sometimes allow these ideas to weaken moral responsibility. The history of misuse of the Judaeo-Christian idea of the afterlife is a leading example of this tendency. In the case of Indian thought, we can see that the idea of a liberation from *samsāra* poses the same kind of threat. Though aimed at easing the moral problems of sin and suffering, the idea of liberation can also serve to enervate moral concern, and in this de-emphasis of positive moral responsibility, we can perhaps see an important instance of this dangerous tendency at work. Still, the severity of the problem here should not be exaggerated, for at least two considerations limit the extent to which Indian moral thought departs from morality's requirements. First, there is the obvious fact that the subordination of moral concern, even in the most world-fleeing sub-traditions of Indian thought, is not extrapolated into a permission for moral license. However illogically, all the major Indian traditions resist the antinomianism or indifferentism implicit within their radical message of salvation from the world, and all continue to insist on at least the important "Do not's" of the moral code. Indeed, it is not uncommon for some specific traditions to raise even this kind of negative injunction to a supererogatory level. Thus, Jainism carries the prohibition on killing so far that it disallows all sorts of daily behavior that can even remotely jeopardize other sentient beings. This may not be the kind of positive supererogation we are familiar with in the West—the active and self-sacrificial reaching out to the other—but in its stern restraint of the self, it is a form of supererogation also.

A second important consideration limiting the scope of this negative tendency is that it is by no means the only, or even the dominant emphasis in Indian religious thought. In contrast to the negative positions I have noted, important Indian traditions and texts seek to develop a more active and other-regarding basis for the moral life, and they do so by employing the fundamental preliminary concepts of *moksha* or *nirvāna* and *samsāra*. In Buddhism, this tendency is represented by the Bodhisattva ideal, and in Hinduism, by the teaching of the *Bhagavad Gītā*. The fact that this ideal and this text are of enormous importance in their respective traditions, points up how central was the effort in Indian religious thought to draw a rich moral conclusion out of not always clearly moral basic beliefs.

The Bodhisattva ideal is commonly associated with Mahayana rather than Hinayana (or Theravada) Buddhism. As a result it is sometimes held to be a less orthodox or a more "popular" Buddhist development. But—quite apart from the difficult question of whether Hinayana and Mahayana can be characterized in terms of their relative orthodoxy—the attribution of the Bodhisattva ideal to Mahayana alone is too facile. Both the term "Bodhisattva" (literally, "enlightenment being" or a "Buddha-to-be") and the ideal it involves are present in the earliest Buddhist texts. Indeed, the Buddha himself prefigured this ideal in his "great renunciation": having, through countless eons, earned merit and prepared himself to abandon rebirth, he refused to go on immediately to *nirvāna*. Instead, he turned back to impart his wisdom—the cause of suffering and the elimination of suffering—to others. As described fully in later Mahayana texts, the Bodhisattva, too, renounces the fruits of his merit. Moved by compassion (*karunā*), he turns back to those mired in *samsāra;* he mingles himself "in the filth of birth and death"; and he vows solemnly not to enter *nirvāna* until all other sentient beings have done so—some texts say until the grass itself does so.[47]

It is sometimes suggested that the Bodhisattva cannot do otherwise. As Mahayana critics of the renunciatory Hinayana position like to point out, an individual quest for *nirvāna* seems to violate the very spirit of Buddhism. How can a state in which the ego with all its desires is renounced be open to one who selfishly desires that state for himself? Must not a readiness for *nirvāna* be displayed, paradoxically, by an unwillingness to accept that state for oneself alone, and is not the Bodhisattva, therefore, the one who most exhibits the Buddhist conception of life? Claims of this sort are persuasive, but not wholly convincing. On the face of it, it seems that the lonely, individual pursuit of liberation espoused by Hinayana conforms at least as closely to the ostensible Buddhist conception of reality. After all, if it is the case, as Buddhism teaches, that there is no such thing as the self, then why struggle to relieve other "selves" from suffering? The answer sometimes given, that others in fact regard themselves as real and suffer accordingly, seems only to force the question once again.[48] Why be morally concerned with an "other" which is nothing more than a collection of causal processes perpetuating itself and its suffering by ignorant self-concern? In other words, the very compassion for others which the Bodhisattva displays seems somewhat pointless in the context of Buddhism's teaching of *anattā*.

None of this diminishes the importance of the Bodhisattva ideal. On the contrary, the development of this ideal and its central place in Mahayana teaching reveals how insistently Buddhism's ultimately moral purposes seek to assert themselves over potentially immoral implications of other aspects of Buddhist belief. If an idea elaborated for moral purposes like "non-self" leads to immoral conclusions, then these must be struck down even at the risk of possible contradiction. A famous statement attributed to the Buddha in the *Diamond Sutra* illustrates this acceptance of possible contradiction in defense of the morally important Bodhisattva teaching:

> Here, Subhuti, one who has set out on the career of a Bodhisattva should reflect in such a wise: "As many beings as there are in the universe of beings, [be they] egg-born, or born from a womb, or moisture born, or miraculously born . . . all these I should lead to Nirvana, into the realm of Nirvana which leaves nothing behind. But, although innumerable things have thus been led to Nirvana, no being at all has been led to Nirvana. And why? If in a Bodhisattva the perception of a 'being' should take place he would not be called a 'Bodhi [enlightenment] being.' He is not called a 'Bodhi-being,' in whom the perception of a being should take place or the perception of a living soul, or the perception of a person."[49]

The inherent tension within Buddhism generated by the Bodhisattva ideal thus expresses itself here in a concern for other beings who, at the same time, are denied essential reality. More fundamentally, this tension expresses itself in the Bodhisattva's involvement in *samsāra,* even though *samsāra* is deprived of any ultimate importance. The moral thrust of Buddhism is revealed, I think, in the acceptance of this ill-fitting series of ideas. Indeed, it is even more strongly revealed in the deliberate employment of this curious constellation of ideas for intensified moral purposes. Thus we learn that the Bodhisattva's freedom from *samsāra* not only does not excuse him from moral responsibility, but is the cause of his supreme moral commitment. Of all beings, only the Bodhisattva is capable of the most purified moral concern. He alone plunges into the world of moral action without any regard for the personal consequences of his performance. Possessing no "self," he is purged of all ego-regarding considerations and is free to do spontaneously and naturally what morality requires. His freedom from the world of "merit" and "demerit," in other words, is interpreted not as a freedom *from* morality but *for* morality, and *nirvāna* is interpreted not as a flight from *samsāra* but as a state of serene and detached activity fully in the center of the world of moral cause and effect.[50] Metaphysically, this understanding is given expression by the teaching that *nirvāna* and *samsāra* are one, *nirvāna* being that state within *samsāra* where one no longer clings to the satisfactions or goals of this world.[51] But metaphysical speculation and development of this sort merely derive from the effort to ensure that the Buddhist devaluation of the world comes to serve the lofty moral purposes for which it was intended.

Though the idea of inner detachment in the midst of committed moral action has a firm place in Mahayana Buddhist thought, it assumes singular importance in the teaching of the Hindu *Bhagavad Gītā*. The great appeal of this text, within Hinduism and without, is partly a reflection of its success in re-establishing morality within the context of a radical devaluation of the world. In fact, the *Gītā* can be interpreted in two ways. It can be seen, rather modestly, as an effort to rediscover some place for those who must perform worldly duties in a tradition where the flight from active responsibility and the life of the solitary recluse have always exerted their appeal. By insisting on the validity of *karma yoga* (the way or discipline of action) alongside *jñāna yoga* and *bhakti yoga* (the disciplines of knowledge and of devotion) it has the effect of placing worldly duty among the available paths to salvation. In a more profound sense, however, the *Gītā* can be read as suggesting a creative synthesis of the whole range of Indian religious concepts, a synthesis in which active moral striving in the world becomes the natural concomitant of liberation from the world. This latter reading of the *Gītā*, I think, accounts for its continuing influence in Indian thought.

The *Gītā* has its point of departure in the very moral problem which, as I argued earlier, first animates the Indian religious effort to retreat from the world: the problem of moral inadequacy and sin. Arjuna, the epic's hero, is called upon, in the fulfillment of his Kshatriya duty, to engage in a bloody battle against his relatives, the Kauravas, whose wicked and unscrupulous behavior has occasioned warfare between his family, the Pāndavas, and theirs. But Arjuna is filled with grief. Seeing fathers, grandfathers, uncles, brothers, and sons in the armies before him, he is overcome by revulsion at the impending slaughter. His limbs grow weak and his body trembles. Casting aside his bow, he sinks down on the seat of his chariot in despair (I. 26-30, 47).[52]

It is sometimes argued that Arjuna's dilemma here is caused by a conflict between the ancient warrior code of honor and the demands of a more universal morality with its rejection of needless violence.[53] Arjuna is thus seen as caught between the need to revenge wrongs against his clan and a developing moral sensibility which repudiates the use of violence for such basically immoral purposes. But this interpretation both seriously distorts the text and, in the process, obscures the profound universal dilemma Arjuna faces. This is not a conflict of custom against morality, but a conflict within morality itself. Arjuna's position is first of all that of the just warrior in a righteous war. As the *Mahābhārata* epic (which the *Gītā* presumes) makes clear, Arjuna's foes, the Kauravas, had violated not only their caste and clan duties, but just about every other ordinary moral duty as well. By cheating at a game of dice, they had treacherously secured possession of the Pandavas' kingdom. Following this, they had broken a promise to return the land if the Pāndavas underwent thirteen years of exile. Finally, by persisting in violence and deceit and by refusing to grant their impoverished relatives even five small parcels of land for subsistence, they had forced the issue to the field of battle. When the *Gītā* thus repeatedly terms Arjuna's cause "righteous," and when it describes the war as a struggle against evil-doers, it is speaking in precise and universally understandable terms.[54]

The reason for Arjuna's despair, therefore, is not that he must uphold honor against right, but that in order to do what is right he must also do evil: he must engage in bloody warfare against his own kinsmen. His is a singular instance of the problem of responsible moral action in a world where others have failed to comply with the moral rules. It is the nature of the choice before Arjuna—and all others who seek to act responsibly in this imperfect world—that in order to do what is right overall, he must perform acts which in isolation amount to grievous moral wrongs. As one commentator has put it, he is placed in a situation where "action for securing order and justice means some sort of involvement in guilt in the absolute sense."[55] And the internecine nature of the struggle only accentuates Arjuna's dilemma. On the one hand, Arjuna's just cause also happens to be one which benefits his own family, thus providing him with a further reason for conscientious moral doubt. (Can he ever really be sure that what he thinks is duty is not merely an excuse for selfish concern for his family's welfare?) On the other hand, in killing his close relatives, Arjuna performs a particularly heinous act within the cosmic understanding of duty (*dharma*) to which he is indebted. In the ruin of a family, he observes, its immemorial laws perish; when lawlessness prevails, the women of a family are corrupted, a mixture of castes arises, and "the eternal laws of the caste and the family are destroyed" (I. 40-43). Since these laws, in turn, are rooted in the natural and cosmic order,

Arjuna, by performing his duty as a righteous warrior, risks contributing to the very degeneration of the universe. Small wonder that he is overcome with grief and eager to flee his responsibility. Not even the prospect of rich kingdoms earned in war or a blessed warrior's afterlife with the gods can console him. As a morally sensitive individual, Arjuna would prefer to suffer death himself rather than take up arms against his kinsmen.

In the midst of this despair, Arjuna's counselor, the avataric god Krishna, speaks. Krishna's words convey some of the most characteristic beliefs of Hindu philosophy. Wise men, he says, do not mourn for the dead or the living, for there is never a time when any of us ceases to be. "As the soul in this body passes through childhood, youth and old age, so (after departure from this body) it passes on to another body." In its course, this soul remains unaffected by objects of sense. It is untouched by what happens to it and by what it does. It is never really born, and it never really dies, but is eternal and everlasting. "He who thinks that this (soul) is a slayer, and he who thinks that this (soul) is slain; both of them are ignorant," says Krishna, and he concludes with this advice to Arjuna: "Therefore fight, O Bhārata" (II. 11-19).

We see here, in special Hindu form, the typical negative move of Indian religious thought: there is no sense in troubling oneself with what one's actions do to others or the self, because these actions have no ultimate importance for any selves. They do not really issue from the self in its most fundamental nature, and they are incapable of really affecting other personalities. Only the ignorant think that their deeds stain themselves morally or seriously injure others. But if this is so, then why fight at all? Why not, as Arjuna is tempted to do, and as generations of renunciates have done before him, abandon active moral striving and flee altogether from the world? In other words, Krishna's consoling wisdom carries with it morally enervating implications that are contrary to that wisdom's very intent. Tackling the problem immediately, Krishna tells Arjuna that there is nothing he can do but perform his warrior's duty. Yet at the same time Arjuna is informed that he need not abandon his moral responsibility.

Arjuna is denied the possibility of being able to flee his duty in several passages which are among the most confusing in the *Gītā*. Contradictory moral and factual arguments are heaped successively upon one another here with no regard for their coherence. Thus, Arjuna is told that all human actions are the work of *prakriti*, Nature or the material principle that controls the world of *samsāra* (III. 5, 27; XVIII. 60). Since we all necessarily participate in *prakriti*, we are helpless before it and are finally compelled to act as our duty requires whether we want to or not. But almost as this is said, moral striving is commended and justified, as though the option not to act remained fully open. "Action is superior to inaction," says Krishna (III. 8). Recommending his own example to the wise, he adds, "If I did not perform action, these worlds would be destroyed, and I should be the author of confusion and destroy these people." Following him, one ought to strive to "maintain the order of the world" (III. 24, 25).

There is little point, I think, in trying to render these divergent arguments coherent on the level that they are presented. They may be seen as growing out of separate aspects of the *Gītā*'s response to the requirements of religious reason. The moral argument is surely closest to the *Gītā*'s intent: morality has value and the ordinary, if difficult, moral duties ought not to be abandoned. But in its effort to ease the despair caused by the awareness of sin, the *Gītā* has already cut the supports out from any clear or persuasive defense of morality. We have just been told, after all, that what I do does not really affect me or others. This may explain the retreat here to a kind of moral determinism—"you can do no other"—which, however ultimately untenable, as the text's lapses back to moral exhortation show, nevertheless serves the argument's larger moral purposes.

With morality thus given something of a rationale, the *Gītā* focuses on the task of energizing the moral life in the face of its own negative teaching. It does this by insisting that there is no need even to consider fleeing from the world and that, indeed, the proper response to the world's ultimate moral unimportance is not flight but committed moral activity. At the center of this argument is the idea of "detached" or "disinterested" actions (*niskama karma*), involving the idea not of a renunciation of moral action but of a renunciation *in* action.[56] Arjuna is told that even as he fulfills his responsibilities, he can and he must free himself from any concern for their effect upon him as a morally responsible individual. Recognizing the fundamental freedom of his deepest self from the world of natural and moral causation, Arjuna should not fear the good or evil karmic consequences of his actions. He should realize, profoundly, that he is beyond the reach of evil. Actions do not "stain" him and he is freed from all sins (IV. 14; VI. 28).

At the same time, in assimilating these awarenesses, Arjuna learns that he must actively translate them into a disciplined moral striving in which no self-interested anxiety about karmic reward or punishment has a place. "In action only hast thou a right and never in its fruits," says Krishna, "Let not thy motive be the fruits of action; nor let thy attachment be to inaction" (II. 47). Indeed, in appreciating the real nature of his self, Arjuna can only be moral. Were he to cling to the "fruits" of his action either by fleeing from responsibility with its prospect of karmic punishment or by hoping somehow for karmic reward, he would reveal his ignorance of the fact that he is not morally touched by the actions he performs. Like the Bodhisattva who cannot be at the same time an "enlightenment being" and still crave his own personal release from *samsara,* Arjuna is prevented by his appreciation of the unimportance of morality from seeking to flee moral responsibility, and, instead, he is impelled to assume a genuinely selfless and purified moral commitment.

Actually, it is once again not quite true that Arjuna must be moral in the face of these awarenesses. Like other efforts to draw a necessarily positive moral commitment out of a prior negation of morality, this teaching of "detached" action does not answer the question of why a systematic but unselfish moral indifference could not as validly express detachment as selfless moral concern. It is evidence of the covert moral intent of this teaching that this conclusion is not drawn. In its place, only the most positive moral implications are stressed, and these are, in fact, quite impressive. By means of the idea of "detached" action, each one of the basic moral problems presented to reason is faced and overcome. Thus, the anguish and despair created by the harsh nature of moral action in a morally blemished world are eased by the perception that one's deeds inflict no lasting evil on the self or others. Renunciation of responsibility is checked by identifying it as a condemnable (and self-condemning) form of egoism. The individual is correspondingly returned to moral striving purged of all tendency to use moral achievement as an instrument of selfish advantage. In this respect, "detached" action works like the analogous Christian idea of grace to combat the danger of moral pride. Whenever moral achievements are publicly acknowledged as praiseworthy, the peril arises that praise will become an object of pursuit to the detriment of clear and truly impartial moral reasoning. By denying any final worth to the self's achievements, therefore, the doctrine of "detached" action serves as an antidote to pride. Finally, by definitively eliminating self-regard from the moral life, this doctrine surmounts the final major problem of a religious ethic: it eliminates all obstacles to autonomous moral choice. It renders the sheer rightness of actions, their suitability for impartial rational approval and not their consequences for the self, the supreme determining ground of action. By pointing to the possibility of a liberation from egoism and heteronomy, therefore, the doctrine of "detached" action frees the individual from the necessity of self-regard and, in the process, becomes a factor in his liberation from the realm of moral cause and effect.[57]

As an isolated religious text, the *Bhagavad Gītā* would undoubtedly be of great religious importance. However, the fact that it gathers together so many important strands of Indian

thought and that its conclusions, though expressed with exceptional lucidity, are shared by so many other Indian religious
movements magnifies its significance. As we have seen, much the
same ideal of non-attached action is present in the Buddhist conception of the Bodhisattva, and the Jain idea of the Jñānin or
"wise person" carries a similar commitment to a state of detached
but active moral exertion.[58] Weber is not wrong, therefore, when
he characterizes this doctrine of "detached" action as "the crown
of classical ethics of Indian intellectuals."[59] By means of it, the
Indian response to the requirements of religious reason is brought
full circle to a satisfactory conclusion. Beginning with the idea of
strict moral retribution, and without ever sacrificing the morally
important implications of that idea, this doctrine provides sufficient freedom from moral determination to facilitate a purified
yet active moral life. In the process, a conceptual structure is
erected in which reason's difficult demand for a union of happiness and virtue is met despite the apparent obstacles posed by an
imperfect world and an imperfect self.

All this is accomplished, moreover, without a significant
employment of the concepts of God or grace. This does not mean
that these concepts are not present in Indian thought. The *Gītā*
itself, in its advocacy of *bhakti yoga,* the way of devotion, cham-
pions both ideas and represents an important contribution to later
Hindu theism. Similarly, Mahayana Buddhism eventually develops out of its Bodhisattva ideal a savior-oriented system of belief
in which concepts of grace and justification by faith strikingly
similar to those of Christianity make their appearance.[60] But
within the orbit of Indian religious thought these ideas are not
necessary, since their religious and moral functions are adequately
performed by the developed concepts of *karma* and *moksha.*
Indeed, the case can be made that theism fits into the Indian religious perspective only with difficulty. As Buddhism recognized,
for example, an all-powerful God, even as redeemer, can be
viewed as hideously immoral in a world of suffering and strict
karmic retribution.[61] As a result, Indian theism tends less to sup-

plement the mainstream religious tradition than to furnish an alternative tradition on the soil of popular culture where the comprehensive but difficult path to purity and happiness afforded by the various technologies of liberation is less readily appreciated.

On the basis of these observations, I would like to re-emphasize here an important lesson drawn from this investigation: it is a mistake to think of religion in terms of subsidiary or derivative concepts. Religion is not to be thought of as necessarily involving belief in concepts such as God and grace, or even *karma* and *moksha*. Rather, religious belief is first of all an effort to respond to the basic and universal requirements of religious reason. The Western understanding of Indian religion has sometimes been hindered by a failure to appreciate this. The fact that Indian religious thought responds to reason's requirements with concepts so different from the Western faiths does not make it irreligious, irrational, or immoral. These differences merely reveal how richly creative individual responses to universal requirements can be, and they point up the need to penetrate the foundational structure of reason which underlies apparent diversity.

Conclusion

Religion is basically irrational; at its worst it is below reason, at its best far above it. It can be studied rationally, and should be and must be, 'for reason is God's scale on earth,' but it can never be understood by reason alone.[1]

This remark by R. C. Zaehner sums up a view shared today by many of religion's critics and defenders—both by those who would dismiss religion as irrational and dangerous and by those who would like to establish a continuing place for religion in a scientific world by seeing it as an important aspect of human experience, although one necessarily beyond rational scrutiny and assault. My aim in this book has been to offer an alternative to this common effort to distance religion from reason. Without denying that religious traditions draw upon experiences and possible satisfactions that are neither rational nor irrational, I have tried to suggest the essential and common rational program to which religions conform. Specifically, I have tried to point up the role of religious belief in completing reason's task of organizing and facilitating man's productive control of his natural and social environments. In addition, by identifying the rational program underlying the development of several important historical traditions of religious belief, I have tried to suggest the essential rationality and intelligibility of these traditions.

Conclusion

One clear result of this investigation is to reveal the enormous complexity of reason in general and religious reason in particular. Indeed, if religion has not been viewed as a rational activity, that is partly because the full complexity of reason itself has not been appreciated. Religion has thus been judged to be irrational because it has been measured against a superficial or inadequate conception of reason. A few illustrations may help make this point clearer. Where reason's deep internal conflict between its prudential and moral employments is not perceived, for example, the voice of impartial, moral reason may seem supremely authoritative and· the difficult problem· of justifying moral commitment may be overlooked. As a result, religion's role in a full rational program can be easily missed. In this kind of context, religion, if it is considered at all, can come to be regarded as, at best, a discretionary but not required supplement to morality. It may be viewed as providing the outgrown historical matrix for morality or it might be seen, more positively, as a still useful emotional stimulant to moral concern. But in either case, religion is denied a necessary place in the moral life and it tends naturally to be shunted aside as an historical curiosity or as a preoccupation of the emotionally led masses. In this connection, it is not accidental that the thinkers of the Enlightenment, who made great strides in elucidating the rational basis of morality and who were not as a rule irreligious, nevertheless prepared the way for the great nineteenth-century critiques of religion.

A superficial understanding of reason can also contribute to the tendency to dismiss as irrational all systems of thought which do not openly confess their adherence to reason. Religious traditions suffer especially at the hands of this tendency not only because they commonly abstain from defending their most important beliefs in rational terms, but also because they sometimes openly criticize reason as an instrument of truth. Despite this, we know that each of these moves has its place within reason's complex total program. The refusal of religions to base their ultimate beliefs on rational argumentation, for example, grows out of impartial reason's recognition of the uncertainty of its own authority and out of its need to ground its most pressing demands in the objective order of reality. Belief in God as the source of all truth, as in the Western traditions, or the reliance on a self-authenticating mystical experience, as in India, both respond to this need for a certainty beyond reason's corrosive influence. A domain beyond rational scrutiny is thus posited or employed by reason to support reason's total program of demands.

Outright castigations of reason within some religious traditions partly respond to this same need, but, in addition, they also reflect the profound rational awareness that a too confident reliance on impartial reason can distort or endanger reason's total program. When Paul ridicules the "wisdom" of the Gentiles, for example, and when he exalts in its place the "foolishness" of the Cross, he is not being irrational. Rather, he can be interpreted, among other things, as pointing to the inadequacy of the Hellenic philosophical reliance on impartial reason as the supreme motivating factor in human behavior, and—by extension—the confidence that when men truly know what is right they cannot rationally choose to do wrong. Against these superficial conclusions, Paul holds up the more profound and more thoroughly rational awareness contained within the symbol of the Cross: that men can, in one of reason's two employments, rationally choose wickedness; that in their freedom they will almost inevitably do so; and that an escape from the misery and self-condemnation that this must entail is reliance on a moral God who has already demonstrated the limitless resources of his forgiveness and compassion.

It goes without saying by now that the same profound logic is also operative in religious castigations of "morality." Here again the displacement or subordination of morality is sometimes offered as evidence that religions work in a realm beyond the ordinary concerns or imperatives of human life. Where the rationality of morality is recognized, religious criticisms of moral striving are also interpreted as proof of the essentially non-rational nature of religious belief. But these castigations, we know, have an important place in reason's total program. By minimizing the importance of moral achievement and by establishing the possibility of a freedom from the dreadful consequences of one's own imperfect moral performance, they aim at combating despair and reinvigorating moral commitment. The fact that traditions which most vehemently criticize moral striving also typically impose lofty moral ideals suggests this to be the case. Here again a too simple conception of reason and morality has blinded observers to the subtle and intricate rational moves made by religious traditions. The ironical result has been a condemnation, as non-rational or irrational, of those very systems of thought which operate at reason's most difficult and demanding frontier.

The complexity of reason not only explains the difficulty many have had in appreciating the rationality of religious belief, but it also helps explain the variegated nature and development of historical religious traditions. The diversity of the world's great religions is so apparent that it has sometimes been questioned whether it is appropriate to gather all these different systems of thought under the one heading, "religion." What, after all, does Hinayana Buddhism, which denies or ridicules belief in a just creator God, have in common with Judaism, for which this belief is the central tenet? The answer to this question, which I have tried to advance in the course of this book, is that all these different traditions represent concrete efforts to respond to the requirements of reason in its religious employment. But implicit in this answer is a broad understanding of why religions display the enormous variety in beliefs that they do. In fact, several different aspects of religious reason work to produce this variety and it is useful as a review to point them out here.

It should be apparent by now that one important cause of

religious diversity is the multiplicity of reason's demands and the difficulty of bringing them all together. Each of the requirements of religious reason calls for attention, and frequently must receive it at the expense of other requirements. In this respect, the construction of religions is no different from the creation of any other complex systems—in politics or engineering, for example—where a series of competing objectives each demands attention. In all these cases there are an enormous number of possible solutions involving different weightings of separate criteria, although it is probably true that the most successful and prevalent solutions will aim at a balanced satisfaction of key objectives. At the same time, no single solution will ever be perfectly satisfactory from all points of view and there will remain ample room for creative diversity.

An illustration from the traditions we have looked at may help clarify this point. We are familiar with the general tension that exists between religious reason's second and sixth requirements, between the demand for a belief that virtue is not unrewarded and the demand that we respect experience, which in this case seems to deny any necessary connection between morality and individual happiness. In choosing how to satisfy these divergent requirements, the Western traditions, Judaism and Christianity, seem generally to have stressed the former: they appear to have chosen to insist on the eventual reality of virtue's reward, even if this has required a corresponding de-emphasis on the significance of present suffering. In characterizing these traditions in this way I of course purposely pass over their important efforts also to recognize and validate present suffering, but I do so because these efforts seem always to presume at least the possibility of a future reward for the righteous. At any rate, for this relative de-emphasis of suffering, these traditions have paid a price: frequently, they have been led to minimize the importance of present hardships to the dismay of morally sensitive minds. The Dostoyevskian protest against a God who would permit the torture of a child and the refusal to accept even an infinitude of promised future blessings in compensation for such an evil reflect modern dissatisfaction with the way these traditions have chosen to handle the facts of experience. Obviously, this is no place to evaluate these criticisms at length. It might be questioned whether they take into account the full range of Judaism's or Christianity's response to the problem of evil, and it might also be asked whether the frequently proposed alternative—dedicated moral commitment stripped of all the traditional religious confidences—is finally even tenable. But the important point here is that no religious tradition is perfectly adequate. Each represents a particular solution to the problem of weighting reason's requirements, a solution that may differ from any number of other solutions.

A comparison with the Indian religions' approach to the weighting of the second and sixth requirements further points this up. Generally in India the claims of experience seem to have been taken very seriously. As a result, the possibility of a future recompense of virtue has been de-emphasized and has been overshadowed by the stress on retreat from a vicious world into the attainable well-being afforded by mystical experience. Although this approach has minimized the conflict with experience, it too has carried a price in terms of the satisfactory completion of reason's total program. As we have seen, the emphasis on experienced bliss in the midst of a perpetually evil and pointless world has sometimes tended to enervate moral commitment or weaken efforts toward the elimination or amelioration of suffering. It is true that Indian religion has thus been spared the task of defending the existence of a just creator God in a world of evil. Indeed, as we know, Buddhism openly rejects the existence of such a God and even in theistic Indian religion, God's relationship to the world is usually conceived in deliberately non-moral terms: creation is a form of divine play. The lesson is that neither creation itself nor anyone's responsibility for the evil in it should be taken too seriously. But if these beliefs lighten the burden placed on our experiential knowledge by presenting the world as it too often seems to be—an ongoing and pointless process—they also render more difficult the task of motivating struggle against the evils experienced in nature and history. The result is that if the Western traditions must work to protect their concept of God from the moral criticisms that concept itself can help nourish, the Eastern traditions must frequently strive to protect morality from their own more immediately tenable beliefs and insistences.

Part of the reason for the diversity of historical religious systems, therefore, is simply that no religious system is perfect. Each one represents a concrete effort to respond to a complex and demanding rational program. The question of whether or not there is such a thing as one objectively superior solution to the requirements of religious reason involves difficult evaluative considerations beyond the scope of this book so that it is impossible to say here whether there is a single religious position to which all this diversity might strive. Nevertheless, it does seem to be true that in the course of their development, religious traditions appear individually to strain toward a more satisfactory general response to reason's demands. Thus, requirements neglected or de-emphasized earlier in the tradition's development receive attention as the tradition grows. Older unsatisfactory responses to particular requirements are replaced by newer ones less in conflict with other aspects of reason's program. And constant efforts are made to increase the religion's responsiveness to each one of reason's demands. Usually, of course, this development works within the framework of those key beliefs first advanced to satisfy reason's needs. Thus the concepts of God's reward and *karma* remain firm features of their respective belief systems even as these systems grow to encompass the difficult problems posed by continued suffering or sin. The different initial responses to reason's most pressing demands, in other words, serve as the template for subsequent religious development, even when that development would seem to counsel a repudiation of the beginning convictions. Quine's observation that our statements about external reality "face the tribunal of sense experience not individually but as a corporate body"[2] seems applicable as well to the way religious systems face the tests of historical experience. This fidelity to original solutions is, thus, a further contributory factor to the diversity of historical religions. In addition to the differences in their points of departure, new differences develop as they seek to overcome or adjust to particular errors or inadequacies in their earliest solutions.

To these explanations of religious diversity, I might finally add the consideration that religions are human products. As such, they not only contain subtle errors—inadequacies or mistakes from the standpoint of impartial reason—but they are also frequently manipulated or abused for immoral purposes. Occasionally in Part II of this book I have tried to suggest the dependency of the great traditions on the specific historical or social contexts in which they take form. This should not surprise us. Almost no human rational achievements—mathematics and natural science are examples—are the creations of single individuals or groups of individuals. Though such creations, because they are rational, are appropriable by single minds, they are usually the work of generations. Religions share this characteristic, but because they are powerful instruments for shaping human behavior, they are also frequently exploited by groups or interests for selfish ends. This point was amply noted in the nineteenth century by social critics such as Marx or Nietzsche. A more balanced view was offered early in this century by Weber who—without being fully clear about the specific rational requirements religion seeks to fulfill—nevertheless sometimes stressed the morally positive and stimulating aspects of religious belief.[3] In any case, the relationship between religions and their historical contexts is something that must always be kept in mind. Human reason does not operate in a vacuum and religious reason is even less prone to do so. If historical religions are so diverse, therefore, this is partly because they have tried to work toward general and impartially sustainable conclusions in cultural and social contexts that have as often impeded as favored that endeavor.

Be this as it may, it has been my aim in this book to suggest that with all their differences, strengths, and weaknesses, the historical religious traditions represent great achievements of human reason. Matured over centuries, subjected to continual critical analysis, and chastened by experience, they remain permanent and important resources for the human mind. It is true that the traditions we have looked at—and some others we have by-passed—are presently in disrepute. Partly, that is the result of continuing inadequacies in their endeavor to meet reason's demands. But more significantly, I think, it is one consequence of mankind's present effort to produce both virtue and happiness here and now, in the world, by means of powerful new scientific, medical, political, and economic technologies. Ironically, the development of these technologies as well as the ideals that sustain their use owe much to the historical religions. As many observers have noted, there are direct connections between the religious interest in nature fostered by Judaism and Christianity and the emergence of modern science in the West. The connection between these faith traditions and the social and political structures of the modern world is perhaps even more evident. In each case, religious rationality has made important contributions to other forms of rational activity.

Contemporary efforts to work within the world to cultivate righteousness and to promote happiness can only be applauded. Moral reason, after all, demands not just a belief in the possible union of virtue and happiness but concrete efforts to unite the two and bring them into reality. Nevertheless, it may be asked whether the two sides of reason's supreme goal, both real virtue and real happiness, can be achieved or even long pursued without nourishment by some of the insights, hopes, and confidences developed over the centuries by the historical religious systems. My claim here, that religious faith is needed to complete reason's total program, suggests that a world which aspires to be rational must eventually draw upon the wisdom of mankind's religious past.

Notes

Introduction

1. For representative positivist statements, see Auguste Comte, *Cour de philosophie positive,* 6 vols. (Paris: Bachelier, 1830-42), Vol. 5, and Edward Tylor, *Primitive Culture,* 2d ed., 2 vols. (London: John Murray, 1873). Feuerbach's view is developed at length in his *The Essence of Religion,* tr. George Eliot (New York: Harper & Bros., 1957). Freud's view is set forth in his *Totem and Taboo,* tr. James Strachey (New York: W. W. Norton & Co., 1950) and *The Future of an Illusion,* tr. W. D. Robson-Scott, rev. ed. (Garden City, N.Y.: Doubleday & Co., 1964). *Karl Marx and Friedrich Engels on Religion* (New York: Schocken Books, 1964) gathers together many of these two thinkers' separate statements on the subject.

2. For a functionalist viewpoint, see J. Milton Yinger, *The Scientific Study of Religion* (New York: Macmillan Co., 1970), esp. pp. 6ff. Rudolf Otto's *The Idea of the Holy,* tr. John W. Harvey (New York: Oxford University Press, 1958), remains a leading statement of the phenomenologist position. Analytic philosophers usually draw upon Wittgenstein's discussion of "the mystical" in the *Tractatus Logico-Philosophicus,* tr. C. K. Ogden (London: Routledge & Kegan Paul, 1922), esp. 6.4, as well as his more general discussion of religious belief in the *Lectures and Conversations on Aesthetics, Psychology and Religious Belief* (Oxford: Basil Blackwell, 1966). For a comparison of Otto and Wittgenstein, see Thomas McPherson, "Reli-

gion as the Inexpressible," in *New Essays in Philosophical Theology,* eds. Antony Flew and Alasdair MacIntyre (New York: Macmillan Co., 1955), pp. 131-43.

3. Fairly general relations of religious belief to morality can be found as far back as the writings of Greek and Roman philosophers. Thus, Cicero, in his *De Legibus* Bk. II. 7, argues that religion is essential to sound public morals. At the beginning of this century, a number of English moral philosophers were stimulated by Kant's "moral argument" to stress the moral function of religious belief. See, for example, W. R. Sorley, *Moral Values and the Idea of God* (Cambridge: Cambridge University Press, 1918), Chs. xiii-xx; Hastings Rashdall, *The Theory of Good and Evil* (Oxford: Clarendon Press, 1907), II, Bk. iii, Ch. 1, Sec. 4; John Baillie, *The Interpretation of Religion* (Edinburgh: T. & T. Clark, 1929), Chs. 5-6; and D. M. Baillie, *Faith in God* (Edinburgh: T. & T. Clark, 1927), Ch. 5.

4. *Critique of Pure Reason,* tr. Norman Kemp Smith (New York: St. Martin's Press, 1965), p. 635. See below, Ch. 1, n. 11 for a full listing of Kant references.

5. Cambridge, Mass.: Harvard University Press, Belknap Press, 1971.

6. A. Macbeath's *Experiments in Living* (London: Macmillan & Co., 1952) offers many provocative indications of the presence of rational moral and religious beliefs in non-literate cultures.

Chapter 1

1. Although his primary aim is to indicate the cognitive abilities needed to make rational judgments, in his *Rationality* (London: Routledge & Kegan Paul, 1964) Jonathan Bennett supports this traditional account of reason.

2. For a good discussion of the terms "reason" and "rational" as significative of the unanimous judgment of the community of intelligent beings, see Bernard Gert, *The Moral Rules* (New York: Harper & Row, 1970), Ch. 2. Also, Marcus Singer, *Generalization in Ethics* (New York: Alfred A. Knopf, 1961), pp. 56f. George Mavrodes, however, explores some difficulties implicit in this idea in his *Belief in God* (New York: Random House, 1970), pp. 38f.

3. Carl G. Hempel, "The Concept of Rationality and the Logic of Explanation by Reasons," in his *Aspects of Scientific Explanation* (New York: The Free Press, 1965), pp. 463-83; Kenneth Arrow, *Social Choice and Individual Values,* 2d ed. (New York: John Wiley, 1963), Ch. 2; J. D. Mabbot, "Reason and Desire," *Philosophy,*

XXVIII (1953), 113-23; and John Harsanyi, "Some Social-Science Implications of a New Approach to Game Theory," in *Strategic Interaction and Conflict,* ed. Kathleen Archibald (Berkeley, Cal.: Institute of International Studies, 1966), pp. 1-18, 138-52.

4. *Treatise of Human Nature,* Bk. II, Pt. 3, Sec. iii.

5. *A Theory of Justice* (Cambridge, Mass.: Harvard University Press, Belknap Press, 1971), Ch. 3.

6. *Ibid.,* pp. 136-42.

7. *Ibid.,* pp. 333-50. Also, Gert, *The Moral Rules,* Chs. 4-6, and David Richards, *A Theory of Reasons for Actions* (Oxford: Clarendon Press, 1971), Chs. 7-10.

8. In his article, "A Critique of John Rawls' Principles of Justice," *Ethics,* LXXXIII (January 1972), 146-50, Leonard Choptiany applies this problem to a criticism of Rawls' emphasis on the possibility of arriving at moral principles within the original position. Choptiany argues that in the original position a rational egoist will not bind himself to any policy which is not guaranteed to maximize his own future expectations. This is less a criticism of Rawls' effort to describe the circumstances of moral choice than an observation of the inherent conflict between particular and impartial rationality.

9. *A Theory of Justice,* pp. 11f. For a similar use of the classical idea of the "state of nature," see Robert Nozick, *Anarchy, State, and Utopia* (New York: Basic Books, 1974), pp. 7-9.

10. "Of the Original Contract," in *Hume's Moral and Political Philosophy,* ed. Henry D. Aiken (New York: Hafner Publishing Co., 1948), pp. 356-72.

11. *Gr.* 393: *Foundations,* p. 9. In order to simplify subsequent references to Kant's writings, I have abbreviated the titles of his major works and of the best available English translations of those works as shown below. I usually cite both the German text and the translation.

GS   *Kant's Gesammelte Schriften,* Hrsg. von der Königlich Preussischen Akademie der Wissenschaften, 26 vols. (Berlin: G. Reimer, 1902-72).

Gr   *Grundlegung zur Metaphysik der Sitten, GS, IV.*
Foundations   *Foundations of the Metaphysics of Morals,* tr. Lewis White Beck (Indianapolis: Bobbs-Merrill, 1959).

KdpV   *Kritik der praktischen Vernunft, GS, V.*
Beck   *Critique of Practical Reason,* tr. Lewis White Beck (Indianapolis: Bobbs-Merrill, 1956).

KdrV	*Kritik der reinen Vernunft, GS,* III.
Kemp Smith	*Critique of Pure Reason,* tr. Norman Kemp Smith (New York: St. Martin's Press, 1965).
KdU	*Kritik der Urtheilskraft, GS,* V.
Meredith	*The Critique of Teleological Judgement,* tr. James C. Meredith (Oxford: Clarendon Press, 1928).
MdS	*Die Metaphysik der Sitten, GS,* VI.
Ladd	*The Metaphysical Elements of Justice,* Part I of "Metaphysics of Morals," tr. John Ladd (Indianapolis: Bobbs-Merrill, 1965).
Gregor	*The Doctrine of Virtue,* Part II of "Metaphysics of Morals," tr. Mary J. Gregor (Philadelphia: University of Pennsylvania Press, 1964).
Rel	*Die Religion innerhalb der Grenzen der blossen Vernunft, GS,* VI.
Greene	*Religion within the Limits of Reason Alone,* tr. T. H. Greene and H. H. Hudson (New York: Harper & Row, 1960).
VE	*Eine Vorlesung Kants über Ethik,* Hrsg. Paul Menzer (Berlin: Pan Verlag Rolf Heise, 1924).
Infield	*Lectures on Ethics,* tr. Louis Infield (New York: Harper & Row, 1963).
VpR	*Vorlesgungen über die philosophische Religions-lehre,* Hrsg. Karl Heinrich Ludwig Pölitz (Leipzig: Verlag der Taubert-schen Buchhandlung, 1830).

12. *KdpV,* pp. 9, 25: Beck, pp. 9, 24. Also, *Gr,* p. 415: *Foundations,* p. 33.
13. *KdpV,* pp. 22, 124: Beck, pp. 20, 129.
14. *Gr,* p. 412: *Foundations,* p. 29.
15. Kant does once state that human reason has a higher purpose than happiness. (*Gr,* pp. 395f.: *Foundations,* p. 11f.) On the basis of this remark, Oliver A. Johnson argues in his article "The Kantian Interpretation," *Ethics,* LXXXV (1974), 65, that Kant's conception of reason differs substantially from Rawls, and he questions whether any contract-type ethical theory which relies on a conception of reason as promoting happiness can really correspond to Kant's ethics. A similar view is expressed by Robert Paul Wolff in his *Understanding Rawls* (Princeton: Princeton University Press, 1977), p. 115. Contrary to Johnson and Wolff's belief, I believe there is too much evi-

dence for Kant's understanding of man as a rational and happiness-seeking being to admit this view. Kant's remark in the *Foundations*, I would argue, is merely an expression of his emphasis on the priority of moral over prudential reason and of the fact that human dignity must derive from morality, not prudence.

16. As Kant puts it, ". . . the concept of happiness . . . is merely the general name for subjective grounds of determination [motives], and it determines nothing specific concerning what is to be done in a given practical problem. . . ." (*KdpV*, p. 25: Beck, p. 24.)

17. Kant points this up in *KdpV*, p. 28: Beck, pp. 27f., when he quotes the bellicose Francis I: "What my brother wants (Milan), that I want too . . ."

18. *Gr*, pp. 413-20: *Foundations*, pp. 30-36. Also, *KdpV*, p. 20: Beck, p. 18.

19. *KdpV*, p. 30: Beck, p. 30. Cf. *Gr*, p. 421: *Foundations*, p. 39, where the imperative has the form, "Act only according to that maxim by which you can at the same time will that it should become a universal law."

20. These considerations seem to underlie John Stuart Mill's criticism of Kant's suggestions that immoral acts are simply illogical. (*Utilitarianism*, Everyman's Library [New York: E. P. Dutton, 1910], Ch. 1, Pt. iv.) For a recent interpretation of Kant as requiring only universalization of maxims and a corresponding criticism, see Robert Paul Wolff, *The Autonomy of Reason* (New York: Harper & Row, 1973), pp. 51, 161-71.

21. Singer, *Generalization in Ethics*, pp. 266-70; John Kemp, *Reason, Action and Morality* (London: Routledge & Kegan Paul, 1964), p. 79, n. 1. R. M. Hare in his *Freedom and Reason* (New York: Oxford University Press, 1965), frequently retreats to universalizability as a sufficient test of principles (though at other times he appears to recognize the importance of impartiality). As a result, he has no adequate way of dealing with the fanatic who is presumably willing to universalize bizarre and eccentric volitions. See his discussion of this problem in Hare, Ch. 9.

22. *Gr*, p. 421: *Foundations*, p. 38, n. 9.

23. Hence, the other formulation of the categorical imperative offered by Kant: "Act as if the maxim of your action were to become through your will a universal law of nature." (*Gr*, p. 422: *Foundations*, p. 39.) The moral importance for Kant of maxims as possible laws of nature is rightly stressed by Paul Dietrichson in his article, "When is a Maxim Fully Universalizable?" *Kant-Studien*, IV (1964),

152. But like other commentators, Dietrichson fails to observe that such constructed laws of nature for a human community must be tested not only for ·their consistency with the considered volition of the willing agent, but for their acceptability to all participants in the system constructed.

24. *Gr*, pp. 433-35: *Foundations*, pp. 51-54.

25. *Gr*, pp. 428-31: *Foundations*, pp. 46-49.

26. Lewis White Beck sums up Kant's view here: "Content (object of desire) without form is blind impulse; form without object of desire is practically ineffective—this is as true of Kant's ethics as the corresponding sentence in the first *Critique* is of his theory of knowledge." (*A Commentary on Kant's Critique of Practical Reason* [Chicago: University of Chicago Press, 1960], p. 96.)

27. Wolff includes Kant among the ranks of the few great philosophers "whose insight into the most profound problems goes so deep that it seems to outreach their capacity for clear, coherent exposition and argument." (*The Autonomy of Reason*, p. 3.) Particularly disappointing in this respect are Kant's efforts to illustrate his moral analysis with examples. Thus, in the *Foundations* he repeatedly confuses the matters of logical and volitional consistency and often too strongly suggests that immoral actions are ruled out on logical grounds alone. (See, e.g., *Gr*, p. 424: *Foundations*, pp. 41f.) Elsewhere, as in his discussions of suicide and sexual behavior, Kant too readily interprets what cannot meet universal acceptance in terms of the received morality of his day. (*Gr*, pp. 421-23: *Foundations*, pp. 39f.; also *VE*, pp. 186-93, 212-15: Infield, pp. 148-54, 167-71.)

Chapter 2

1. Recent progress made in rational ethical theory may account for the growing number of discussions of this question in the literature. These include Kurt Baier, *The Moral Point of View* (Ithaca, N.Y.: Cornell University Press, 1958), Ch. 12; Bernard Gert, *The Moral Rules*, Ch. 10; G. J. Warnock, *The Object of Morality* (London: Methuen & Co., 1971), Ch. 9; John Hospers, *Human Conduct* (New York: Harcourt, Brace and World, 1961), pp. 194-95; Marcus Singer, *Generalization in Ethics*, pp. 319-27; and David Richards, *A Theory of Reasons for Actions*, Ch. 14. Rawls deals with this question obliquely when considering whether it is good for the individual to develop a sense of justice. (*A Theory of Justice* [Cambridge, Mass.: Harvard University Press, Belknap Press, 1971], pp. 567-77.)

Important articles include Kai Nielsen, "Why Should I Be Moral?" *Methodos,* XV (1963), 275-306; D. A. Lloyd Thomas, "Why Should I Be Moral?" *Philosophy,* XLV (April 1970), 128-39; Marvin Glass, "Why Should I Be Moral?" *Canadian Journal of Philosophy,* II (December 1973), 191-95; and Michael D. Bayles, "The Complexity of 'Why Be Moral?' " *The Personalist,* LIV (Autumn 1973), 309-17.

2. Thus, Gert's proposed answer to the question "Why should I be moral?" emphasizing the moral rules' protection of persons is not satisfactory, since a concern for persons can easily prompt violations of the moral rules. (See his *The Moral Rules,* pp. 201ff.)

3. Kai Nielsen, in his article "Why Should I Be Moral?" p. 301, identifies the area of sex as providing frequent occasions for violations of an individual's conscience.

4. *Human Conduct,* pp. 194-95.

5. *The Moral Point of View,* pp. 308-15.

6. Hence, Singer is mistaken when he comments "to ask whether one ought to be impartial is one question, and a senseless one." (*Generalization in Ethics,* pp. 50f.) Thomas Nagel is considerably more cautious in his *The Possibility of Altruism* (Oxford: Clarendon Press, 1970). He recognizes the claims of both "subjective" reason and "objective" reason, the latter involving an impersonal standpoint. Nevertheless, perhaps because he does not see that objective reason is necessarily partial in the moral case, he too strongly affirms that only objective reasons are finally acceptable (e.g., p. 96).

7. Marvin Glass, "Why Should I Be Moral?" p. 195.

Chapter 3

1. Kant's argument here is paralleled by his less exhaustive discussions in the first *Critique* (*KdrV,* pp. A804-31, B832-59: Kemp Smith, pp. 635-52); in the *Religion* (*Rel,* p. 108: Greene, p. 307) and the *Critique of Judgement* (*KdU,* pp. 442-85: Meredith, pp. 108-63).

2. *KdpV,* pp. 110-11: Beck, pp. 114f.; *KdU,* p. 450: Meredith, pp. 118f.; *Rel,* pp. 6-8: Greene, pp. 5-7. Kant's discussion of the Highest Good has drawn the attention of many Kant scholars. Recent treatments include Joseph Bohatec, *Die Religionsphilosophie Kants in der 'Religion innerhalb der Grenzen der blossen Vernunft' mit besonderer Berücksichtigung ihrer theologischdogmatischen Quellen* (Hamburg: Hoffman und Campe, 1938); Michael Despland, *Kant on History and Religion* (Montreal: McGill-Queen's University Press,

1973); Carl A. Raschke, *Moral Action, God and History in the Thought of Immanuel Kant* (Missoula, Mont.: American Academy of Religion, 1975); and Allen Wood, *Kant's Moral Religion* (Ithaca, N.Y.: Cornell University Press, 1970).

3. Lewis White Beck, in his *Commentary on Kant's Critique of Practical Reason,* pp. 244f.

4. A. S. Pringle-Pattison, *The Idea of God in Modern Philosophy,* 2d ed. (Oxford University Press, 1920), pp. 32-33. Erich Adickes' effort to show that Kant "repudiated" the moral argument in the *Opus Posthumum* is based partly on the view that the doctrine of the Highest Good reverses some of Kant's most important ethical insistences. See his *Kants Opus Postumum, dargestellt und beurteilt, Kant-Studien, Ergänzungshefte* 50 (1920), 702ff., 769-85, 810ff.

5. *KdpV,* p. 110: Beck, p. 115.

6. John R. Silber, "Kant's Conception of the Highest Good as Immanent and Transcendent," *Philosophical Review,* LXVIII (1959), 478ff., and Gerald Barnes, "In Defense of Kant's Doctrine of the Highest Good," *The Philosophical Forum,* XI (Summer 1971), 448f. It is true that later in the *Critique of Practical Reason* (*KdpV,* pp. 125ff.: Beck, p. 130) Kant affirms that it is our duty to promote the Highest Good and, hence, a necessity that we assume the possibility of doing so. But the duty to promote this end may simply be secondary and derivative from our own (and everyone's) need to count upon this end if we are to be moral. Thus, Yirmiahu Yovel distinguishes between a universal level of the Highest Good, to which the duty pertains, and a personal level of this concept where it is bound up with a descriptive analysis of the conditions of human willing. ("The Highest Good and History in Kant's Thought," *Archiv für Geschichte der Philosophie,* LIV [1972], 258.) I believe Yovel errs, however, in relating this descriptive aspect to *human* willing rather than willing per se.

7. Beck observes, for example, that proportioning happiness to desert is not *my* task as a moral agent: ". . . *my* task is to realize the one condition of the *summum bonum* which is within my power [to act out of respect for the moral law]." He adds that The Highest Good may form an ideal of reason, but it is a mistake to hold its attainability as "directly necessary to morality." (*A Commentary on Kant's Critique of Practical Reason,* p. 245.)

8. The personal rational dimensions of this problem for Kant are suggested by his repeated relation of the Highest Good not to the duty to promote this end so much as each individual's needs as a rational

but self-interested agent. See, for example, the emphases of his discussions of the Highest Good in *KdpV*, pp. 110, 124: Beck, pp. 114,
129; *KdrV*, p. A809, B837: Kemp Smith, p. 638; *KdU*, pp. 452f.;
Meredith, pp. 120f.; *VE*, pp. 102, 115: Infield, pp. 82, 92 and *MdS*,
Zweiter Theil, p. 482: Gregor, pp. 155f.

9. *KdV*, pp. 11f., 115f.: Beck, pp. 115, 119-21. For a discussion of
Kant's differences with Greek ethics on the matters of duty and the
good, see John R. Silber, "The Copernican Revolution in Ethics: The
Good Reexamined," *Kant-Studien*, LI (1959), 85-101.

10. *KdpV*, pp. 88, 111, 118: Beck, pp. 91, 115, 123.

11. *VE*, p. 31: Infield, p. 25.

12. P. 527. It is not clear that Kant himself ever advances the idea that
the "freedom" associated with the performance of moral duty is an
adequate recompense for moral sacrifice, but he does place high value
on moral freedom in the third section of the *Grundlegung* (*Gr*, pp.
454, 455, 457: *Foundations*, pp. 74, 77).

13. What Kant, in the *Metaphysical Elements of Justice*, calls "negative"
freedom to distinguish it from "positive" freedom or the determination by pure (moral) reason. (*MdS*, p. 213: Ladd, p. 13.)

14. Sartre, *Nausea*, tr. Lloyd Alexander (New York: New Directions,
1969), p. 157.

15. *KdpV*, pp. 113f.: Beck, pp. 117f.

16. *KdpV*, p. 114f.: Beck, p. 119.

17. This is the sense of Kant's well-known remark (*KdpV*, p. 5, n.: Beck,
p. 4, n. 1) that freedom is the *"ratio essendi* of the moral law"
while the moral law is the *"ratio cognoscendi* of freedom." Very
similar is his statement that "freedom and unconditional practical
law reciprocally imply each other." (*KdpV*, p. 29: Beck, p. 29.)

18. The existence of this kind of causality does not of course obviate, in
Kant's view, the need for human striving to bring about happiness
with virtue wherever possible. See Y. Yovel, "The Highest Good and
History in Kant's Thought," pp. 241ff.

19. *KdU*, p. 452: Meredith, p. 212.

20. *KdpV*, pp. 119ff.: Beck, pp. 124-26.

21. *KdpV*, p. 120: Beck, p. 125.

22. This is the strong position taken by A. J. Ayer in his *Language,
Truth and Logic*, 2d ed. (London: Victor Gollancz, 1946). Anthony
Flew, in his contribution to *New Essays in Philosophical Theology*,
pp. 96-99, stresses the non-falsifiability and, hence, vacuity of such
beliefs. Somewhat differently, Albert Camus bases his rejection of
theism on the sacrifice of intellectual ludicity and honesty that he

believes it to involve. (*The Myth of Sisyphus and Other Essays,* tr. Justin O'Brien [New York: Alfred A. Knopf, 1955].)

23. For an extensive effort in this direction, see Raeburne S. Heimbeck, *Theology and Meaning* (Stanford, Cal.: Stanford University Press, 1969). John Hick, in his *Faith and Knowledge* (Ithaca, N.Y.: Cornell University Press, 1957), holds up eschatological verification as a way of meeting the unfalsifiability charge. Ian Ramsey in his *Religious Language* (London: S.C.M. Press, 1957) and in several of the essays in his *Christian Empiricism* (London: Sheldon Press, 1974) has sought to emphasize the factual or empirical elements within religious belief.

24. *KdpV,* pp. 120f., 143, n.: Beck, pp. 125, 149, n. 6.

25. *KdpV,* p. 120f.: Beck, p. 125; *KdrV,* p. B xxv: Kemp Smith, p. 27.

26. *KdpV,* pp. 135f.: Beck, p. 141.

27. Kant even concedes that these moral-religious beliefs may "waver." (*KdpV,* p. 146: Beck, p. 151.) In the third *Critique,* he characterizes this rational-religious belief as a "Zweifelglaube" or doubtful faith. (*KdU,* p. 472: Meredith, p. 147.)

28. *KdpV,* pp. 121, 126: Beck, pp. 126, 130f. Kant's most systematic discussion of the epistemological status of this moral faith appears in the first *Critique* in the section entitled "Opining, Knowing, and Believing." (*KdrV,* pp. A820-31, B848-58: Kemp Smith, pp. 645-52.) For a discussion of the distinction made by Kant between "knowledge" and "faith," see Allen Wood, *Kant's Moral Religion,* pp. 13-25. Also, Rodney Needham, *Belief, Language and Experience* (Oxford: Basil Blackwell, 1972), pp. 53-55.

29. *KdpV,* p. 122: Beck, p. 126.

30. *A Commentary on Kant's Critique of Practical Reason,* p. 47. Kant's abrupt resolution of this issue is another example of a defect in style noted by Wolff: "Although Kant tends to run on when he is discussing matters of minor importance, he can be startlingly brief in his treatment of the most crucial issues." (*The Autonomy of Reason* [New York: Harper & Row, 1973], pp. 138f., n. 18.)

31. Kant criticizes "dogmatic" empiricism of this sort in the first *Critique.* There, he characterizes it as "reprehensible" because of the "irreparable injury" it inflicts on the interests of practical reason. (*KdrV,* p. A471, B499: Kemp Smith, p. 427.)

32. *KdpV,* p. 121: Beck, p. 126.

33. In the third *Critique,* Kant speaks as often of a moral "world cause" (Weltursache) as of God. (*KdU,* pp. 452-59: Meredith, pp. 108-30.)

34. Albert Camus, *A Happy Death,* tr. Richard Howard (New York:

Vintage Books, 1971), p. 45. Similarly, Kai Nielsen observes that "many people, at least, can remain happy even after 'the death of God' . . . [because] even in a purely secular world there are permanent sources of human happiness for anyone to avail himself of." (*Ethics without God* [London: Pemberton Books, 1973], p. 51.)

35. *The Theory of Good and Evil*, II, Bk. 3, Ch. 1, Sec. 4. Kant himself terms the individual who adopts such a position a "visionary" because he pursues a goal he knows to be unreachable. (*VpR*, p. 140.)

36. Kant characterizes his own position correctly when he states, "This moral argument is not intended to supply an *objectively* valid proof of the existence of God. It is not meant to demonstrate to the skeptic that there is a God, but that he *must adopt* the assumption of this proposition as a maxim of his practical reason, if he wishes to think in a manner consistent with morality." (*KdU*, p. 450, n.: Meredith, p. 119, n.) John E. Smith captures the sense of Kant's position well when he observes that the "so-called moral argument" is not a deduction of God's existence from the empirical fact of morality but rather an effort at "finding the conditions for the intelligibility of morality." (*Reason and God* [New Haven: Yale University Press, 1961].)

37. A. Hazard Dakin observes that for Kant, in disobeying conscience "we feel . . . not only that we have committed something heedless, imprudent, or cowardly, but that we have betrayed our own true nature." ("Kant and Religion," in *The Heritage of Kant,* eds. George T. Whitney and David F. Bowers [Princeton: Princeton University Press, 1939], p. 412.) Compare this with Paul Tillich's remark in *The Courage to Be* (New Haven: Yale University Press, 1952), p. 53, that the anxiety of moral self-condemnation produces "the despair of having lost our destiny."

38. Adickes, *Kants Opus Postumum,* pp. 720ff., 769-85, 810f. But see the reply by George A. Schrader, "Kant's Presumed Repudiation of the Moral Argument in the *Opus Postumum:* An Examination of Adickes' Interpretation," *Philosophy,* LVI (1951), 228ff.

39. *KdU*, p. 471, n.: Meredith, p. 146 n. Cf. Kant's characterization in the *Religion* of our predisposition to good as that "which announces a divine origin." (*Rel,* pp. 49f.: Greene, p. 45.) This natural movement by Kant between the sense of a compelling moral duty dominating one's being and a posited belief in God is given provocative expression in the *Religion:* "Though it does indeed sound dangerous, it is in no way reprehensible to say that every man *creates a God* for himself, nay, must make himself such a God according to moral con-

cepts . . . in order to honor in Him *the One who created him."* (*Rel*, pp. 168f., n.: Greene, p. 157, n.)

40. Walter Lippman, *A Preface to Morals* (New York: Macmillan Co., 1929), p. 137.

41. See above, Introduction, n. 1. For a comparison of Kant and Freud on the relationship between religion, human wish, and reason, see Wood, *Kant's Moral Religion*, pp. 184-87.

Chapter 4

1. For a discussion of this problem, see Gert, *The Moral Rules,* pp. 68, 180.

2. W. G. Maclagan offers an insightful discussion of this demand of morality in his *The Theological Frontier of Ethics* (London: George Allen & Unwin, 1961), Ch. 4. On p. 105 he observes that "The moral Rubicon is crossed when, and only when, the willing of our particular duties is enclosed within a general and unqualified devotion of the will . . ."

3. *Rel*, pp. 36.: Greene, pp. 31f.

4. This point is forcefully made by Paul Taylor in his *Principles of Ethics* (Belmont, Cal.: Dickenson Publishing Co., 1975), pp. 223ff. See also my article "Niebuhr's Critique of Rationalism: A Limited Validation," *Harvard Theological Review*, LXV (1972), 561-75.

5. This problem, I believe, underlies Kant's well-known moral rigorism, his refusal, for example, to permit benevolent lies or a right of rebellion. See his essay "On A Supposed Right to Lie from Altruistic Motives," *GS*, VIII, 423-30, tr. by Lewis White Beck in *Critique of Practical Reason and Other Writings in Moral Philosophy* (Chicago: University of Chicago Press, 1949), pp. 346-50, and his discussion of a right to rebel in his *The Metaphysical Elements of Justice, MdS,* Erster Theil, pp. 318-22; Ladd, pp. 84-89.

6. It is perhaps for this reason that utilitarianism has seemed an acceptable rule for minor matters of social policy, where benefits and losses to individuals are not extreme. However utilitarianism, anticipating the difficulty that besets all moral reasoning, becomes seriously deficient when decisions of life and death are at stake. For a discussion of this problem see Rawls, *A Theory of Justice,* pp. 170ff.

7. *The Concept of Dread,* 2d ed., tr. Walter Lowrie (Princeton: Princeton University Press, 1957), p. 29.

8. *Rel*, pp. 19-44: Greene, pp. 15-39.

9. *Ibid.,* pp. 32f.: Greene, pp. 27f.

10. *Ibid.,* p. 68: Greene, p. 62.
11. *Ibid.,* p. 67: Greene, p. 60.
12. *Ibid.,* pp. 71f.: Greene, p. 66.
13. Kant observes that it is not only my own past experience but the experience of anyone in all major respects like myself that is pertinent to my estimate of how firm my moral disposition might be. He uses this insight to validate the Christian assertion of the enduring significance of Adam's sin. (*Ibid.,* p. 42: Greene, p. 37.)
14. I follow the French existentialist tradition here in employing cases drawn from war and related forms of armed violence to illustrate the ambiguity of moral choice. See, for example, Simone de Beauvoir, *Le Sang des Autres* (Paris: Gallimard, 1946); Sartre, *Les Mains Sales* (Paris: Gallimard, 1948); Camus, *Les Justes* (Paris: Gallimard, 1946); and Elie Wiesel, *Le Jour* (Paris: Editions du Seuil, 1961).
15. These considerations form the core of the religious and secular "just war" tradition. For a review of the development and teachings of this tradition, see James T. Johnson, *Ideology, Reason and the Limitation of War* (Princeton: Princeton University Press, 1975). For a briefer statement, see William V. O'Brien, *Nuclear War, Deterrence and Morality* (New York: Newman Press, 1967), Ch. 3.
16. Thus, Kant observes that ". . . man cannot so scrutinize the depths of his own heart as to be quite certain, in even a single action, of the purity of his moral purpose and the sincerity of his attitude, even if he has no doubt about the legality of the action." (*MdS,* Zweiter Theil, p. 392: Gregor, p. 52.)
17. What I say here puts me in agreement with those writers on the problem of "dirty hands" who hold that on the strictly normative level genuine moral dilemmas do not exist. If an action is right in a specific case, although it may be ideally objectionable, performing it in that case is right and not worthy of punishment. This seems generally to be the utilitarian position, and is properly the position of any moral theory—even a Kantian one—which contains a single principle or procedure for deriving moral rules in specific cases. For a statement of this view see R. B. Brandt's article, "Utilitarianism and the Rules of War," in *War and Moral Responsibility,* eds. Marshall Cohen, Thomas Nagel, and Thomas Scanlon (Princeton: Princeton University Press, 1974), pp. 24-45. The real problem of moral inadequacy, I believe, arises not on the normative level nor even on the level of psychology, as R. M. Hare suggests in his article, "Rules of War and Moral Reasoning" (*Ibid.,* p. 59). Rather, it develops in connection with rational assessments of moral worth, when the presence of self-

regarding motives in all instances of moral choice makes affirmation of the rectitude of any agent's volition difficult, if not impossible.

18. *The Nature and Destiny of Man* (New York: Charles Scribner's Sons, 1941), I, pp. 259f.

19. This is a further reason for Kant's objection to the making of moral exceptions. It misjudges Kant, I think, to term his sensitive, if incomplete, rational analysis of this problem "repellent fanaticism" as does W. I. Matson in his article, "Kant as Casuist," *Journal of Philosophy*, LI (1954), 859.

20. W. D. Ross gives this point expression by means of his well-known distinction between *"prima facie* duties"—the abstract moral rules—and "duty proper"—the final moral choice one makes in concrete situations. See his *The Right and The Good* (Oxford: Clarendon Press, 1930), Ch. 2 and *Foundations of Ethics* (Oxford: Clarendon Press, 1939), pp. 83-86.

21. Kant observes that the tendency to view suffering or hardship as a deserved punishment for past transgressions "lies in all probability very near to human reason which is inclined to knit up the course of nature with the laws of morality." (*Rel*, p. 73: Greene, pp. 67f., n.)

22. My account here can be contrasted with that of Freud for whom guilt, though not without social value, is essentially an infantile and irrational phenomenon. See his *Civilization and Its Discontents*, tr. Joan Riviere (London: The Hogarth Press, 1963), Ch. 7. Also, Philip Rieff, *Freud: The Mind of the Moralist* (Garden City: Doubleday & Co., 1959), pp. 300f.

23. Kierkegaard expresses this well when he describes the process of moral despair: ". . . [S]o it is with men in this world: first a man sins from frailty and weakness, and then . . . he despairs over his weakness and becomes, either a Pharisee who in despair manages to attain a certain legal righteousness, or he despairs and plunges again into sin." (*The Sickness unto Death* [Princeton: Princeton University Press, 1954], p. 213.)

24. *Rel*, pp. 75, 171: Greene, pp. 70, 159. This stress on grace as a means to the perfection of virtue in the *Religion* replaces the emphasis on immortality in the second *Critique*. This reflects Kant's deepened awareness of the problem of sin. For a discussion of the development of Kant's thought on this subject, see Wood, *Kant's Moral Religion*, pp. 182, 231.

25. *Rel*, pp. 70f.: Greene, p. 65.

26. *Ibid.*, pp. 66f.: Greene, pp. 60f.

27. *Ibid.*, pp. 72f.: Greene, p. 66.

28. I follow Gert here (*The Moral Rules*, pp. 93-100) in holding a willingness to penalize infractions in some way as a distinguishing feature of one attitude we take toward genuine moral rules.

Chapter 5

1. The misinterpretation of Kant's stress on duty as involving the necessary exclusion of other motives is common. Kant himself helped
foster this misinterpretation by (correctly) emphasizing the moral
preferability of action done from duty without benevolent intention
to benevolent actions done in violation of duty. (*Gr*, pp. 397f.: *Foundations*, pp. 13ff.) Unfortunately, what was meant to be an illustration of a difficult point has frequently been interpreted as a moral
requirement.

2. Kant's definition of religion as "the recognition of all duties as divine
commands" (*KdpV*, p. 129: Beck, p. 134) suggests a willingness to
accept motives for moral obedience of at least equal stature to the
respect for the moral law itself, so long as these motives are in no
way opposed to the moral law. This interpretation is not contradicted
by Kant's assertion that morally worthy actions must be performed
not only in conformity to duty ("according to duty") but for the
sake of duty ("from duty"). (*Gr*, pp. 390, 398: *Foundations*, pp. 6,
14.) Actions done "according to duty" are morally insufficient, it
would seem, because the motives behind these actions are usually
contingent and can easily conduce to immoral behavior. But where
the determining ground necessarily leads to conformity with the
moral law—as in the case of obedience to the will of a God defined
as absolutely righteous—then this problem of possible divergence
cannot arise.

3. For a schematic presentation of the range of issues and requirements
associated with a complete moral position, see Rawls, *A Theory of
Justice* (Cambridge, Mass.: Harvard University Press, Belknap Press,
1971), p. 109.

4. W. D. Ross, *Foundations of Ethics* (Oxford: Clarendon Press, 1939),
pp. 156ff.

5. This, of course, is precisely the logic of Kant's use of theism as a
solution to the antinomy of pure practical reason. His effort here involves the use of a supra-empirical postulate to avoid a resolution (in
favor of experience) of the apparent contradiction between moral
reason and our non-moral experience of the world. Borrowing from
Kant's description of a noumenon (any purely intelligible object), in

the first *Critique,* we can say, therefore, that religious objects have "only . . . a negative employment"; their primary function is a limiting concept "to curb the pretensions of sensibility [sense experience]." (*KdrV,* p. A255, B311: Kemp Smith, p. 272.)

6. Compare here Reinhold Niebuhr's characterization of religious myth as aiming at a unity of meaning in the face of a multifarious and discordant experience of reality. See his essay "The Truth in Myths," in *Faith and Politics,* ed. Ronald H. Stone (New York: George Braziller, 1968), p. 17.

7. *The Idea of the Holy,* tr. John W. Harvey (New York: Oxford University Press, 1958), pp. xxi, 5, 10, 180. On pp. 5, 112ff. Otto criticizes Kant for having neglected the "irrational" in the concept of the Holy.

8. Allen Wood defends Kant against the objections of the Otto school by observing that for Kant "the rational validity of any judgment rests on its *universal* communicability." Kant's disinterest in accounts of religious feelings, and his objection to views of religion based primarily upon them, therefore, rest not on a denial of the possible reality of such feelings, but on the *unjustifiability* of claims made regarding them. (*Kant's Moral Religion,* p. 202.)

9. In his *Lectures & Conversations on Aesthetics, Psychology and Religious Belief,* Wittgenstein states many of the themes that have characterized analytic philosophy of religion, including the relative unshakability of religious beliefs, the role of these beliefs in regulating the conduct of life (in providing a "picture" for a "form of life"), and their derivation from "an entirely different kind of reasoning" from that found in science. See also the *Philosophical Investigations,* tr. G. E. M. Anscome (Oxford: Basil Blackwell, 1967), p. 266. For a fuller discussion of Wittgenstein's approach to religion, see W. Donald Hudson, *Wittgenstein and Religious Belief* (New York: St. Martin's Press, 1975). Similar views, with some important differences, are offered by R. B. Braithwaite, *An Empiricist's View of the Nature of Religious Belief* (Cambridge: Cambridge University Press, 1955), and Peter Winch, "Understanding a Primitive Society," in *Ethics and Action* (London: Routledge & Kegan Paul, 1972), Ch. 2, and *The Idea of a Social Science* (London: Routledge & Kegan Paul, 1958), pp. 100ff.

10. Without denying the contribution made by those moral philosophers who have concerned themselves with the uses of moral language, rationalist philosophers like Rawls and Gert have recently refocused attention on the specific logic and justification of moral judgments.

For a discussion of this matter see Rawls, *A Theory of Justice,* pp. 404-7 and Gert, *The Moral Rules,* Ch. 9.

11. In his *Reason and Commitment* (Cambridge: Cambridge University Press, 1973), Chs. 2-5, Roger Trigg develops an insightful criticism of the priority analytic philosophers place on the commissive or affective aspects of religious and moral discourse. He observes that commitment is logically based on reasons and that these presume both standards of correctness and the "propositional element" of factual beliefs about the nature of reality. Although Trigg is certainly right here, no more than the analytic philosophers does he appear to recognize that the "standards of correctness" as well as the postulated factual beliefs which underlie religious discourse and commitment derive from the operations of practical reason.

Chapter 6

1. *Aspects of Rabbinic Theology* (New York: Schocken Books, 1961), p. 46. My debt to Schechter in this chapter is clear. I follow him both in treating Rabbinic thought as forming a single and reasonably coherent tradition and in regarding that tradition as the central core of Jewish faith. Though it is true that the Rabbis were influenced by their cultural and historical contexts and frequently disagreed, as Ephraim Urbach emphasizes in his *The Sages* (Jerusalem: Magnes Press of the Hebrew University, 1975), pp. 10ff., I nevertheless assume that on most of the major theological issues discussed in this chapter there is enough agreement among the Rabbis to permit us to speak of a single body of Rabbinic teaching.

2. Thus, in *Sifre,* Numbers, ed. H. S. Horovitz (Leipzig, 1917), Sec. 143, p. 191, all the sacrifices enjoined by Torah are derived from the command of God. Jacob J. Petuchowski notes that Rabbinic thought accepted both the idea of a moral law known to all mankind—the Seven Laws of the Sons of Noah—as well as the importance of "reasonable argument" in the derivation of authoritative laws, independent of scripture. But Petuchowski adds that revelation still remained primary to the tradition, with the Noachide legislation being only a special case of revelation, and interpretive reason largely limited to explicating the content of revealed documents. ("The Dialectics of Reason and Revelation," in *Rediscovering Judaism,* ed. Arnold Wolff [Chicago: Quadrangle Books, 1965], pp. 34-37.)

3. *The Ethics of Judaism,* tr. Henrietta Szold (Philadelphia: The Jewish Publication Society of America, 1900), pp. 113f. Also, Emil G.

Hirsch, "Ethics," *The Jewish Encyclopedia* (New York: Funk and Wagnalls, 1906), V, p. 246.

4. *Genesis Rabbah* 8:8, 13; 27:4; *Exodus Rabbah* 28:5; and *Lamentations Rabbah*, Proem 24, pp. 43f., all in *Midrash Rabbah*, eds. H. Freedman and Maurice Simon, 10 vols. (London: Soncino Press, 1939). Also Tractate *'Abodah Zarah* in the *Babylonian Talmud*, ed. I. Epstein, 35 vols. (London: Soncino Press, 1935-52), 3b. Henceforth, all references to this edition will be identified with the letters TB.

5. In the last of these passages, especially vv. 2ff., Rabbinic commentators identified eleven distinct moral attributes. (*Tanna de Be Eliyyahu*, ed. M. Friedmann [Vienna: 1900], p. 65.)

6. *Religion of Reason out of the Sources of Judaism*, tr. Simon Kaplan (New York: Frederick Ungar Publishing Co., 1972), p. 254. As a student of Kant, Cohen is perhaps foremost among those scholars who have sought to interpret Judaism in terms of Kant's philosophy of religion.

7. Schechter, *Aspects*, p. 204.

8. *Ibid.*, pp. 230f.

9. TB *Sotah*, 5a. For a fuller discussion of this, see my article "Jewish Ethics and the Virtue of Humility," *Journal of Religious Ethics*, I (1973), 56f.

10. TB *Shabbath*, 31a.

11. Schechter, *Aspects*, p. 120.

12. Very typical is Kant's characterization of Jewish faith as "a collection of mere statuatory laws." (*Rel*, p. 125: Greene, p. 116.) Perhaps the classic rationalist defense of the precepts of the law is that of Maimonides in his *Guide for the Perplexed*. See *The Reasons of the Laws of Moses*, tr. James Townley (reprint ed., Westport, Conn.: Greenwood Press, 1975).

13. TB *Aboth*, 2:1; *Jerusalem Talmud*, Tractate *Pe'a*, ed. R. Krotoschin (Berlin, 1866), 1:1. Henceforth, references to the *Jerusalem Talmud* will be prefaced with the letters TJ.

14. TJ *Yoma*, 45b; TB *Shabbath*, 150a.

15. TB *Yoma*, 85b. For a discussion of this see A. Büchler, *Studies in Sin and Atonement* (New York: KTAV Pub. House, 1967). See also TB *Kiddushin*, 40a, and *Gittin*, 55a for a distinction between the religious and moral requirements of the law and the priority of the latter. It remains true, however, that the religious sin of idolatry, just because it represented a repudiation of the whole system of be-

lief, was considered more serious than any particular moral infraction. (*Sifre,* Numbers, Sec 111, p. 116.)

16. Jacob B. Augus summarizes the Rabbinic position when he states, "The divine law itself may be nonrational and amoral, though not antirational and immoral." (*The Evolution of Jewish Thought* [London and New York: Abelard-Schuman, 1959], p. 61.)

17. Lazarus, *The Ethics of Judaism,* p. 24.

18. TB *Makkoth,* 23b.

19. *Aspects,* p. 146.

20. TB *Makkoth,* 23b-24a.

21. TB *Berakoth,* 45b; *Baba Kamma,* 99b; *Baba Mezi'a,* 83a; *Yebamoth,* 20a.

22. TB *Kiddushin,* 40b; cf. TB *Nazir,* 23b; *Horayoth,* 10b; *Yoma,* 38b.

23. George Foot Moore is thus correct when he maintains, "The almighty power of God was not in Judaism a theological attribute of omnipotence which belongs in idea to the perfection of God; it was, as in the prophets, the assurance that nothing can withstand his judgment or thwart his purpose." (*Judaism,* 2 vols. [Cambridge, Mass.: Harvard University Press, 1927], I, 375.)

24. Very typically, the Rabbis represent their pagan antagonists as challenging the Jewish claim of God's omnipotence, a challenge made all the sharper by the destruction of the Temple. (TB *Gittin,* 56b; *Num. Rab.,* 18:22; *Aboth de R. Nathan,* Yale Judaica Series, Vol. X, *The Fathers According to Rabbi Nathan,* ed. Judah Goldin [New Haven: Yale University Press, 1955], p. 8.)

25. Hence, the use of the term *Gevura* ("Might") as a common epithet for God in the Rabbinic writings. For a discussion of this attribute see Urbach, *The Sages,* Ch. 5.

26. *Gen. Rab.,* 1:1.

27. *Song of Songs Rab.,* 3:10; *Num. Rab.,* 12:4.

28. *Gen. Rab.* 24:1; *Midrash Tehillim,* Yale Judaica Series, Vol. XIII, *The Midrash on Psalms,* tr. William G. Braude (New Haven: Yale University Press, 1959), 14:1.

29. *Tanhuma,* ed. S. Buber (Wilna, 1885), IV, 14b-15a.

30. *The Hirsch Siddur,* tr. Samson Raphael Hirsch (Jerusalem and New York: Feldheim Publishers, 1969), p. 657.

31. TB *Menahoth,* 13:11; *Baba Mezi'a,* 58b; *Sanhedrin,* 106b.

32. TB *Kiddushin,* 40a.

33. *Gen. Rab.,* 9:3; *Exod. Rab.,* 21:3.

34. II:1; 1:7. All quotations from the *Aboth* are from the edition and

translation by R. Travers Herford, *The Ethics of the Talmud: Sayings of the Fathers* (New York: Schocken Books, 1962).

35. *Gen. Rab.*, 26:6; *Lev. Rab.*, 28:1.
36. *Aboth de R. Nathan*, 32, pp. 130f. See also Urbach, *The Sages*, pp. 28ff. for a good discussion of the Rabbinic understanding of the relationship between atheism and the denial of God's retributive power.
37. The foresight of God is a favored motif of Haggadah. See, for example, *Gen. Rab.*, 1:5; 6:1; 8:4; 9:11; 17:4; 74:2; *Exod. Rab.*, 3:3; 40:1.
38. TB *Berakoth*, 33b; *Megillah*, 25a; *Niddah*, 16b.
39. 3:19. A succession of interpreters, including Maimonides, have regarded this text as a discussion of the problem of free will and divine foresight. Urbach contends, however, that the knowledge referred to here involves God's ability to perceive even secret sins, so that the entire text aims merely at underscoring human moral responsibility. (*The Sages*, pp. 256-60.) For a more traditional interpretation, see Julius Guttman, *Philosophies of Judaism* (New York: Holt, Rinehart, and Winston, 1964), p. 40.
40. Leviticus 26.
41. See D. S. Russell, *The Method and Message of Jewish Apocalyptic* (Philadelphia: Westminster Press, 1964), pp. 430-36, for a more detailed bibliography on this subject.
42. TB *Kethuboth*, 111a; *Shabbath*, 63a; *Gen. Rab.*, 12:6.
43. Thus, Mishnah *Sanhedrin*, 10:1, lists those who deny the resurrection among those who "have no share in the world to come."
44. TB *Menahoth*, 44a; TB Berakoth, 34b. For a fuller discussion of Jewish eschatology, see Joseph Klausner, *The Messianic Ideal in Israel* (New York: Macmillan Co., 1955).
45. TB *Berakoth*, 17a. Also *Mekilta de-Rabbi Ishmael*, tr. Jacob Lauterbach (Philadelphia: The Jewish Publication Society of America, 1949), I, 89ff., 253f.
46. TB *Aboth* 1:3; 4:2, 22. Cf. *'Abodah Zarah*, 19a.
47. For a good discussion of the Rabbinic concept of the fear of God, see H. Travers Herford, *Talmud and Apocrypha* (London: Soncino Press, 1933), pp. 133ff. Also, Urbach, *The Sages*, Ch. 14.
48. Schechter, *Aspects*, pp. 159ff.
49. See, e.g., TB *Sukkah*, 49b.
50. TJ *Berakoth*, 9:7. Also, TB *Berakoth*, 61b.
51. Thus Nelson Pike affirms in his article "Hume on Evil," in *God and Evil*, ed. Nelson Pike (Englewood Cliffs, N.J.: Prentice-Hall,

1964), pp. 95ff., that the prior acceptance of God's existence and justice renders a theistic position *logically* insusceptible to attack based on the experience of evil. But to say that a problem can in principle be resolved is not to dispense with the pressing task of offering concrete ways of doing so.

52. Drawing on Weber, Yinger terms this a "theodicy of good fortune." See his *The Scientific Study of Religion,* pp. 288f.

53. Job 8, 11, 15, 18, 20, 22.

54. *Seder Eliahu zuta* in *Seder Eliahu rabba und Seder Eliahu zuta,* ed. M. Friedmann (Vienna, 1900), Ch. 23, p. 41.

55. TB *Baba Kamma,* 60a.

56. TB *Aboth,* 4:19. As might be expected, the precise meaning of this passage has been a matter of dispute.

57. *Midrash Tehillim,* 94:2; *Gen. Rab.,* 32:3; *Song of Songs Rab.,* 2:16, 2,2. TB *Berakoth,* 5a.

58. TB *Berakoth,* 5a.

59. *Mekilta,* II: 280.

60. TB *Berakoth,* 5b.

61. This distinction is implicit in the characteristic way in which discussions of the relationship between sin and suffering refer always to the suffering of the self. See Cohen, *Religion of Reason,* pp. 226f.

62. A similar transvaluation of experience occurs when the Rabbis interpret the prosperity of the wicked as evidence of God's mercy. (TB *Gittin,* 56b.)

63. Emil Hirsch maintains in his article "Ethics," in *The Jewish Encyclopedia,* p. 255, that Judaism neither teaches nor recognizes "the consciousness of sin, and the helplessness of the sinner," and a similar view is advanced by Simon Bernfield in *The Foundations of Jewish Ethics* (New York: Macmillan, 1929), p. 102. For a richly documented refutation of these claims, see F. R. Tennant, *The Sources of the Doctrines of the Fall and Original Sin* (New York: Schocken Books, 1903, 1968).

64. Hence, the oft-repeated saying attributed to R. Eliezer HaGadol according to which even Abraham, Isaac, and Jacob could not withstand an indictment before God. (TB *'Arakin,* 17a and *Sanhedrin,* 46b, 101a.) No less indicative of the imperfection of the righteous are the frequent tales concerning respected Rabbis succumbing to illicit sexual temptations. (TB *Kiddushin,* 81a; *Sukkah,* 52a.)

65. For a discussion of the Biblical view of sin in Jewish perspective, see Mordecai M. Kaplan, "A Philosophy of Jewish Ethics," in *The Jews,*

ed. Louis Finkelstein (New York: Schocken Books, 1971), pp. 32-64.

66. *Aboth de R. Nathan,* 15, p. 85; TB *Yebamoth,* 103b; *Lev. Rab.,* 14:5.

67. TB *Berakoth,* 61a.

68. Schechter, *Aspects,* p. 269.

69. *Tanḥuma,* 7, 10a. Cf. *Gen. Rab.,* 22:6.

70. This union of body, mind, and will in wrongdoing is colorfully suggested by the tale of the blind man and the cripple who conspire in theft and who, despite their efforts to blame each other for making the essential contribution to the wrongdoing, are jointly convicted. (TB *Sanhedrin,* 91a; *Lev. Rab.,* 4:5.)

71. TB *Aboth,* 3:18; *Rosh Hashanah,* 17a; *Gen. Rab.,* 39:6.

72. TB *Baba Bathra,* 16a; *Kiddushin,* 30b.

73. For a survey of Rabbinic teaching on this see A. Marmorstein, *The Old Rabbinic Doctrine of God* (Oxford: Oxford University Press, 1927), Vol. I. Also, Urbach, *The Sages,* pp. 448-61.

74. *Num. Rab.,* 15:16. Cf. TB *Yoma,* 39a.

75. TB *Berakoth,* 23a.

76. *Sifre,* Numbers, Sec. 134, p. 180.

77. TB *Berakoth,* 7a.

78. *Pesikta Rabbati,* ed. M. Friedmann (Vienna, 1880), 184b-85a.

79. *Deut. Rab.,* 2:20; TB *Sanhedrin,* 103a. The Perek Helek or "Chapters on the Share" of this tractate contain a series of discussions on the fate of unrepentant sinners and the question of who is to be denied a share in the world to come. For a summary of Rabbinic attitudes toward repentance, see Maimonides *Mishneh Torah,* Hilkoth T'shuvah (reprint ed., New York: Otzea Harambam, Inc., 1960).

80. TJ *Sanhedrin,* 10:2; *TB Sanhedrin,* 103a; *Eccles. Rab.,* 4:1, 1; *Sifre,* Numbers, Sec. 8, pp. 10ff.

Chapter 7

1. This theme finds special expression in the many Rabbinic elaborations on the topic of God's love for Israel. See, for example, *Song of Songs Rab.,* 2:16, 1; 3:2, 2; *Exod. Rab.,* 30:24; 41:1.

2. This prophetic motif is carried over into Rabbinic thought where it appears especially as the concept of *Kiddush ha-Shem,* the sanctification of God's name to the non-Jewish world through acts of moral purity, religious piety, or even martyrdom. (TB *Yoma,* 86; *Aboth de R. Nathan,* 31, p. 161.)

3. See B. J. Bamberger, *Proselytism in the Talmudic Period* (New

York: KTAV Pub. House, 1939, 1968) and W. G. Braude, *Jewish Proselyting in the First Five Centuries of the Common Era* (Providence, R.I.: Brown University Press, 1940).

4. Kierkegaard's claim that repentance is at once "the highest ethical expression" and "the deepest ethical self-contradiction" reflects his grasp of the fact that genuine and complete repentance, though morally demanded may also be morally beyond the reach of a conscientiously sensitive wrongdoer. (*Fear and Trembling* [Princeton: Princeton University Press, 1941], p. 108 n.)

5. *Aboth de R. Nathan*, 39, p. 161: TB *Yoma*, 86a, 87a.

6. Schechter, *Aspects of Rabbinic Theology*, Ch. 11, esp. pp. 150f.

7. Though the Rabbis almost never relinquish their insistence on the minimal requirement that each individual endeavor to repent, they were prepared to accept even the slightest change of heart as a basis for acceptance by God. (See *Song of Songs Rab.*, 5:2, *Pesikta Rabbati*, 184b.)

8. Ephraim Urbach, *The Sages* (Jerusalem: Magnes Press of the Hebrew University, 1975), pp. 462-69.

9. At various times and by various scholars, the authenticity of Colossians, Ephesians, and II Thessalonians has been questioned. Romans, I and II Corinthians, Galatians, Philippians, I Thessalonians, and Philemon are generally accepted as Pauline. In the remainder of this chapter, I rely on these authentic epistles, and I refer to the disputed letters only when a particular point contained within them is amply supported in the authentic epistles. All subsequent New Testament quotations are drawn from the Revised Standard Version.

10. For a good review of the literature on this issue, see Victor Paul Furnish, "The Jesus-Paul Debate from Bauer to Bultmann," *Bulletin of the John Rylands Library,* XLVII (1965), 342ff.

11. In Rom. 13:8-10, Gal. 5:14 Paul offers the Golden Rule as a synopsis of the law. For a discussion of these uses of the law by Paul, see W. D. Davies, *Paul and Rabbinic Judaism,* 2d ed. (New York: Harper & Bros., 1955), pp. 112f.

12. Morton Scott Enslin, *The Ethics of Paul* (New York: Abingdon Press, 1957), p. 85. Of course, Paul's rejection of the law in both these senses also puts him decisively *out of* Rabbinic Judaism, as Samuel Sandmel observes (*Judaism and Christian Beginnings* [New York: Oxford University Press, 1978], Part IV, ch. 2).

13. Robin Scroggs points out the continuity between Paul's teaching here and that of the Rabbis. (*The Last Adam* [Philadelphia: Fortress

Press, 1966], pp. 78f.) See also, E. P. Sanders, *Paul and Palestinian Judaism* (Philadelphia: Fortress Press, 1977), pp. 111-16, 175, 203f. Sanders, however, contends that Paul's theology does not begin with his analysis of man's plight before the law, but with the proclamation of universal salvation in Christ. The diatribes against the law merely seek to explicate why a new means of salvation was needed (Ch. V, Sec. 4). This analysis strikes me as too one-sided and inattentive to the emphasis Paul places on the law as a problem.

14. The position that the "I" in this passage is not biographical but rhetorically general is taken by Rudolf Bultmann in his article "Romans 7 and the Anthropology of Paul," in *Existence and Faith*, tr. Schubert M. Ogden (New York: Meridian Books, 1968), pp. 147-57.

15. St. Augustine, for example, records some of the vehement criticisms marshaled against his own strong doctrine of the enslaved will. (*Anti-Pelagian Works, Treatise on Man's Perfection in Righteousness,* in *Nicene and Post-Nicene Fathers,* ed. Philip Schaff, 14 vols. (New York: Christian Literature Co., 1887-94), V, p. 160.) A position very similar to Augustine's is reaffirmed by Luther in response to the medieval return to a semi-Pelagian view. (See his *Bondage of the Will.*)

16. I have stressed here the specific moral source of this problem, but, of course, it also finds expression on the religious level, where moral failure takes the form of a vivid sense of inadequacy before God and a consequent sense of alienation from or perhaps even hatred of God. It may be that it is this religious expression of inadequacy that is at the forefront in Paul's writings—it is certainly so in the writings of Luther—but since the religious and ethical go together this does not mean, as Herman Riderbos maintains in his *Paul: An Outline of His Theology,* tr. John R. DeWitt (Grand Rapids, Mich.: Eerdmans, 1975), p. 139, that Paul's concept of sin "does not bear only or primarily an ethical character."

17. Hence Bultmann's observation that for Paul justification has a "forensic" quality and amounts to God's free bestowal of a verdict of acquittal on the sinner. (*Theology of the New Testament,* tr. Kendrick Grobel, 2 vols. [New York: Charles Scribner's Sons, 1951-55], I, 271ff.)

18. Calvin merely elaborates this fundamental idea when he builds his own Reformation ethic on the insistence that the Christian must first "grasp Christ's righteousness" but that one cannot appropriate this "without at the same time grasping sanctification also." (*Institutes of the Christian Religion,* III, xvi, 1.)

19. *The Protestant Ethic and the Spirit of Capitalism* (New York: Charles Scribner's Sons, 1958).

20. This view is suggested by Aquinas when he compares the reception of grace to vision. Just as seeing requires the eye to be turned toward the source of light, so must the recipient of grace make an initial effort to turn his will toward God. ("Treatise on Grace," *Summa Theologica*, I-IIae. Q. 109, Art. 6.) The Council of Trent later elevates this to the status of official Church doctrine, eclipsing other, less voluntarist motifs in the teaching of Aquinas.

21. This problem may lie behind Kierkegaard's remark that "[a]n ethic which disregards sin is a perfectly idle science; but if it asserts sin, it is *eo ipso* well beyond itself." (*Fear and Trembling*, p. 108.)

22. Augustine gives classic expression to this awareness when he asks, "How is it then that miserable men dare to be proud, either of their free will before they are freed; or of their own strength if they have been freed?" (*On the Spirit and the Letter*, in Schaff, *Nicene and Post-Nicene Fathers*, V, p. 106.)

23. The issue of whether Paul holds a universalist position has long been disputed. For a discussion of the various possible eschatologies in Paul's writings, see Floyd Filson, *St. Paul's Conception of Recompense* in *Untersuchungen zum Neuen Testament*, XXI (1931).

24. *Institutes of the Christian Religion*, III, xxiii, 7.

25. Enslin, pp. 50, 58.

26. The difficulty of resolving this problem rationally on any superficial level has long been apparent in the writings of commentators on Paul's ethics. Albert Schweitzer's view (in his *The Mysticism of Paul the Apostle*, tr. William Montgomery [London: Adam and Charles Black, 1931], pp. 225, 294f.), that it is logically impossible to derive any kind of an ethic from Paul's doctrine of justification, forms a major pole in the debate. On the other side of the debate are the many theological efforts to develop a relation between Paul's preaching of justification by faith and his unexpected and urgent moral exhortations. For a review of the literature on this problem, see Victor Paul Furnish, *Theology and Ethics in Paul* (Nashville and New York: Abingdon Press, 1968), Appendix, pp. 242-79. In distinction from these theological efforts to resolve this tension in Paul's thought, I am arguing that these two sides of his thinking can be fully understood only by tracing them to their source in two related and necessary aspects in the structure of religious reason.

27. My debt here to Niebuhr's penetrating discussion of the atonement is evident. (See his *The Nature and Destiny of Man*, II, 54-57.)

28. John Hick rightly characterizes this as "an evil than which no greater can be conceived." (*Evil and the God of Love*, Fontana Library [1968], p. 279.)
29. *The Nature and Destiny of Man*, II, 56.
30. *Exod. Rab.* 15:29; *Lamentations Rab.*, Proem, 24, pp. 43f. God's suffering as a result of the (perhaps justified) suffering of his people is also a common theme in the Rabbinic literature. See *Exod. Rab.* 30:24; *Song of Songs Rab.* 5:2, 2.
31. I draw these virtues not from the lengthy "virtue lists" present in Paul's writings, (e.g., I Cor. 13:4ff.; II Cor. 6:6-7; Gal. 5:22-23; Phil. 4:8; I Thess. 5:8) but rather from an independent reading of those particular and distinct dispositions of the moral life emphasized by Paul in the course of his letters. Commentators have rightly cautioned against efforts to use these unsystematic lists as a basis for interpreting Paul's moral teaching. (See Enslin, *The Ethics of Paul*, pp. 161ff. and Eric Wahlstrom, *The New Life in Christ* [Philadelphia: Muhlenberg Press, 1950], pp. 218ff. and pp. 281ff.) There is also the question of whether many of the virtues identified on these lists are properly understood as moral as opposed to "theological" virtues.
32. Hence, Reinhold Niebuhr's insistence that Christian love, or *agape*, is the "final law of human existence." (*Faith and History: A Comparison of Christian and Modern Views of History* [New York: Charles Scribner's Sons, 1949], p. 175.)
33. There has been considerable discussion of the significance and content of the Pauline idea of *imitatio Christi*, with views ranging from the position that Paul had in mind here the full moral pattern of Jesus' life to the position of those who evacuate this concept of all but the idea of radical obedience to God. For a review of this debate, see Furnish, *Theology and Ethics in Paul*, pp. 219-24.
34. Also, Eph. 4:15; 5:23 and Col. 1:18; 2:19 where Christ is termed, somewhat differently, the head of the body. The concept of the body of Christ has received extensive consideration in the theological literature. For a brief review of these discussions, see Ernst Käsemann, "The Theological Problem Presented by the Motif of the Body of Christ," in *Perspectives on Paul* (Philadelphia: Fortress Press, 1971), Ch. 5.
35. For an account of Christian employments of the body metaphor, see Ernst Troeltsch, *The Social Teachings of the Christian Churches*, tr. Olive Wyon, 2 vols. (New York: Harper & Bros., 1960), I, 284-305.
36. Cf. Acts 23:6; 26:6-8, where Paul's preaching of Christ is presented as a reaffirmation of the Pharisaic doctrine of resurrection.

37. The baptismal rite Paul refers to here involves the total immersion and near-asphyxiation of the participant. Liturgy thus supports the moral belief structure.

38. Günther Bornkamm observes that this emphasis on suffering gives a deeply paradoxical character to the Pauline proclamation of salvation. (*Paul* [New York: Harper & Row, 1971], p. 170.)

39. In his *Religion Without Revelation,* tr. John Gordon Smith, 2d ed. (New York: Macmillan & Co., 1968), Dietrich Bonhoeffer extends this motif beyond the problem of suffering to the general theological problem of God's "hiddenness." The suffering God becomes for him the affirmation and support of man's autonomy and "aloneness" in the world.

40. Thus, Furnish observes that for Paul, justification has not only a "declarative" but also a "causative" meaning. (*Theology and Ethics in Paul,* p. 152.)

41. Paul does not elaborate on the nature of the agency of the Spirit. Paul Wernle, in *Der Christ und die Sünde bei Paulus* (Freiburg: J. C. B. Mohr, 1897), p. 89, observes that Paul sometimes refers to the Spirit as a supernatural power, while at other times, he seems to refer to it as an indwelling potentiality which man can, and should, exercise through his will.

42. Martin Buber voices a moral criticism of Christianity for its disconcern with the concept of peoplehood. See his *Eclipse of God* (New York: Harper & Row, 1953), p. 106.

43. Thus, Niebuhr observes, "The problem of the meaning of history according to prophetism is how history can be anything more than judgment, which is to say whether the promise of history can be fulfilled at all." Or again, "The problem of history, according to prophetism, is not that God should be revealed as strong enough to overcome the defiance of the evil against His will, but as having resources of mercy great enough to redeem as well as judge all men." (*The Nature and Destiny of Man,* II, 27, 29f.)

44. Rudolf Bultmann, *Kerygma and Myth,* ed. Hans W. Bartsch (New York: Harper & Row, 1961), esp. pp. 22-43. For a discussion of Bultmann's understanding of the relationship between history and faith, see John Macquarrie, *An Existentialist Theology* (New York: Harper & Row, 1955), pp. 166-80. Bultmann's position is anticipated by Kierkegaard in his *Concluding Unscientific Postscript,* tr. David F. Swenson (Princeton: Princeton University Press, 1941), pp. 24-47.

45. Kant misses this and reflects his debt to a more superficial rationalist background when he maintains that the redemptive significance of

Christian faith is independent of historical revelation. (*Rel*, pp. 119f.: Greene, pp. 110f.) D. M. MacKinnon correctly describes Kant's interpretation of Christianity as a "protest against the morally destructive effects wrought on human life by competing religious authoritarianisms." ("Kant's Philosophy of Religion," *Philosophy*, L [1975], 134.) For a good discussion of Kant's moralized Christology, see Wood, *Kant's Moral Religion*, p. 246. In accepting Kant's approach to religion, one does not have to adopt his particular interpretation of any one faith, and it is clear that my account of the significance of Christ draws more heavily on Kant's discussion of radical evil than Kant did himself.

Chapter 8

1. *Karma*'s status as a virtual dogma of Indian religion is emphasized by Surendranath Dasgupta, *A History of Indian Philosophy*, 2 vols. (Cambridge: Cambridge University Press, 1922), I, 87; Louis Renou, *Hinduism* (New York: Washington Square Press, 1963), p. 26; Max Weber, *The Religion of India* (New York: The Free Press, 1958), pp. 117f.; and R. C. Zaehner, *Hinduism* (New York: Oxford University Press, 1966), p. 5.

2. Good discussions of the *karma* doctrine may be found in Dasgupta, *A History of Indian Philosophy*, I, 71-74; L. De La Vallé Poussin, "Karma," *Encyclopaedia of Religion and Ethics*, VII, 673-76; and John McKenzie, *Hindu Ethics: A Historical and Critical Essay* (London: Oxford University Press, 1922), pp. 79ff.

3. Tr. Irving Babbitt (New York: New Directions, 1965), v. 127, p. 21.

4. The Buddhist stress on mental *karma* places volition, and not outward actions, at the center of the process of karmic determination. (Dasgupta, *A History of Indian Philosophy*, I, 108.)

5. K. N. Jayatilleke, *Ethics in Buddhist Perspective* (Kandy, Ceylon: Buddhist Publication Society, 1972), p. 54. Also, P. T. Raju, *The Philosophical Traditions of India* (London: George Allen & Unwin, 1971), pp. 206f.

6. See, for example, the derisory Buddhist treatment of the deterministic views of Makkhali Gosāla, head of the Ājīvaka school, and of the similar view of Pūrana Kassapa in the *Sâmañña-Phala Sutta* (The Fruits of the Life of a Recluse) in *The Sacred Books of the Buddhists*, tr. T. W. Rhys Davids, 31 vols. (London: Henry Frowde, 1895), II, 69-73.

7. The *Satapatha-Brāhamana,* tr. J. Eggeling (Oxford: Clarendon Press, 1897), 10. 4, 3, mentions the prospect of "re-death" for those who perform ritual actions imperfectly. But the first clear statement of the essential ideas of the *karma* doctrine appears in the Upanishads. In the *Brihad-Āranyaka* Upanishad (III.ii.13) there is the suggestion that this doctrine was initially the esoteric teaching of a class of religious virtuosi.

8. Dasgupta, *A History of Indian Philosophy,* I, 21f., 71ff. Also Raymond Pannikar, "The Law of *Karman* and the Historical Dimension of Man," *Philosophy East and West,* XXII (1972), 35ff., and M. Hiriyanna, *Outlines of Indian Philosophy* (New York: Macmillan Co., 1932), p. 79.

9. I use the later term "caste" here for what are more correctly the four *varnas* of the early Indian religious and social order. Castes themselves (*jātis*) are subdivisions of the four *varnas.*

10. For a discussion of the relationship between the concepts of *rita* and *dharma,* see John M. Koller, "*Dharma:* An Expression of Universal Order," *Philosophy East and West,* XXII (1972), 131-44.

11. Louis Dumont, in his *Homo Hierarchicus* (Chicago: University of Chicago Press, 1970) and his *Religion/Politics and History in India* (Paris and The Hague: Mouton Publishers, 1970), convincingly documents the contemporary religious basis of caste distinctions, particularly their relation to ritual dietary and pollution beliefs. Nevertheless, Dumont repeatedly observes instances where class and social factors exert continuing pressure on what have become largely religious distinctions.

12. J. Muir, *Original Sanskrit Texts,* 3d ed. (London: Trübner & Co., 1890), I, 140ff. For a similar relation of *varna* to *karma* see *Chāndogya* Upanishad (V. x. 7).

13. For a representative statement of this position, see I. C. Sharma, *Ethical Philosophies of India* (New York: Harper & Row, 1970), pp. 89f. In the nineteenth century, this position was actively supported by social reformers like Dayananda Sarasvati. See Raju, *The Philosophical Traditions of India,* pp. 208f.

14. *Chāndogya* Upanishad (IV. iv. 13).

15. *The Religion of India,* p. 121.

16. There may be some positive moral significance to this teaching in its elimination of causes for bitterness and envy. See Hiriyanna, *Outlines of Indian Philosophy,* p. 79 and Dumont, *Homo Hierarchicus,* pp. 103ff.

17. Weber, *The Religion of India,* p. 105. Also, David G. Mandelbaum, *Society in India* (Berkeley, Cal.: University of California Press, 1970), II, p. 319.
18. *Hinduism,* p. 4.
19. Quoted in Sharma, *Ethical Philosophies of India,* p. 108.
20. *Mysticism and Morality* (New York: Basic Books, 1972), p. 45.
21. *Ibid.,* pp. 26, 41.
22. Quoted by William Hume in the introduction to his *Thirteen Principal Upanishads* (London: Oxford University Press, 1921), p. 55.
23. *The Religion of India,* p. 167.
24. This is Weber's suggestion in *The Religion of India,* p. 133.
25. Danto, *Mysticism and Morality,* pp. 47f. Zaehner, *Hinduism,* p. 61.
26. See, for example, *Rig-Veda* 1. 24. 9d; 3. 7. 10d; 7. 86. 3a, 4d; 7. 88. 6c; 7. 89. 5c,d. Also, *Atharva-Veda* 6. 97. 2d; 6. 115. 1, 2, 3; 6. 116. 2, 3.
27. Thus, Weber observes that the inscription literature left by Indian princes has as a common theme the interest in maintaining class status in future lives. (*The Religion of India,* p. 121.) For a vivid description of the ruler's fear of moral pollution, see the "Temiya Jataka," in Elizabeth Wray and Clare Rosenfield, *Ten Lives of the Buddha* (New York and Tokyo: Weatherhill, 1972), pp. 23-30.
28. *Chāndogya* Upanishad (IV. xiv. 3).
29. Weber, despite his own deep appreciation of the moral significance of *karma,* makes this distinction between Western and Indian salvation striving. (*The Religion of India,* pp. 167.) For a similar view, see Melford Spiro, *Buddhism and Society* (New York: Harper & Row, 1970), p. 38.
30. See above, pp. 110-12.
31. This is the basis of Kant's remark that the absence of certainty of God's existence is beneficial since it allows for the development of morally purer motives than the hope of reward—*KdpV,* pp. 146f.: Beck, p. 152.
32. The *Upanishads* sometimes reveal the presence of this kind of experiential basis to their speculative discussions. See, for example, *Katha* Upanishad (VI. 10), *Svetāsvatara* Upanishad (II, 8-13), and *Maitri* Upanishad (VI. 30).
33. Zaehner, *The Comparison of Religions* (Boston: Beacon Press, 1962), pp. 10, 16ff., 24f., 30, stresses this mystical, as against historical focus.
34. Pannikar, "The Law of *Karman* and the Historical Dimension of Man," p. 44.

35. I. 5. I draw here on Hume's translation.
36. Hence the famous *neti, neti* ("Not this, not that") passages of the *Brihad-Āranyaka* Upanishad (II.iii.6; III.ix.26; IV.ii.4; IV.iv.22; IV.v.15).
37. *Brihad-Āranyaka* Upanishad (IV.iii.21).
38. *Māndūkya* Upanishad (7).
39. For a good review of Western discussions of this problem, see Guy Richard Welbon, *The Buddhist Nirvana and Its Western Interpreters* (Chicago: University of Chicago Press, 1968).
40. For example, the *Milinda-pañha* (III.iv.8 and IV.viii.76).
41. Jayatilleke, *Ethics in Buddhist Perspective*, p. 19.
42. For discussions of these various codes see D. Bhargava, *Jaina Ethics*, 1st ed. (Delhi: Motilal Barnarsidass, 1968); Sharma, *Ethical Philosophies of India*, Chs. 6, 7, and 9; Dasgupta, *A History of Indian Philosophy*, I, 199f., 270f.; H. Saddhatissa, *Buddhist Ethics* (New York: George Braziller, 1970), Ch. 4.
43. The classical explication of the *anattā* doctrine is found in the *Milinda-pañha* (II.i.1).
44. "Emptiness and · Moral Perfection," *Philosophy East and West*, XXIII (1973), 362.
45. *The Comparison of Religions*, p. 95.
46. *Path of Perfection*, tr. Bhīkkhu Ñānamoli (Lake House, Colombo, Ceylon, 1956), p. 308.
47. For a concise description of the Bodhisattva, see the discussion by Nagarjuna quoted at length by D. T. Suzuki in his *Outlines of Mahayana Buddhism* (New York: Schocken Books, 1963), pp. 292ff.
48. This is the answer given by Santideva in his *Bodhicaryāvatāra* (VIII.103).
49. *Vajracchednikā Sutra*. Translation from *Buddhist Texts Through the Ages*, tr. and eds. Edward Conze *et al.* (New York: Harper & Row, 1964), pp. 172f.
50. *Ratnagotravibhaga* I, vv.69-78 in Conze *et al.*, eds., *Buddhist Texts through the Ages*, eds. Conze *et al.*, pp. 130f.
51. For a discussion of this teaching in Mahayana Buddhism, see Suzuki, *Outlines of Mahayana Buddhism*, pp. 352-57.
52. All quotations are from the translation by Eliot Deutsch (New York: Holt, Rinehart, and Winston, 1968).
53. Zaehner, *Hinduism*, pp. 111, 116, 121. Weber, *The Religion of India*, pp. 64f. and 144ff.
54. K. N. Upadhyaya points out that the Kauravas, in the course of the *Mahā-bhārata* had committed all of the crimes which the law books

Gītā on War and Peace," *Philosophy East and West,* XIX [1969], 163-65.) For a thorough account of the ethical perspective of the epics, see Dhairyabula Vora, *Evolution of Morals in the Epics* (Bombay: Popular Book Depot, 1959).

55. A. Janaki Ram, "Arjuna and Hamlet: Two Moral Dilemmas," *Philosophy East and West,* XVIII (1968), 28.

56. Hiriyanna, *Outlines of Indian Philosophy,* p. 121.

57. The correspondence between this implication of the *Gītā's* teaching and Kant's doctrine of autonomy has occasionally been noted by commentators on the *Gītā,* but these commentators have failed to see how the *Gītā's* total religious and moral position, not just the stress on detached action, conforms to the Kantian religious program. See, for example, Balbir Singh Gauchhwal, "Moral Religion of Kant and Karmayoga of the Gītā," *Kant-Studien,* LV (1964), 394-409 and Sarvepalli Radhakrishnan, "The Ethics of the Bhagavadgita and Kant," *International Journal of Ethics,* XXI (1911), 467-75.

58. Sharma, *Ethical Philosophies of India,* pp. 142f. Also, Hiriyanna, *Outlines of Indian Philosophy,* pp. 166ff.

59. *The Religion of India,* p. 185.

60. For a succinct account of these developments, see Edward Conze, *Buddhism: Its Essence and Development* (New York: Harper & Row, 1959), Ch. 6.

61. Jayatilleke, *Ethics in Buddhist Perspective,* p. 31.

Conclusion

1. Zaehner, *The Comparison of Religions,* p. 12.

2. *Methods of Logic,* rev. ed. (New York: Henry Holt & Co., 1959), p. xii.

3. *The Protestant Ethic and the Spirit of Capitalism* as well as Weber's other writings on economics seek to demonstrate this positive effect of religious belief on the process of modernization.

Further readings

The following books and articles include primary readings and further discussions of major issues, problems, or methods dealt with in each chapter. Some of these discussions present opposing viewpoints to those developed in the text. This list is not complete and indicates only some of the more important works available in English. References for more specific issues may be found in the Notes.

Introduction

Feuerbach, Ludwig. *The Essence of Religion.* Harper & Bros., 1957.

Freud, Sigmund. *The Future of an Illusion.* Doubleday & Co., 1964.

———. *Totem and Taboo.* W. W. Norton & Co., 1950.

Marx, Karl, and Friedrich Engels. *Karl Marx and Friedrich Engels on Religion.* Schocken Books, 1964.

McPherson, Thomas. "Religion as the Inexpressible," Antony Flew and Alasdair MacIntyre, eds. *New Essays in Philosophical Theology,* pp. 131-43. Macmillan Co., 1955.

Otto, Rudolf. *The Idea of the Holy* (tr. John W. Harvey). Oxford University Press, 1923, 2d edition (paper), 1958.

Further readings

Yinger, J. Milton. *The Scientific Study of Religion*. Macmillan Co., 1970.

Wittgenstein, Ludwig. *Lectures and Conversations on Aesthetics, Psychology and Religious Belief*. Basil Blackwell, 1966.

Chapter One

Baier, Kurt. *The Moral Point of View*. Cornell University Press, 1958.

Gert, Bernard. *The Moral Rules*. Harper & Row, 1970.

Hare, R. M. *Freedom and Reason*. Oxford University Press, 1965.

Nagel, Thomas. *The Possibility of Altruism*. Clarendon Press, 1970.

Rawls, John. *A Theory of Justice*. Harvard University Press, Belknap Press, 1971.

Richards, David. *A Theory of Reasons for Actions*. Clarendon Press, 1971.

Kant, Immanuel. *Foundations of the Metaphysics of Morals* (tr. Lewis White Beck). Bobbs-Merrill, 1959.

————. *Critique of Practical Reason* (tr. Lewis White Beck), Part I, Bk. I. Bobbs-Merrill, 1956.

Wolff, Robert Paul. *The Autonomy of Reason*. Harper & Row, 1973.

Chapter Two

Baier, Kurt. *The Moral Point of View,* Ch. 12.

Gert, Bernard. *The Moral Rules,* Ch. 10.

Hospers, John. *Human Conduct*. Ch. IV, Sec. 11. Harcourt, Brace and World, 1961.

Nielsen, Kai. "Why Should I Be Moral?" *Methodos,* XV (1963) 275-306.

Singer, Marcus. *Generalization in Ethics,* Ch. 10, Section 3. Alfred A. Knopf, 1961.

Taylor, Paul. *Principles of Ethics: An Introduction,* Ch. 9. Dickenson, 1975.

Warnock, G. J. *The Object of Morality,* Ch. 9. Methuen & Co., 1971.

Chapter Three

Beck, Lewis White. *A Commentary on Kant's Critique of Practical Reason*. University of Chicago Press, 1960.

Kant, Immanuel. *Critique of Practical Reason,* Part I, Bk. II; Part II.
———. *Critique of Judgment* (tr. James Meredith), Part II. Clarendon Press, 1928.
Raschke, Carl A. *Moral Action, God and History in the Thought of Immanuel Kant.* American Academy of Religion, 1975.
Wood, Allen. *Kant's Moral Religion.* Cornell University Press, 1970.
Yovel, Yirmiahu. "The Highest Good and History in Kant's Thought," *Archiv für Geschichte der Philosophie,* LIV (1972) 258.

Chapter Four

Cohen, Marshall; Thomas Nagel; and Thomas Scanlon, eds. *War and Moral Responsibility.* Princeton University Press, 1974.
Kant, Immanuel. *Religion within the Limits of Reason Alone* (tr. T. M. Greene and H. H. Hudson). Harper & Row, 1960.
Maclagen, W. G. *The Theological Frontier of Ethics,* Ch. 4. George Allen & Unwin, 1961.
Pa'il, Meir. "The Dynamics of Power: Morality in Armed Conflict after the Six Days War," *Modern Jewish Ethics: Theory and Practice,* Marvin Fox, ed. Ohio State University Press, 1975.
Tillich, Paul. *The Courage to Be.* Yale University Press, 1952.

Chapter Five

Kant, Immanuel. *Religion within the Limits of Reason Alone.*
Otto, Rudolf. *The Idea of the Holy.*
Outka, Gene, and John P. Reeder, Jr. *Religion and Morality.* Doubleday & Co., 1973.
Trigg, Roger. *Reason and Commitment.* Cambridge University Press, 1973.
Winch, Peter. "Understanding a Primitive Society," *Ethics and Action,* Ch. 2. Routledge & Kegan Paul, 1972.
Wittgenstein, Ludwig. *Lectures & Conversations on Aesthetics, Psychology and Religious Belief.* Basil Blackwell, 1966.

Further readings

Chapter Six

Büchler, A. *Studies in Sin and Atonement.* Oxford University Press, 1928; reprinted by KTAV Pub. House, 1967.

Cohen, Abraham. *Everyman's Talmud.* E. P. Dutton & Co., 1949.

Cohen, Hermann. *Religion of Reason out of the Sources of Judaism.* Frederick Ungar Pub. Co., 1972.

Herford, R. Travers. *The Ethics of the Talmud: Sayings of the Fathers.* Schocken Books, 1962.

————. *Talmud and Apocrypha.* Soncino Press, 1933.

Kadushin, Max. *The Rabbinic Mind.* Jewish Theological Seminary of America, 1952.

Katz, Steven T. *Jewish Ideas and Concepts.* Schocken Books, 1977.

Lazarus, Moritz. *The Ethics of Judaism.* 2 vols. Jewish Publication Society of America, 1900.

Marmorstein, A. *The Old Rabbinic Doctrine of God.* Oxford University Press, 1927; reprinted by KTAV Pub. House, 1968.

Montefiore, Claude G., and H. Lowe. *A Rabbinic Anthology.* Schocken Books, 1974.

Schechter, Solomon. *Aspects of Rabbinic Theology.* Schocken Books, 1961.

Urbach, Ephraim. *The Sages.* University of Jerusalem, Magnes Press, 1975.

Chapter Seven

Bornkamm, Günter. *Paul.* Harper & Row, 1971.

Bultmann, Rudolph. "Romans 7 and the Anthropology of Paul," *Existence and Faith.* Meridian Books, 1968.

Davies, W. D. *Paul and Rabbinic Judaism.* Harper & Bros., 1955.

Enslin, Morton Scott. *The Ethics of Paul.* Abingdon Books, 1957.

Furnish, Victor Paul. *Theology and Ethics in Paul.* Abingdon Books, 1968.

Houlden, J. L. *Ethics and the New Testament.* Oxford University Press, 1977.

Käsemann, Ernst. *Perspectives on Paul.* Fortress Press, 1971.

Sanders, E. P. *Paul and Palestinian Judaism.* Fortress Press, 1977.

Sandmel, Samuel. *Judaism and Christian Beginnings.* Oxford University Press, 1978.

Weber, Max. *The Protestant Ethic and the Spirit of Capitalism.* Charles Scribner's Sons, 1958.

Chapter Eight

Bhagavad Gītā (tr. Eliot Deutsch). Holt, Rinehart and Winston, 1968.

Conze, Edward. *Buddhism: Its Essence and Development.* Harper & Row, 1959.

———— *et al.,* eds. *Buddhist Texts through the Ages.* Harper & Row, 1964.

Danto, Arthur C. *Mysticism and Morality.* Basic Books, 1972.

Dasgupta, Surendranath. *A History of Indian Philosophy.* 2 vols. Cambridge University Press, 1922.

Dhammapada (tr. Irving Babbit). New Directions, 1965.

Dumont, Louis. *Homo Hierarchicus.* University of Chicago Press, 1970.

Jayatilleke, K. N. *Ethics in Buddhist Perspective.* Buddhist Publication Society, 1972.

Mandelbaum, David G. *Society in India.* 2 vols. University of California Press, 1970.

Renou, Louis. *Hinduism.* Washington Square Press, 1963.

Saddhatissa, H. *Buddhist Ethics.* George Braziller, 1970.

Sharma, I. C. *Ethical Philosophies of India.* Harper & Row, 1970.

Suzuki, D. T. *Outlines of Mahayana Buddhism.* Schocken Books, 1963.

Upadhyaya, K. N. "The Bhagavad Gītā on War and Peace," *Philosophy East and West,* XIX (1969) 159-69.

Weber, Max. *The Religion of India.* Free Press, 1958.

Zaehner, R. C. *Hinduism.* Oxford University Press, 1966.

Index

Index

Index

Index

Index